STUDIES IN ROMANCE LANGUAGES: 42

John E. Keller, Editor

Dramas of Distinction

A Study of Plays
by Golden Age Women

TERESA SCOTT SOUFAS

THE UNIVERSITY PRESS OF KENTUCKY

Publication of this book was assisted by grants from
The National Endowment for the Humanities and from
The Program for Cultural Cooperation between
Spain's Ministry of Culture and United States Universities.

Copyright © 1997 by The University Press of Kentucky

Scholarly publisher for the Commonwealth,
serving Bellarmine College, Berea College, Centre
College of Kentucky, Eastern Kentucky University,
The Filson Club Historical Society, Georgetown College,
Kentucky Historical Society, Kentucky State University,
Morehead State University, Murray State University,
Northern Kentucky University, Transylvania University,
University of Kentucky, University of Louisville,
and Western Kentucky University.

Editorial and Sales Offices: The University Press of Kentucky
663 South Limestone Street, Lexington, Kentucky 40508-4008

01   00   99   98   97   5   4   3   2   1

Library of Congress Cataloging-in-Publication Data

Soufas, Teresa Scott.
   Dramas of distinction: a study of plays by Golden Age women /
Teresa Scott Soufas.
       p.   c.m.   (Studies in Romance languages ; 42)
   Includes bibliographical references and index.
   ISBN 0-8131-2010-1 (cloth: alk. paper)
   1. Spanish drama—Women authors—History and criticism.
   2. Spanish drama—Classical period—History and criticism.
   I. Title.
PQ6055.S58   1996
862'.30809287—dc21   96-44394

This book is printed on acid-free recycled paper meeting
the requirements of the American National Standard
for Permanence of Paper for Printed Library Materials.

Manufactured in the United States of America

For Chris
for everything

CONTENTS

ACKNOWLEDGMENTS

I am most appreciative of the staff of the rare books and manuscripts section in the Biblioteca Nacional de Madrid for helping me obtain copies of the plays I have studied. Thanks also to the Committee on Research at Tulane for grant support to visit the appropriate archives in Spain during the late stages of my project

I also want to thank my husband, Chris, my parents, my sister and her family, and all the members of my family who believed with me in the value of my work. And special thanks to my son Paul, who, during the period of research and composition of this book, kept me mindful of all the things that are truly important.

INTRODUCTION

My aim in this volume is to examine the works of some women dramatists in Golden Age Spain on their own textual terms and not necessarily in relation to the male-dominated canon already in place in theatrical, academic, and theoretical circles. I am not interested, therefore, in a direct comparison between how one of these women depicts, for example, a cross-dressed woman in pursuit of her male lover and how Pedro Calderón de la Barca depicts such figures. What I am interested in is a gender-centered reading of plays that are part of the literary production of Golden Age Spain and that were shaped by and contributed to the social, political, and artistic conventions of the period.

The five dramatists whose works I examine are Angela Azevedo, Ana Caro Mallén de Soto, Leonor de la Cueva y Silva, Feliciana Enríquez de Guzmán, and María de Zayas y Sotomayor, women grouped for consideration not from an essentializing move that universalizes them because of their sex but in order to interrogate the simultaneity of time, geography, and strategies of expression that they share. These women's plays are products of the period beginning as early as 1628 to perhaps as late as the 1660s, the majority having been composed (and staged, if at all) during the 1630s and 1640s. They evince a multiplicity of subject positions as the authors negotiate ways to do what most women did not do in their society: that is, write for a public—specifically, a theatrical one.

Little is known about the lives of these five women authors.[1] Angela Azevedo, a native of Lisbon, Portugal, was born around 1600 to Juan de Azevedo Pereira and his second wife, Isabel de Oliveira, a couple who must have occupied a position of nobility and comfort high enough to educate their child so that she "tuvo fama de ingeniosa, discreta y hermosa."[2] After moving with her family to Madrid, Azevedo

1

became a member of Philip IV's court; Manuel Serrano y Sanz records that she "vivió protegida por Doña Isabel de Borbón, mujer de Felipe IV, de la cual fué dama," and that she married "un caballero de ilustre alcurnia" (268: 10). Diogo Barbosa Machado likewise affirms that the marriage was "digno de seu nacimento" (175). María Isabel Barbeito Carneiro reports that the widowed Azevedo retired with a daughter to a Benedictine convent, a place for which "debió sentir especial veneración" (3), where she spent the remaining years until her death. Azevedo's dramatic texts are left to us in seventeenth-century printed documents without information about place or date of printing. All three plays demand the use of stage machinery, indication perhaps of the advantage that court patronage afforded this dramatist.

Recent bio-bibliographical studies that include entries on Ana Caro provide the rather scant information we have about the life of this woman, the only one among the five to have gained the status of professional playwright.[3] As recorded in studies by Frederick de Armas ("Ana Caro"), Amy Kaminsky, Ruth Lundelius, and Lola Luna, Caro was born sometime around 1600, probably in Granada, but she spent the majority of her life in Seville.[4] Information about her brother, Juan, reveals that at his death in 1655 he left grandchildren, and the supposition that the siblings were chronologically close in age leads to the speculations about her birthdate.

In his *Varones ilustres de Sevilla*, Rodrigo Caro, the Sevillan poet and presumably a distant relative of Caro's, lauds her as "insigne poetisa que ha hecho muchas comedias, representadas en Sevilla y Madrid y otras partes, con grandísimo aplauso, en las cuales casi siempre se le ha dado el primer premio" (73). Diego Ortiz de Zuñiga also includes Caro in his late seventeenth-century *Annales eclesiasticos y seculares de la muy noble y leal ciudad de Sevilla* in which he identifies her as "escritora de comedias." Luna likewise draws attention to Caro's place "en la primera bibliografía de la literatura española," compiled by Nicolás Antonio and containing the entry: "D Anna Caro, Hispalensis, tempore nostro poesim coluit, et nonnullas comedias in publicum proponi permisit quae non sine plausu, recitate sunt" (cited in *Ana Caro: "El conde,"* 3). Her contemporary Juan de Matos Fragoso cites her play *El conde Partinuplés* in his own drama *La corsaria catalana*, in a passage about the play texts in the hands of a depicted theater manager. To the question asked by the character León, "Qué comedias traes?" the *autor* replies:

> De las plumas milagrosas
> De España . . .
> *La bizarra Arsinda,* que es
> Del ingenioso Cervantes,
> *Los dos confusos amantes,*
> *El conde Partinuplés.*[5]

Adding to these allusions to undocumented performances of her secular plays is Kaminsky's assertion that between 1641 and 1645 "Caro earned money as a playwright," in the amount of 300 reales each for *autos sacramentales,* religious plays celebrating the Corpus Christi festival (87).[6] Luna comments upon the significant fact that in seventeenth-century Spain "una mujer recibiera la aprobación del Cabildo a sus piezas breves para el Corpus, y que esta aprobación se tradujera en un pago de 300 reales por cada auto." She also reports that Caro also rceived "unas libranzas anuales . . . exiguas [pero] no por ello despreciables, en 1641, 1642, 1643, 1645 y una de mayor importancia en 1637" (*Ana Caro: Valor,* 11).

This means that Caro is the only dramatist among those studied here who verifiably enjoyed professional outlets for her theatrical works. Compared with that of her male colleagues, this activity is not extensive, but it is noteworthy in relation to what was considered the norm for women's literary aspirations and to the more limited avenues of public representation her female peers enjoyed: "La figura pública de esta autora contrasta con el de la dama de letras 'aficionada,' poetisa lírica ocasional, o con el de la escritora 'aristócrata.' Y contrasta también con el de la escritora espiritual, que escribe generalmente para una audiencia conventual ampliada excepcionalmente a la corte" (Luna, "Ana Caro, una escritora," 18). Caro's professional status as a writer is likewise noteworthy in a period of intensified competition among the growing ranks of those (mostly male) subjects able to take advantage of Hapsburg educational reforms and expansion (Luna, *Ana Caro: Valor,* 11–12). The scant biographical information available affords few answers about just how she obtained access to avenues of print, distribution, and representation for her works. That her dramas, poems, *loa*, and *autos* existed in published form, for the most part, attests to her success, if not to her process of accomplishment.

Caro enjoyed a close friendship with María de Zayas, with whom she shares mutual references in their works.[7] In one of Caro's own poems—written, as Lundelius recounts, to mark "the ostentatious festivities in Madrid . . . which celebrated the arrival [there] of María, the Bourbon princess of Cariñán (Carignano), and the election of Ferdinand III of Hungary, brother-in-law of Philip IV, to the succession of the Holy Roman Empire"[8]—Caro claims to have wanted to see the Spanish court and to have made her entry into Madrid on January 1, 1637, during a snowstorm (Lundelius, 239 n. 9). Alonso de Castillo Solórzano praises these circumstantial verses in his novel *La garduña de Sevilla* (1642) and affirms Caro's presence in Madrid in Zayas's company. Speculation about Caro's participation in an apocryphal literary *academia* in Seville is based on references in Luis Vélez de Guevara's picaresque novel *El diablo cojuelo,* allusions whose historical and geographical grounding have led some scholars to speculate that Caro did enjoy association with such a group.[9] Lundelius notes that Caro's last known composition is a sonnet in praise of Tomás de Palomares's book *Estilo nuevo de escrituras públicas,* published in 1645 (231). Her play *El conde Partinuplés* was published in an anthology of dramatic works in 1653, a date suggesting that it was composed a few years earlier if Caro followed the usual practice of Golden Age dramatists that John Varey describes: "vendió la obra a un autor de comedias y éste, después de haberla representado muchas veces, la vendió a un impresor" (102). With this in mind and considering the dates of her performed *autos* and six poetic works between 1628 and 1645, the majority appearing in the 1630s, it is reasonable to assume that her two extant *comedias* are also products of the decade and a half 1630–45.

Kaminsky comments that within a six-year period both Zayas and Caro (1647 and 1653 respectively) "disappear from literary and historical records" (87); Lundelius speculates that Caro may have perished "in the terrible plague which decimated Seville during the years 1649–1652" (231). Of her two secular plays studied here, *El conde Partinuplés* and *Valor, agravio y mujer,* the first exists in its 1653 edition in an anthology titled *Laurel de comedias: Quarta parte de diferentes au-*

tores and in a handwritten copy as well. The latter was probably based on the printed text, since, as Alberto Blecua asserts, the printed version of a play usually followed by a few years its composition and representation, and the theatrical manuscripts "proceden (habitualmente) de copias de las partes impresas" (213). The earliest text of *Valor, agravio y mujer* is a manuscript in seventeenth-century script, contemporary with the playwright.

Leonor de la Cueva y Silva also left behind few details about her life and no information about her activity as a dramatist except the autograph manuscript text of her one extant play.[10] She is better known as a poet because of her more extensive body of poetic compositions, also found in her own handwritten manuscript and as yet unpublished in its entireity. Cueva was born in the early seveneenth century to Agustín de la Rúa and Leonor de Silva, members of the minor nobility in Medina del Campo, and she seems to have spent her whole life there. On the basis of the amorous poems Cueva includes in her collection and lists as commissioned pieces, Julián Olivares and Elizabeth Boyce speculate about her participation in literary circles in her native city. They contend that she was singled out for such commissions because of "la muy probable existencia en Medina del Campo de un círculo literario en que doña Leonor fuese la persona más capacitada para escribir poesía" (48).[11] Such a literary assembly must have been the reading audience for her dramatic work as well. There is no record that she ever married, nor is the date of her death fixed. Serrano y Sanz asserts that she probably died after 1650, but Olivares and Boyce point to the sonnet composed by Cueva for the death of Queen María Luisa de Borbón, who died in 1689, as proof of a longer life span (268:106).[12]

The autograph manuscript of Cueva's *La firmeza en la ausencia* is decorated (like that containing her poems) with her hand-drawn geometrical pattern. This manuscript, now housed in the Biblioteca Nacional de Madrid, was once part of the personal library of the Duques de Osuna. Although it is impossible to determine the exact date of the play's composition, some historical references in the plot help establish its probable chronological place in Cueva's oeuvre. The historical background is the early sixteenth-century invasion of Spanish-held territory in the region of Naples. In particular, dialogue is devoted in Act 3 to the male protagonist's participation in an important battle that took place historically in 1503 near the Garigliano River. There the Spanish troops, under the leadership of Gonzalo Fernández de Córdoba (also known as the Gran Capitán), won a resounding victory against the French, who were forced to retreat. The celebration of this prominent indication of Spain's past strength and besting of her French antagonists may have been connected to Cueva's efforts to bolster her nation's sagging self-image. Her theatrical representation about mid-seventeenth century would coincide with the last decade of the Thirty Years' War (1618–48), a period marked by a renewal of intense struggles between Spain and France. In the year 1647, moreover, the kingdom of Naples itself revolted against Spanish domination. The revolt was quelled in 1648, but rivalry with France on multiple fronts as well as the steadily deteriorating effectiveness of the Hapsburg monarchs in Spain may have motivated Cueva to choose a renowned Spanish victory as the background for her play. Such a context suggests a date of composition from the 1630s to as late as the 1660s.

In consistent reiteration of an unfortunate pattern, a recent commentator on Feliciana Enríquez's life and works begins his introduction: "Little information is available about [her] life" (Pérez, *Dramatic Works,* 1). Relying on Santiago Montoto's earlier study of Enríquez, Louis C. Pérez places her probable birth date prior to 1580, in Seville. Born to Diego García de Torre and María Enríquez de Guzmán, the playwright and her sisters Magdalena and Carlota used their mother's maiden name, a common practice at that time and one which in this case is attributed by Pérez to the connection to Andalusian nobility it afforded (*Dramatic Works,* 1). Enríquez's first marriage in 1616 was to Cristóbal Ponce Solís y Farfán, an older widower who, after three years of marriage, in turn left his wife a widow and patron of a chaplaincy that supported her economic needs.[13] Four months after Ponce's death, Enríquez married Francisco de León Garavito, a union which like her first brought her no children but lasted much longer. After Garavito's death in 1630 widowed her for a second time, neither her chaplaincy nor a subsequent arrangement that afforded her directorship of a *patronazgo* secured her financial well-being. She spent the last part of her life in conditions of poverty, forced to accept charity from an Augustinian order with which her late husband's brother, Lorenzo Ribera de Garavito, was affiliated. Like Caro, she may have died around 1647 during the epidemic that killed so many people in Seville (Pérez, *Dramatic Works*, 2–3).

Also interesting, not for its historical validity but rather for its mythic quality, is the connection traced and accepted by numerous nineteenth-and early twentieth-century scholars between Enríquez and the figure Feliciana, praised by Lope de Vega in his *Laurel del Apolo*.[14] In one section of this long poem, Lope writes of a woman so named who donned male clothing and went to study at the University of Salamanca, where she lived as a male student until she fell in love with a certain Don Félix and abandoned her disguise. As Pérez notes, critics as noteworthy as Marcelino Menéndez Pelayo, Emilio Cotarelo y Mori, and Blanca de los Ríos have accepted the equivalence of Enríquez with the character Lope describes, and "they also see a very strong similarity between [the dramatist] and Doña Jerónima, one of Tirso de Molina's heroines" (*Dramatic Works*, 5). Yet others, such as Mario Menéndez Bejarano contend: "It's unbelievable that Menéndez y Pelayo could have accepted such an absurd legend" (quoted in Pérez, 7).[15] The fantastic and legendary quality associated with the woman Lope describes bespeaks the equally implausible and preposterous value attributed to Enríquez by the earlier scholars of Golden Age literature who find a woman's presence among the canonical writers so phenomenal.

Also important in Enríquez's dramaturgy are her theoretical tracts, which are either woven into her dramas directly—as in her "Prólogo" to *Primera parte*—or appear as separate pieces such as those found in her "Carta ejecutoria" and "A los lectores," following *Segunda parte* in the 1627 edition of the plays. As discussed in Chapter 5, Enríquez interrogates the relationship of a female dramatist like herself to the Lopean *comedia nueva* and its predominantly male proponents. In her clever arguments about positioning herself as a supporter of the classical precepts of dramatic composition, she depends upon rhetorical ambiguities and contradictions in order to reveal the problematical nature of the woman author's claim to fame. Enríquez's two-part play and its accompanying *entremeses* and *coros* were published in two seventeenth-century editions, 1624 and 1627. The later edition, upon which is based my own anthologized edition of the *Segunda parte* and its two-part *entremés* and the aforementioned theoretical pieces (T. Soufas, *Women's Acts*), also incorporates numerous textual changes and corrections.[16]

María de Zayas's life is also, as two scholars recently note, "shrouded in mystery" (Welles and Gossy, 505). She was born probably around 1590 to María de Barasa and Fernando de Zayas y Sotomayor. Her father was a military officer who received the prestigious knighthood in the order of Santiago in 1638. The family seems to have accompanied him during his service to the Count of Lemos in Naples between 1610 and 1616. Madrid was the author's home for most of her adult life, and from 1621 to 1639 she was active in literary circles in that city, as recorded in her own occasional poems and in laudatory references to her by noted writers such as Juan Pérez de Montalbán, Lope de Vega, and Alonso de Castillo Solórzano. Pérez de Montalbán, for example, extols her in his *Para todos,* published in 1632: "Décima musa de nuestro siglo, ha escrito á los certámenes con grande acierto; tiene acabada una comedia de excelentes coplas, y un libro para dar á la estampa, en prosa y verso, de ocho novelas ejemplares" (359r). Her greatest fame rests on the two collections of prose works she published respectively in 1637 and 1647, but Montalbán's reference to her play indicates that if not actually performed, it must at least have circulated in manuscript form among her literary peers. Most of her life is undocumented; no evidence remains about a marriage, nor is her date of death certain.[17] The fact that she did not closely edit and correct her second collection of *novelas,* as she did her first, has led more than one scholar to speculate that she died in 1647.[18] Her play *La traición en la amistad* has been left to us in her autograph manuscript. Taking into account Pérez de Montalbán's 1632 reference to this drama and its own internal references to the War of Succession of Mantua (1628–30) as its background, one can reasonably assume that Zayas composed the play between 1628 and 1632.

I have arranged this study in chapters that allow consideration of similarities among the women's negotiations of social and artistic conventions. The issues I examine do not divide or separate themselves easily, however. Thus, whereas Chapter 2 deals with the dramatized representations by Caro and Cueva of women's difficult relationships to monarchy and monarchs, it also raises issues treated directly in Chapter 3 concerning the commodification of women as prizes to be bid on in the upper-class marriage markets within the troubled economic field of seventeenth-century Spain. The often portrayed cross-dressed woman on the Golden Age Spanish stage is a subject of Chapter 4, in which I also scrutinize, through a variety of cross-gendered characters in three plays, the fluidity of gendered identity—which, more firmly rooted in the orthodoxy of male political privilege than in biological sex—resonates throughout the other chapters as well. Chapter 5 examines one dramatist's more theoretical engagement of male authorial privilege, a cultural dimension that she and all the authors considered here had to confront and contend with while trying to locate and occupy a legitimate space in the intellectual and theatrical circles of early modern Spain.

As a starting point, I cite the words of one of María de Zayas's narrators in her second collection of short prose pieces: "Pues ni comedia se representa, ni libro se imprime que no sea todo en ofensa de las mujeres, sin que se reserve ninguna" (*Desengaños*, 124). This voice articulates an awareness of how popularized art forms such as the seventeenth-century theater and the more widely accessible sorts of printed literature reinforce and intersect with the cultural expectations of gender constructs that are promoted as natural. This juncture interests me as well, and I am mindful of the need to engage a critical and theoretical strategy that allows interpretive projects to bypass both an essentialist feminist approach that tends to measure women authors and their works against male models and a psychoanalytic approach that does look to woman as the focus of analysis but can fall into universalization without historicizing differences between women. Like Theodora Jankowski, I endorse the principle that "if we accept the fact that gender is a social construct, then we accept the fact that what is constructed can be 'deconstructed'" (4). Thus, I have based my approach to the plays of these five dramatists on new historicist practices that enable one to consider artistic literary texts within the context of a historical and ideological framework that includes nonartistic documents and cultural practices as well. It is here that this late twentieth-century critical undertaking must examine the issue of and demands for female silence with as much vigor as that with which the seventeenth-century women dramatists wrote their plays. Throughout this study I refer to the many Renaissance exhortations to silence and enclosure that appear in the treatises of philosophers and moralists from many European nations, including the seemingly progressive manuals about women's education.

Reiterated in those works is the insistence that women be excluded from the realm of public communication and relegated to the domesticity that occupies and develops within a very narrow range her physical and mental strengths. Citing an ancient Greek proverb, for example, Juan Luis Vives remarks at one point in his "Formación de la mujer cristiana" on the importance of keeping women away from discursive participation in society: "La tarea de la mujer es la tela y no los discursos" (1123).

In his *La perfecta casada,* Fray Luis de León expounds further the circular argument that imposes silence upon women: "Porque, así como la naturaleza . . . hizo a las mugeres para que encerradas guardasen la casa, así las obligó a que cerrasen la boca. . . . Porque el hablar nasce del entender . . . así como a la muger buena y honesta la naturaleza no la hizo para el estudio de las sciencias ni para los negocios de dificultades, sino para un solo oficio simple y doméstico, así les limitó el entender, y por consiguiente, les tasó las palabras y las razones" (175–76).

Proclaiming before the fact the limitations of a woman's intellect, patriarchal notions restrict her training and imply that her only strengths lie in quietly running the home and refraining from discursive participation in the social dimensions outside. A space is left open in such arguments, however, for the exception: that is, the woman who does exceed these expectations of "la mujer buena y honesta." Such a woman, by implication, would be exiled from the ranks of the respectable, since, as Ann Jones concludes about such issues in Renaissance culture, "in a woman, verbal fluency and bodily purity are understood to be contrary conditions" ("Surprising Fame," 78). Therefore, as I discuss further in Chapter 1, simply by writing their dramatic texts, these female dramatists transgressed the acceptable use of language that their society defined for them. Lacking the extensive access to the representational dimension of Spanish Golden Age theater that their male colleagues enjoyed, they seem at most—with the known exception of Caro's *autos*—to have been able to circulate their manuscripts among the members of intellectual circles; no real evidence about stagings of their plays has come to light. And so, a professional silence has enveloped their dramas.

With this in mind, therefore, I return to the coincidence of my approach to these works with that of Jankowski concerning the early modern English drama. Considering feminist postures, such as Elaine Showalter's encouragement about recourse to feminist theorizing as long as its basis remains women's experience, Jankowski focuses at one point on Ellen Messer-Davidow's suspicion of theoretico-critical language as yet another tool of patriarchal dominance that permits misreadings of female-authored texts. Messer-Davidow recommends approaching such texts "through a new biolanguage or rebellious silence" (65). Countering this position, Jankowski responds that "since language is as implicated in patriarchal ideology as literature or criticism, how can we, as women whose gender was constructed under such an ideology, create a language free of the masculinst taint?" Or, she continues, "if, as women, we accept a 'rebellious silence' as our critical alternative, we implicate ourselves still deeper in patriarchal ideology, an ideology that has for generations constructed our gender as 'silent.'" She concludes that an invocation to silence at any level becomes, in effect, an endorsement of "prevailing male critical methodologies no matter how sexist they may be" (3). My approach, then, is based on new historicist practices that permit not only opening up the discourse of and about a dramatic text as one among many textual productions within a historico-cultural framework but also considering gender as an important dimension in the representation of power relationships. I want to extend what we understand as the spatial and aural configuration of Spanish Golden Age theater so that criticism of it can include the dramas written by these no longer silent authors: Azevedo, Caro, Cueva, Enríquez, and Zayas.[19]

1

COMEDIA, GENDER, CONVENTION

... y ponen delante de los ojos las mujeres deshonestas, sus meneos y melindres, ¿ de qué otra cosa sirven sino de encender en lujuria a los hombres?

—Juan de Mariana

No salga a ver las mujeres de la tierra, no sea danzadora, ni juegue juegos de burlas, no vaya a públicos convites, no beba vino . . . ni salga fuera de casa.

—Gaspar de Andrade y Astete

Definitions of woman's nature and how she should fulfill the roles of constructed appropriateness were written and published by male humanists of the sixteenth and seventeenth centuries throughout Europe. Golden Age Spain is no exception to this field of discursive production, which inscribes the female in the symbolic as it institutionalizes her participation in culture and the limitations to her public agency. Seventeenth-century female dramatists, however, engaged the discourse on womanhood through representations of the social institutions in which the depicted women—royal, aristocratic, or from the middle nobility—lived and positioned themselves in compliance with or against the expectations of their portrayed society. What emerges from my reading of these plays as texts (albeit with speculative attention to their performability) is an encoded pattern of disruption for the ideological category "Woman," challenging the patriarchal insistence on the inherently natural quality of the two-gendered hierarchy that assigns women to enclosure and silence and men to public and vocal exercise of agency. Whereas the universalization of women to "woman" is scrutinized and resisted in dramatizations of female characters attending to the chaos that results from their male companions' abuse of the essentializing hierarchized system, these same depicted women resort to demonstrating the construction of gender roles in order to reestablish the abandoned order and privilege they are able to enjoy under the system that invokes the naturalness of femininity and masculinity.

The approach I take to these plays, to their place in the network of dramatic production in seventeenth-century Spain and the ideological assumptions they encode, interrogates these matters within a larger context of the concerns of Renaissance thinkers, which anticipate the feminist debates so strongly argued in our postmodern era over essentialism and constructionism. As Constance Jordan demonstrates in her discussion of the history of feminist social issues, there is a "fundamental discrimination between a feminism that finds its rationale in a conception of the individual . . . and a second kind of feminism that posits as its point of critical departure the essentially different experience of women in contrast to men" (7). Following Karen Offen's arguments in this regard, Jordan explains that the first sort described, termed "individualist," is grounded in "a concern for the autonomy of the female subject, particularly in relation to law and politics"; the second, or "relational" type appreciates "what women are and do in contrast to what men are and do" (7). Offen adds that relational feminism, which is older, "proposed a gender-based but egalitarian vision of social organization . . . that featured the primacy of a companionate, non-hierarchical, male-female couple as the basic unit of society, whereas individualist arguments posited the individual, irrespective of sex or gender, as the basic unit" (135). These two positions are evident in Renaissance feminism, which "can fairly be analyzed in individualist and relational terms" (Jordan, 8).

The individualist model resonates in the work of current proponents of the constructionist stance, who "take the refusal of essence as the inaugural moment of their own projects and proceed to demonstrate the way [that] previously assumed self-evident kinds (like 'man' or 'woman') are in fact the effects of complicated discursive practices" (Fuss, 2). Renaissance feminists, in an age that "saw little meaning in sexual—that is, physiological—difference," understood a human being as biologically male or female "but behavioristically both masculine and feminine if virtuous" (Jordan, 8). Still operative is the classical and medieval epistemological system in which everything in the universe is explicable with reference to its relationship to something else.[1] Thus, Galen "cited homologies in the genital structure of the sexes to show that male and female were versions of the same unitary species. The female genitals were simply the male genitals inverted, and carried internally rather than externally" (Orgel, "Nobody's Perfect," 13).

In concert with such thought, Thomas Laqueur has recently explicated "the corporeal theatrics of a world where at least two genders correspond to but one sex, where the boundaries between male and female are of degree and not of kind, and where the reproductive organs are but one sign among many of the body's place in a cosmic and cultural order that transcends biology. . . . The one-sex/one-flesh model dominated thinking about sexual difference from classical antiquity to the end of the seventeenth century." (25). Stephen Orgel argues for the "interchangeability of sexes" as an "essential assumption of [Renaissance] culture as a whole" (12); Laqueur adds that into the seventeenth century, "to be a man or a woman was to hold a social rank, to assume a cultural role, and not to *be* organically one or the other of two sexes. Sex was still a sociological, not an ontological, category" (142).

What is played out in the dramatic works under examination is a recognition of the social roles assumable according to one's determined bodily assignment. A female body gave one a certain range of possibilities within the sociopolitical arena; a male body afforded a different and, generally, wider range. This is not to say, however, that the roles were not interchangeable. If the social conditions were altered or the sex of the body disguised, then the person's gendered identity and privileges could be called into question and at times even exchanged. The tension resulting from "the proper relation between the biological functions of the female body and behavior . . . designated culturally as feminine" became the focus of many Renaissance feminist writers, among them the Spanish dramatists considered here, as they investigated the ideological grounding that Jordan explains in the following terms: "A woman's experience is obviously both of her femaleness and of her femininity; Renaissance feminists would also add that she has or can have an experience of masculinity" (82 n. 20). The individualist model is not easily separated from the relational model in such a system of thought, and what Diana Fuss contends in discussing the interconnection of essentialism and constructionism in postmodern feminist arguments is evident in an anticipatory manner in the Renaissance arguments about women.

Modern notions of essentialism invoke an Aristotelian definition of essence as "that which is most irreducible, unchanging, and therefore constitutive of a given person or thing" (Fuss, 2). As numerous scholars explain, essentialism presents problems in its nod to the stability across time and cultures of what is understood by "man" and "woman." For some feminist theoreticians, however, essentialism invokes an original or female essence invulnerable to the pressures of patriarchal influence. Constructionists, on the other hand, inquire into essence as a historical construction produced by discursive practices that attribute naturalness or self-evidence to what for them are processes of social determination. Passing through a number of intriguing critical strategies, Fuss ponders the ways essentialism is "embedded in the idea of the social and lodged in the problem of social determination" and undergirds antiessentialist and deconstructive discourse. She questions "the essentialist/constructionist divide" by interrogating the "'constructionist' assumption that nature and fixity go together (naturally) just as sociality and change go together (naturally). In other words, it may be time to ask whether essences can change and whether constructions can be normative" (6). Confronting the notion of the "risk of essence," a term coined by Stephen Heath in a 1978 essay, Fuss turns to Derrida's particular invocation of "risk" in daring to speak as a woman. She writes: "For a male subject to speak as a woman can be radically de-essentializing; the transgression suggests that 'woman' is a social space which any sexed subject can fill." She continues: "But because Derrida never specifies *which* woman he speaks as (a French bourgeois woman, an Anglo-American lesbian, and so on), the strategy to speak as woman is simultaneously re-essentializing. The risk lies in the difficult negotiation between these apparently contradictory effects" (19).[2]

Fuss likewise takes up the issue of the distinction between "deploying" or "activating" essentialism and "falling into" or "lapsing into" essentialism (20). As she argues, the latter two terms imply an accidental or mistaken step into a reactionary stance, whereas the former two terms suggest strategy or intervention:

What I am suggesting is that the political investments of the sign "essence" are predicated on the subject's complex positioning in a particular social field, and that the appraisal of this investment depends not on any interior values intrinsic to the sign itself but rather on the shifting and determinative discursive relations which produced it. . . . The radicality or conservatism of essentialism depends, to a significant degree, on *who* is utilizing it, *how* it is deployed, and *where* its effects are concentrated. [20]

Borrowing from as well as critiquing Gayatri Spivak's challenge to and sanction of the Subaltern Studies group's strategic recourse to essentialism as a provisional gesture, Fuss also invokes a Foucauldian poststructuralist notion of subject position, which allows her to urge that "in the hands of a hegemonic group, essentialism can be employed as a powerful tool of ideological domination; in the hands of the subaltern, the use of humanism to mime (in the Irigarian sense of to undo by overdoing) humanism can represent a powerful displacing repetition" (32). Spivak indeed provides a way to insert the notion of choice and a way to move between subject positions, in spite of poststructuralism's deconstruction of agency and free will, by asserting, says Fuss, that the "social vacancies . . . are of course not filled in the same way by different individuals" (34). Urging her own readers to resist the tendency toward taxonomies and stereotyping of Michel Foucault's subject positions in the context of the theory of reading, Fuss reiterates the benefits of such a theory and the "shifting grounds of subjectivity" (35).

Turning to the theoretical feminist strategies operative in the arguments and literary works of the early feminists in seventeenth-century Spain, one finds their invocation of Renaissance culture's blurred boundaries of sexual identity that empowers a human being to occupy the social space of either gender. This move simultaneously deessentializes through its transgression of the constructed norm and reessentializes by means of validating the sexed category for imitation. The early modern feminists take an admittedly classist position that accords validity to certain individualist/constructionist strategies and performances in order to reestablish their version of the relational/essentialist social model; in that version, "what women are and do and what men are and do" can remain distinct but avoid the potentially abusive distortions of the gendered hierarchy that the patriarchal version of the relational/essentialist model promotes. In these approaches, one finds in the work of seventeenth-century female authors a dimension of convergence with twentieth-century feminist minds. Additionally, as has been argued recently, the epistemological grounding of Spanish thought in that period shares assumptions common to postmodern theoretical attacks on subjectivity and autonomous individuality. Post-formalist understanding of textuality conceives of texts not as self-referential artifacts but rather as components woven into an all-encompassing and interreferential textual network and part of the inescapable structure of language; the context of the Spanish *comedia,* for example, is also a macrocosmic structure (Soufas and Soufas, *"Vida,"* 295). This configuration understands all things, including texts, as means rather than as ends in themselves that refer only to the possibility of an awaiting closure—not a self-referential closure but the resolution of death, which becomes the definitive closure to the performance of life on earth. Dramatic characters find success or ruination in proportion to their recognition that they are by themselves insufficient means to accomplish a resolution. This model, often invoked as the evidence of Spanish theocentric difference from the rest of (secular) Europe, can instead be seen as evidence of Spain's engagement of the emerging secular ideology of seventeenth-century Europe through a premise that anticipates postmodern culture's proclamation of the insufficiency of ideologies that place great value on the autonomy of the individual.[3]

Expressions of individual subjectivity and difference from the norm were, above all, not encouraged in Renaissance women. Instead, silence, invisibility, and chastity were the qualities that Renaissance gender ideology demanded as evidence of female respectability. These gender constructs transcended the potential subdivisionary categories of class distinction: the male-dominated discourse inscribed a definable model of the gentleman from among the members of *man*kind, but as Ruth Kelso asserts about the Renaissance concept of the gentleman's class-privileged female counterpart, "There [was] no such thing as the lady so far as theory went, no formulated ideal for the lady as such, distinguished either from the gentleman or from any other woman" (1). She continues:

> Many books of a theoretical sort were written for and on the lady . . .
> but beyond the dedications to ladies, duchesses, or queens, the contents,
> it is scarcely an exaggeration to affirm, apply to the whole sex rather than
> to any favored section of it. . . . The purposes of these writers are too dis-
> parate and the elements too antithetic to each other; they have no
> central figure in common as the writers on the gentleman have. . . . The
> result is not the building up steadily from start to finish of an integrated
> ideal, as was the case with the gentleman, but a series of fresh starts and
> stops. [1–3]

The implications for this leveling of differences and divisions between
and among women of varied Renaissance social and cultural contexts
point to a conceptual commonality with regard to the gender constructs. As Emilia Navarro contends about the treatises on womanhood,
"taken as a constituting body of knowledge, these texts codify 'woman,'
i.e., a de facto univocal and supposedly universal term, a 'natural' term
if you will . . . [that] underscores gender and elides class" (19).[4]

One of the most obvious contexts of this leveling is apparent in the
humanist's advice about women's education. Although the most liberal
male humanists advocated instruction for women, their recommenda-
tions generally articulated a well-delineated restraint to this enterprise,
always with a view toward training the female for the domestic life and
wifehood and her function as a complement to the male. In Castiglione's imagined dialogue among male figures in the *Courtier,*
Giuliano de Medici, for instance, supports women's training and education within the context of the Renaissance court and urges that a
woman balance cleverness and charm (a "ready liveliness of wit") with
virtue and bodily purity ("sober and quiet manners") in order to prove
herself both *arguta* and *discreta* (343). As Ann Jones points out, the
female courtiers "were habitually seen and heard, as the onlookers and
the admiring chorus for men's self-display," and "the tension between
public accessibility and private chastity was acute" ("Surprising Fame,"
78). De Medici's insistence that a laudable woman must "keepe a certain mean very hard, and come just to certain limits" (Castiglione, 343)
implies not only that her speech and her bodily purity are contradictory
phenomena but also that however capable she may be of fuller intellectual and linguistic participation in public life beyond the "certain

limits," any attempt by her to exercise free expression automatically calls into question her social and moral reputation.

Kelso reminds us, moreover, that "education for the gentleman was a wide-flung subject, involving all that was called liberal and drawing on the best pedagogical advice of the time," whereas education for a woman "looked to her proficiency in domestic affairs and what in moral and religious training would keep her safely concerned only with them." Occupations for men included the spheres of government and warfare, as well as scholarly, mercantile, and agricultural pursuits, but "for women only one occupation was recommended—housewifery" (Kelso, 4). Despite the social reality that imposed different economic privilege or hardship on women from various class backgrounds, royal, aristocratic, bourgeois, and peasant women shared many aspects of the female's lack of choice. As the Renaissance dramatists depict it, however, marriage (and frequently preparation for marriage), even though considered a "natural" state for females, was a trouble-filled dimension that caused rather than resolved difficulties. The problems dramatized in many works arise in spite of the female characters' adherence to the caveats about silence, enclosure, and chastity. Moreover, in most of the plays studied here there is no represented anagnorisis for the female protagonists, a fact that underscores the limited range of options available to a woman or her dramatized counterpart, since to resume or to continue her life as it was before the depicted chaos threatened its stability, she must be free of the taint of conventionalized dishonor. A male character whose libertine ways are eventually brought under control is not ostracized from respectable social contexts, as his female peers can be and often are. The playwrights, therefore, have less leeway in dramatizing social disruption where their female characters are concerned. They can thus be located in the Renaissance feminist tradition that Jordan identifies, which organizes its definition of society's problems around male figures who have more opportunity both for transgression and for social redemption.

It is in this regard that a theoretical position emerges from the women dramatists' plays. Their critique of the construction of gendered differences presents a recognition of qualified interchangeability between the sexes, which the women figures invoke when necessary in order to cope with the injustices their male companions cause through a represented lack of respect for the constructed sociopolitical roles available to them in the imagined societies. The plays focus not so much on a need to eliminate the constructed groupings for men and women as on the ways gendered hierarchies could better serve cultural ends if the males would meet their responsibilities with more integrity. Again, such a perspective is in keeping with the concerns Jordan outlines as the Renaissance feminist project: "Renaissance feminists spoke of powerlessness and objectification, but they tended to see the wretched condition of women as a consequence of the moral perversion of men, who failed to live up to the challenge of being fully human. They sought recognition for women as females and exponents of the feminine but also as a reason to reform the distorted humanity of men, to bring the other half of the human race into line" (9).

This double focus sharpens the reader/spectator's reception of the depicted limitations and dangers for women both in the essentializing tendencies of humanistic discourse about their natural place in society and in the deessentializing construction of cultural identities that permits a fluidity of role assumption. In a pattern that is repeated in play after play, the men fail to live up to the best interpretation of the role assigned to them, and the women must step in to assume that role, only to fulfill it more successfully and to provide a model of comportment for the males around them. The assumption of a cross-gendered role or quality is not presented as a revolutionary suggestion for overthrowing the social system depicted; instead, the socially assigned roles are resumed at the end of the plays. Nevertheless, the counterdiscourse of flexible boundaries between the roles has been expressed.

The inability of society to maintain without effort and insistence the fixed status of women is theatrically and dramatically demonstrated by female characters, played in Spain by female actors, who exhibit their ability to step out of femininity and into masculinity. Since the reverse move is not generally enacted (one exception is an unconventional cross-dressed male in Azevedo's *El muerto disimulado*), the playwrights discussed here suggest their recognition of a useful and positive register for the so-called masculine exercise of agency through access to language and physical intervention.[5] Their own undertaking results in the production of texts and the dramatic proposition of an alternative to social and artistic convention that finds a parallel in the actions they portray through their female characters.[6] The changeability and instability of the subject positions as represented in the female-authored *comedias,* however, reveal the early modern understanding of ways in which identity depends upon circumstances, just as our present-day "intellectual discourse has redefined consciousness as something that cannot exist within a self-defining monadic ego independent of a circumstantial structure" (Soufas and Soufas, *"Vida,"* 300).

The drama as a visual and verbal representation makes particularly complex the presence of women on stage who are not silent or enclosed. On the basis of ancient authority such as Aristotle's exhortation "Silence is the virtue of woman as eloquence is of the man" (A. Jones, "Surprising Fame," 79), the humanists systematically denied to women the aspects of education that would train them in rhetorical argumentation and persuasion. This is a significant omission, as Joan Gibson argues, since "those aspects of rhetoric pertaining to delivery or to an active life were exactly the ones forbidden to women; women are to form an audience, not to seek one" (19). In Spain, Fray Luis de León expressed what others of his countrymen also advocated: "Como son los hombres para lo público, así las mujeres para el encerramiento y como es de los hombres el hablar y el salir a leer, así de ellas el encerrarse y encubrirse" (181–82). Vives likewise reiterated that "[d]el bien hablar no tengo ningún cuidado; no lo necesita la mujer . . . ni parece mal en la mujer el silencio" (1000). Such insistence in the manuals of behavior suggests the culturally imposed nature of this gender-specific silence and the fact that silence was to be learned by woman and imposed upon her by those who made themselves responsible for her instruction. Dramatic representation subverted this constraint by the very nature of the appearance and speech of female cast members on the public stage.

The Renaissance social organization and its underlying gender ideology, furthermore, posited the "fundamental assumption of the whole ideal of gentility . . . that some must rule and some be ruled. The first law of woman . . . was submission and obedience, exemplified in the beginning and for all time by our Mother Eve. Theory does not divide women into two groups, the rulers and the ruled, and prescribe to each a different set of laws on the basis of that relationship. Practice did just that, but not theory. Theory said that all women must be ruled" (Kelso, 3).

Citing studies by Robert Weimann and Louis A. Montrose, Ania Loomba contends that in Renaissance Europe "an increasing focus on discontinuous identity and on female changeability" were coterminous with interrogations about theatrical space and its regulation and limitation. Montrose's consideration of the connection between authority and the Renaissance stage is, argues Loomba, "analogous to that between authority and women" (130). She continues:

> The drive to limit and contain theatre space was concurrent with and similar to the effort to limit and contain women. In both cases transience, mobility, alteration, disguise and changeability are seen as subverting a dominant need for stability . . . Both women and theatre are seen to stray from their allotted spaces in various ways . . . Social and political boundaries are defied by the drama and women as they dress in the garments of their superiors, and if women are seen as attempting to usurp authority, the players are accused of inciting political trouble or rebellion. Ideologically, women threaten the demarcation of the "private" sphere and popular theatre resists the confinement of dramatic performance. [131][7]

The public individuated voice was not raised in any modern sense by anyone in the general population. The playwrights studied here, therefore, questioned the boundaries of the private and the public nature of intellectual activity as they composed dramas more likely to be read than to be performed publicly. A reading audience is a relatively more educated one that can consume dramatic texts through the private act of reading, rather than in a public playhouse heavily populated with the uneducated *vulgo*. Navarro contends that in Spain "and in other Counter Reformation countries, the emergence of reading as a private activity and its subversive potential was not lost on the Church, which forbade all individual readings of the Bible in the vernacular, precisely because it recognized its possible liberatory effects" (21). The enclosure and admonition against public speech directed toward women thus also posed transgression by the women who wrote for private intellectual circles.

Spanish Golden Age dramatic theory, in general, reasserted the seventeenth-century ideological construction of woman's silence in a variety of ways: through frequent portrayals of women as problematical instigators of a represented dilemma because of their use of oral and written language; through a dramatized male imposition of and obsession with the young woman's silence before her marriage; and through a relative lack of depiction of married women and an almost complete elimination of mothers, their absence reaffirming their silence and enclosure because in effect they disappear from dramatic representation once they become married women characters.[8] The gender constructs of Renaissance Europe are evident in the writings of moralists and philosophers such as Fray Luis and Vives, who, like their contemporaries in many countries, invoked the argument that a woman's sexual purity could be assured only by her silence and her invisibility to public gaze. The staging of a story necessarily interfered with such demands, since the female characters spoke and gestured before an interior and an exterior audience composed in part or even primarily of men whose represented gaze and listening faculties objectified and critiqued this public display. Much sixteenth-and seventeenth-century criticism of the *comedia* in the numerous rounds of debate about its appropriateness attacked the presence of women on the stage, almost invariably connecting their appearance with suspicions about lascivious practices and the inspiration of lustful desire in the men who viewed them. On similar issues in Elizabethan theater, Sue-Ellen Case comments, "The female gender had become the custodian of male sexual behaviour, which it instigated and elicited. The female body had become the site for sexuality. If women performed in the public arena, the sexuality inscribed upon their bodies would elicit immoral sexual responses from the men, bringing disorder to the social body" (*Feminism* 20).

It is thus not surprising to find that in the then contemporary denunciations of the *comedia,* the target of condemnation is actually a variety of supposed consequences of the female presence both on the stage and in the theater. Most frequently, the sight and sound of the woman enacting her role are said to incite men to lustful thoughts and actions. In his *Tratado de la comedia* of 1613, for example, Juan Ferrer compares what he perceives to be the greater danger of hearing and seeing a romantic plot performed as compared to the act of reading amorous poetry: "Pues si la poesía (en materia de amores), leída tiene la fuerza que dicen estos autores, ¿qué será oída y representada, dándole los vivos colores y subiéndola de punto con el donaire del decir, con la desenvoltura en los meneos y gestos, con la suavidad de la música y instrumentos, con lustre de buenos y gallardos vestidos, en boca de una mujercilla de buena cara, de no buenas costumbres y mucha libertad y desenvoltura, qué efectos podrá causar?" (Cotarelo y Mori, 252).

In keeping with Case's observations, this disparaging image of the female actor as a *mujercilla* is enhanced by the description of her as illicitly free and wanton, as a physically appealing model of gestures and sound invested with an inescapable power of attraction, as the object of patriarchal desire who nevertheless is said to bear the guilt for this attraction. Ferrer's insistence upon the lack of restraint evident in the woman performer's behavior and morals indicates his circular argument that the male observer thus cannot control himself after having witnessed the woman's performance. The influence of her *desenvoltura* emanates further still, for Ferrer claims that these women "van cobrando más gracia y más donaire, mayor libertad y desenvoltura, y así van estragando y dañando cuando más va, más a la república" (Cotarelo y Mori, 252). The moral danger that the publicly displayed woman represents for men becomes as well a political danger for the nation whose active male citizens can be thus distracted from civic and patriotic duty—yet are not derided here for their own lack of restraint.

In the contemporary, anonymous *Diálogo de las comedias* of 1620, the freedom from enclosure, silence, and social control becomes the focus of attack with regard to women's presence and influence in the theater. One discussant contends that it is not "la hermosura, ni la sabiduria, ni la nobleza, ni la discrepción destas mugercillas lo que hace el daño." The affected men who "tienen mugeres muy discretas y hermosas y nobles y de iguales partes con ellos . . . las dejan por esotras." Familial stability is also put at risk, then, and the *Dialogo's* author encourages factionalism among women, breaking them into categories of *muy discretas* and *nobles*—by implication, more like their male companions and relatives than like *esotras*. The conclusion drawn is therefore that "lo que les lleva es la desenvoltura y la desvergüenza y el brío y libertad de las tales, y sólo la apariencia y representación es lo que con esta desenvoltura los arrebata" (Cotarelo y Mori, 216).

Similarly, Juan Bautista Fragoso writes in 1630, "En las comedias escritas en nuestra vulgar se mezclan muchas cosas impúdicas y obscenas, porque se introducen mujeres de no mucha edad á danzar y cantar, las cuales con su garbo y movimiento y con la desenvoltura de su semblante introducen en los que las ven y oyen el amor torpe" (Cotarelo y Mori, 320). The presence of women in the performance is presented as the source of obscenity ("*porque* se introducen mujeres"), but as in the moralistic writings generally, here too she is characterized as the passive object of observation, discussion, critique, and disapproval and yet the active agent of lust.

Also presented, moreover, is the argument that female participants in the dramas seem not to perform as subjective agents but to have been sent into dramatizations for commercial reasons by those who control the acting companies. In his *Agricultura christiana* of 1589, Juan de Pineda's interlocutor charges: "que porque salgan más gustosas las representaciones meten mugeres en ellas, porque como con cebo más atractivo concurrirán más mujeriegos. Y también aquí ha lugar la doctrina de los santos, que con tal cebo pesca el diablo muchas almas" (Cotarelo y Mori, 505). Through such arguments, women in the theater become associated with a dual function as both entrepreneurial and diabolical bait for unwary male clients and their souls.

The effect on women, young and old, of attending a theatrical performance was likewise a concern recorded on the negative side of the debate about the *comedia*. It was claimed that witnessing the fictitious portrayals of adultery, tricks against husbands and male guardians, and participation in love affairs would inspire the women in the audience to imitate the artistic depiction in their real life attitudes and behavior. A late seventeenth-century treatise by José Saenz de Aguirre contains the following assertion: "A cada paso sucede que los que van al teatro honestos y continentes salen absolutamente trocados. ¡Cuántas doncellas y castas matronas que sostuvieron íntegra su virtud se ven allí arder en el amor impuro, del que antes no habían sufrido sensación alguna, y perdiendo insensiblemente el pudor y recato, llegan á corromperse!" (Cotarelo y Mori, 49). The author of the anonymous *Diálogo* of 1620 also refers to the corrupting effect of the female actor upon the women spectators: Oírla decir palabras en público que nunca en hecho de verdad se atrevió muger á ser tan sinvergüenza . . . ¿no es cosa llana que todas estas vistas y palabras son provocativas á mal, son lazo, son veneno? ¿Qué han de aprender allí las doncellas que en su vida tal vieron ni oyeron, qué las casadas que se criaron con vergüenza y recogimiento? (Cotarelo y Mori, 213).

Ferrer likewise agrees that women can only be led astray by going to the theater: "¿Qué han de hacer después sino repetir y practicar la lición que en la comedia aprendieron?" (Cotarelo y Mori, 253). García de Loaise y Girón envisions a sort of negative metamorphosis for the women who view *comedias*: "Y lo peor es que la matrona ó doncella que por ventura vino á la comedia honesta, movida de la suavidad de conceptos y ternura de palabras, vuelve deshonesta" (Cotarelo y Mori, 393). According to Juan de Mariana, an additional result of women's presence in the audience is their neglect of what he considers their more proper duties: "Quitada la vergüenza y menospreciado el cuidado de la casa, concurrirán, sin poder tenerlas, lo que sabemos hacerse en este tiempo, y que muchas veces, antes del mediodía, dejan las casas por tomar lugar á propósito para ver la comedia que á la tarde se representa" (Cotarelo y Mori, 432–33). Juan de Pineda complains, furthermore, that "las mugeres que dicen ir por ver las tales representaciones, más van por representarse á sí mesmas y ser vistas de los que allí se hallaren" (Cotarelo y Mori, 506).

These diatribes against the female presence in the audience for theatrical performances evince the fact that there *were* women in attendance in the *corrales,* a point that Jean Howard (34) and Orgel ("Nobody's Perfect," 8) make about the theater in Renaissance England as well. In response to another anonymous treatise from the mid-seventeenth-century that offers an apology for the *comedia,* a contemporary invective comes from Gonzalo Navarro Castellanos in his *Discursos políticos y morales:* " Pues si tantas virtudes halla en las comedias, si son tan honestas y decentes y la escuela mejor de las virtudes, diga ¿por qué razón . . . las mujeres castas se avergüenzan de asistir á ellas en público? ¿Por qué . . . guardan sus frentes . . . con sus mantos? ¿Por qué no van con la cara descubierta á los teatros como á los templos?" (Cotarelo y Mori, 150). Such a passage alludes to techniques of disguise—masks and covered faces—that women used in order to have freer access to theatrical performances. This ploy made attendance itself a performance; it allowed female audience members to be watched but not recognized and also to assume the role of observer and thus remain a step beyond the male control that sought to monitor and enclose them.

Despite proscriptions to the contrary, the public presence of women on stage and in the audience was simultaneously acknowledged and hailed as a threat to the rigidity of culturally determined gender categories. Likewise, the critics voiced their concerns over the "femnization" of men as a result both of their enacting *comedia* parts and of their idle viewing of plays. Navarro Castellanos, in fact, included "los hombres graves" who hid behind "las celosías" with the masked "mujeres castas" at the theater as examples of inappropriate audience members (Cotarelo y Mori, 150). In such arguments a point of juncture for the varying debates over morals, political concerns, and gender ideology is evident. The supposed shift from the militaristic and physically powerful traits traditionally associated with masculinity to the culturally termed negative feminine characteristics of vanity, superficiality, and physical inactivity reflects the nationalistic views of conservative Spaniards who—for religious, economic, and political reasons—feared and resisted the influence of foreign countries. Attacks on the *comedia* often reveal combinations of anxieties that equate misogyny and xenophobia, both of which must be met, according to the arguments proffered, by a strong response from the traditional male defenders of culture.[9] A sixteenth-century treatise by Pedro de Rivadeneira (1589), for example, cites the stereotypical attributes of femininity introduced by theatrical performances as a detriment to the entire nation: "Pero no solamente se estragan las costumbres y se arruinan las repúbicas . . . esta manera de representaciones; pero hácese la gente ociosa, regalada, afeminada y mujeril" (Cotarelo y Mori, 522). Others who complain in similar terms about Spain's effeminate courtiers—too much given to excesses in fashion, entertainment, and vice—and the corrupting influences from external sources include Juan de Mariana, Pedro de Guzmán, Fray Juan de Santa María, and Juan Pablo Mártir Rizo (Elliott, 247, 251).

Some commentators make a clear distinction between the moral value of the appearance and demeanor of theatrical males and females in terms that continue the derision against women and their effect upon men. About the women's habit of wearing low-necked bodices and ornate attire, Ignacio de Camargo writes: "No se puede negar que las mugeres de este siglo han excedido infinito en la profanidad de los vestidos." He lists such characteristics as "la demasía de los adornos y afeites," "la superfluidad de las galas," and "la desnudez indecente de los trajes" (Cotarelo y Mori, 126). These are not his real target of complaint however, since, as he claims, "no es en realidad tan monstruoso, ni de tanto que hacer á la admiración por ser como natural achaque de un sexo fragil y vano." He continues: "Mas, ¿quién jamás pensara ver á los hombres nacidos solo para nobles y varoniles empresas abatidos á tan bajos y afeminados empleos que apenas se distinguen de las mugeres? . . . De dónde pueden nacer estos viles y afeminados afectos sino . . . de los patios de las comedias" (Cotarelo y Mori, 126).

Orgel's further comments about the English theater are pertinent here as well. He contends that the dread of effeminization is of central importance in the period's discussions of manhood, and that such a fear "also, in a much more clearly pathological way, underlies the standard arguments against the stage in anti-theatrical tracts from the time of the church fathers on." As Camargo's words quoted above show, this explanation applies to Spain as well as to England, which is Orgel's stated focus of examination: "In this context, the very institution of theater is a threat to manhood and the stability of the social hierarchy, as unescorted women and men without their wives socialize freely, and (it follows) flirt with each other and take each other off to bed" ("Nobody's Perfect," 15).

Such concern for guarding the gender categories and resultant limitations upon the feminine, however, meant that in addition to seeking to restrict or eliminate women's presence on the stage, critics simultaneously denigrated the practice—fully institutionalized in England, for example—of having boys and young men enact female parts. Melveena McKendrick notes that the Council of Trent "had clearly been convinced that it was better for women to appear on stage than for boys to dress up and act as women" (*Theatre*, 203). Decades later, the 1620 *Diálogo* contains an exchange between the two discussants about the possibility that "sólo representasen hombres, y las figuras de muger hiciesen mozuelos sin barba." The option is quickly discounted, however, with reference to "tiempos pasados" when "se quitaron las mujeres y se experimentaron graves peligros en que entrasen mozuelos" (Cotarelo y Mori, 217). The composers of *Consulta del Consejo* of Castile, writing to Philip III in 1600 about the restrictions that ought to be imposed on the recent reinstatement of theatrical presentations in Spain, cautiously support the use of female actors in appropriate parts: "Parece al Consejo que es de mucho menos inconveniente, que mugeres representen, que muchachos en hábito de mugeres" (Cotarelo y Mori, 164).

Censure of this sort again provides evidence that the practice warned against was current.[10] Spanish companies included both women actors and boys who played female parts, but most vehement are the invectives against female actors appearing dressed as men. Ignacio de Camargo (1689) writes: "¿Qué cosa más torpe y provocativa que ver á una muger de esta calidad que estaba ahora en el tablado dama hermosa afeitada y afectada, salir dentro de un instante vestida de galán airoso, ofreciendo al registro de los ojos de tantos hombres todo el cuerpo que la naturaleza misma quiso que estuviese siempre casi todo retirado de la vista? ¿Pues qué sería si en este traje danzase como lo hacen muchas veces?" (Cotarelo y Mori, 124). Ferrer likewise complains that the contemporary custom of women being seen "en hábito de hombres por las calles y por las casas, con tanto daño de sus almas y de las ajenas" is a direct result of "el verse cada día en las comedias mujeres representar en hábito de hombres," a practice that "ha hecho perder el miedo y la vergüenza á cosa en que tanta la había de tener de buena razón" (Cotarelo y Mori, 253). An earlier treatise by Fray José de Jesús María (1600) similarly attacks "una cosa tan vedada y detestable por leyes divinas y humanas, como es que la mujer se vista en traje de hombre" (Cotarelo y Mori, 381). Mariana (1609) complains in comparable terms about the effect of such masquerade upon the men who view these female actors playing their assigned roles "en forma y traje y hábito . . . aún de hombres, cosa que grandemente despierta á la lujuria y tiene muy gran fuerza para corromper los hombres" (Cotarelo y Mori, 431).

As is the case with much of the writing by Renaissance moralists, from the most conservative traditionalist to the most broad-minded humanist, the authors of such tracts are frequently addressing a male readership with whom they share ideas about what is proper, appropriate, and good for women. Passages written by the cleric José de Barcía y Zambrana in the late seventeenth century, for instance, exemplify male-to-male communication about female behavior. Writing directly to the "padres cristianos" with regard to daughters, he urges:

> ¿No viste a tu hija antes que viese comedia con una dichosa ignorancia de estos peligros que vivía como inocente paloma? ¿No la viste después, que abriendo los ojos a la malicia, supo lo que debiera ignorar? ya pide gala, ya desea salir, ya quiere ver y ser vista, y ya te da qué llorar o el casamiento desordenado ó el escándalo con que vive. . . . Pues no te quejes de los disgustos que recibes de tu hija, puesto que regaste el veneno de su apetito con las aguas del teatro. [Cotarelo y Mori 83]

What emerges from a consideration of seventeenth-century theatrical practices and critical discourse on the theater is an understanding of the *comedia* at the levels of both performance and literary form as a site of tension and struggle over license to express and represent transgressive alternatives to established cultural relationships and the exercise of power. The capacity of the dramatic experience to encompass the erasure of division lines between genders, social classes, and majority-minority relationships constitutes an implicit, if not explicit, concern for the moralists who argue against the theater's legitimacy. But the representational strategies of the Spanish women playwrights studied here challenge the socially constructed demands for women's silence and invisibility, and investigate the notion of interchangeability of genders as well. Within the conventions and traditions of dramatic portrayal, their dramas articulate and depict their resistance to the dramatized myth of woman as the compliant object of desire and exchange among men, which finds frequent portrayal on the *comedia* stage. Dramatized consistently in their works is the impossibility of adhering to the dichotomous demands made by the portrayed societies on the unmarried woman during the transition period between her availability for marriage and her entry into the role of wife. To be sure, the female protagonists in these plays are aristocratic or royal, and their particular privileges connected with an upper-class life carry with them the ambiguous advantages of education and freedom from the drudgery of a lower-class struggle or even a more middle-class involvement in family business undertakings. The upper-class woman's opportunities for more developed intellectual concerns, however, become an ambivalent entitlement, since the expectation is that she become an educated listener, an appropriate spouse for the man to whom she is matched. In commenting on the humanistic impulse to promote women's learning, Joan Kelly describes the women so educated as "daughters in revolt against fathers who schooled some of them for a society they forbade all women to enter" (69).

Also central to the dramatized transgression of the role of the unmarried, female aristocrat is the interrogation of the value of gendered differences within the tropological dimension of the world as theater. The elements that José Antonio Maravall associates with the baroque topos of the "mundo como teatro" include aspects that the playwrights challenge from the standpoint of gender—not only the transitory nature of the role assigned to each member of society but also its "rotación en el reparto, de manera que lo que hoy es uno mañana lo será otro." Likewise, Maravall argues, emphasis on appearance and insistence on the lack of coincidence between the surface and the "núcleo último de la persona" are elements contributing to the social tendency to "desvalorizar el mundo, sus pompas, sus riquezas, su poderío," but without forcing those who enjoyed these privileges to relinquish them (320–31). The women playwrights' sensitivity to such issues frequently leads to their dramatization of the tensions generated in seventeenth-century culture over the loss of confident dependence upon the socially hierarchized system. This suggests a further valorization of the critique of gender hierarchies. They put into play the period's anxieties over changes (or potential changes) in the exercise of control in what John Beverley identifies as the "paradoxical conjunction of the principle of submission to authority with the practical and theoretical ideal of the self-willed, independent individual" (225). Beverley continues with reference to the world-as-theater topos: "The Spanish Baroque is similarly aware of the 'semiotic' or arbitrary and contingent character of social authority and roles; on the other hand, it will also insist on the necessity of these remaining as they are" (221).

The women writers of Golden Age Spain considered here were persons of sufficient privilege to be able to take advantage of an education and exposure to artistic and literary expressions in composing their own works. From what can be termed a protofeminist posture they push numerous conventional categories to the limits in their plays but they do not advocate revolutionary change in the modern feminist sense. Rather, they critique from within by portraying the inadequacy of a social system that operated on the basis of adherence to hierarchical roles and power relationships at the same time that those roles were becoming obsolete with the emergence of the individual in Western culture: "Far from restoring the Scholastic principle of *comunitas,* based on the natural reciprocity of the hierarchically differentiated orders of society, Baroque culture tends precisely to interpellate the human subject as a solitary individual" (Beverley, 224). But the "solitary individual" is made a problematical entity in seventeenth-century Spanish thought and letters, which do not celebrate but engage dialectically and critically the "presence of the 'new man' on the European scene, the ascendant bourgeois individual whose materialistic philosophy is premised on the right of free thinking" (Soufas and Soufas, *"Vida,"* 301).

Likewise, although the female playwrights scrutinize and criticize the community through female characters, the women they portray do not approach their problems as a group or cohere in any sort of organized allegiance but, rather, insist on the need to restore the integrity of the ordered and hierarchical social patterns. Thus, the authors' target for dramatized challenge is the sector of society—the portrayed men—whose practice does not uphold the theory of the gender ideology undergirding the social differentiation that sets categories of people apart on the basis of wealth and rank. The women dramatists join their male colleagues in turning attention to the deterioration of morals, ethical values, and attendant rules of courtesy and interaction. Among the social problems frequently dramatized in the *comedia* are ignored promises, and elements such as a woman's sexual purity before marriage and the territorial and political integrity of the nation that are placed in the trust of male figures who prove more inclined to violate than to safeguard that custody.

Golden Age dramatic works can be understood as a discursive field incorporating dialectical images and practices generated by social and political institutions that promoted the predominant definitions of appropriate gendered behavior. Dramatic conventions reflect gender ideology with regard to woman's retirement from public view and as audience for rather than agent of speech. One result of the demand for women's silence, chastity, and enclosure appears in the dramatic representation of the role of wife and mother, a phenomenon considered by Emilie Bergmann within the context of "the process of women's disappearance from cultural discourse." Mothers, Bergmann writes, "virtually disappear as cultural protagonists in literary representation, and most notably in the multitude of treatises concerning women's behavior published in the sixteenth century. . . . [In the *comedia*] the near-absence not only of mothers but of any responsible adult women has thus far been invisible" (124–25). In fact, the *comedia* frequently includes references to mothers who have died in childbirth.

Jordan considers the challenge of the Italian humanist writer Beatrice Pia, who participated in the "struggle to come to terms with patriarchalism [that] resulted in an evaluation of the physical nature of women which contested what education and culture held was the inherent frailty of the sex" (142). The humanist exempla that provided laudatory accounts of masculine virtues and male strength were recast by Pia and others through interpretations suggesting that for "a woman to act like a man is for her to experience the virile dimension of her person, . . . [and the] heroines of the classical past are important to her less for their moral qualities than for their feats of physical endurance" (143). In particular, writes Jordan, Pia focused on the biological demands of childbirth and provided anecdotal evidence of the energy with which it is met that "defies processes of acculturation which have persuaded women to see themselves as weak" (143). "The Gaditine women," wrote Pia, "have been praised by historians because immediately after giving birth, they rose from their beds and proceeded with domestic tasks and they did not customarily lie in bed thirty or forty days as we do, emptying the larder of delicacies, robbing the henhouse and eating a ton of boar's meat. Because of this we do not know how to do such wonderful deeds as did the German women, who restored to battle order the army that was in flight from the enemy" (quoted in Jordan, 143).

A dual resonance of such a counterdiscourse on women is discernible in the women's plays of the Spanish Golden Age. Just as Pia indicates, although they dramatize that it is fully within the woman's capabilities to fulfill feats of strength culturally determined as masculine, when her male companions fail to do so, childbirth and motherhood are not necessarily the representational means for this display. Nevertheless, through their encoding of the conventional absence of a woman once she is married and becomes a mother—that is, she disappears from other spheres of social participation—the women dramatists recognize, evaluate, and emphasize the problem that the mother's absence creates for her children, both male and female. In all but one of the plays studied here, the mothers of the principal characters are dead (several are said to have expired in childbirth), and in each case the gender imbalance in the familial configuration is noted and lamented, daughters especially being depicted as suffering because of a mother's absence.

In particular, the dichotomy between marriage and the courtship and preparations that led to it mixes private and public attitudes that in sixteenth-and seventeenth-century European culture rested heavily upon the woman's calculated economic, moral, and social value—determined publicly by what she did not do or say except in private and what was arranged for her between the interested men. Margaret King's study of women during the Renaissance, for example, addresses marriage as a problematical area for the fathers of daughters. King points out that the daughters had to relinquish their rights to paternal property, other than the dowry, and the ability to choose a partner according to sexual choice: "Parents chose husbands for their daughters and negotiated property settlements largely without their participation" (32). The value of woman as a commodity of exchange between men "was predicated on the value of the woman as a vessel that would generate legitimate children," Jordan points out, and so pregnancy as an involuntary signifier of sexual activity was a useful symbol for misogynists: it indicated woman's dependency or, if linked with scandalous and unsanctioned union, her "inherent moral debility." A woman's body can reveal her sexual activity, whereas a man's does not, and so her procreative potential becomes an argument in support of efforts to restrict her (29).

The plays by the five women playwrights studied here show a significant shift in the politics of marriage arrangements. Dramatized frequently is a mishandling of marriage contracts by the males involved. This state of affairs entails a range of issues that the female characters must confront in order to overcome the depicted bias against their exercise of agency in matters of the heart. Even when their activities are not regulated by a male relative, the women characters contend with a portrayed society that restricts the ways in which they can respond to the abusive entitlement of male authority and its posture of superiority with regard to women's intellectual, physical, and moral capacities. In comparison with other literary undertakings, the theater was a risky site of moral contention among forms of artistic creativity to which a woman might contribute her own works. A performed play is a most public medium for expression, providing roles and represented moments in which female actors speak and move in front of onlookers. Breaking the rules of silence and enclosure put into question the involved woman's views on chastity and propriety, and thus the theater was a more difficult arena for participation on the part of women authors than were other means of composition.[11]

It is indeed the case that little is known about the performance, if any, of the plays studied here. In seventeenth-century Spain, where manuscripts circulated freely but protected published works were much less the norm than today, it is highly likely that plays by women passed from one to another of their literary peers, as did male-authored dramas. But for the women's plays, unlike the men's, there is no information about stagings, successful or otherwise. Such a silence reiterates the general silencing of women and suggests that what was written into female-authored *comedias* was experimental just because of its authorial source. Enríquez de Guzmán made of these conditions the very requirements for the reception of her two-part play, renouncing the public *corrales* in favor of the salons and palaces where she intended her works to be read, if not staged. The plays by Zayas and Cueva quite likely had the same fate, though they were perhaps not so determinedly directed to such a medium of exposure. Because Caro was a recognized professional among the writers of her time, it is inviting to speculate about the staging of her two secular plays, but so far no records of these performances have surfaced. As a court attendant to Philip IV's wife, Isabel de Borbón, Azevedo quite possibly secured palace audiences for her works.

The presumed private or textual consumption of these plays suggests the prevalence of the humanistic vision of the educated woman as a decorative adornment and a participant in the leisure activities of the increasingly more decadent and politically inactive courtly and upper-class elite. What the five dramatists consider through their compositions are different ways to configure the traditional components of secular dramas by theorizing the disruption of an assigned and internalized gendered category. They present women characters whose words and actions unsettle any potential cohesion among themselves and their female peers. The universalization of the category Woman is dislocated and deessentialized, yet simultaneously the characters' efforts move them and their male companions toward a reestablishment of the relational union of men and women which in turn reessentializes the gendered norms and their basis in class hierarchies and privilege. Such a phenomenon dramatizes the possibility and the capability of an overlap of the theatrical and the dramatic.

2

BODIES OF AUTHORITY

El conde Partinuplés (Caro)
and *La firmeza en la ausencia* (Cueva)

Por grande que sea en estado, y por generosa que sea en sangre una
muger, tam bien le parece en la cinta una rueca como al cavallero una
lança y al letrado un libro, y al sacerdote su hábito.
—Pedro Luján, *Coloquiales matrimoniales*

The world finds no usefulness in women except the bearing of children.
—Baldassare Castiglione, *The Courtier*

En la mujer nadie busca la elocuencia, ni el talento, ni la prudencia, ni el
arte de vivir, ni la administración de la República.
—Juan Luis Vives, "De la formación de la mujer cristiana"

Essentialist tenets underlay early modern monarchical authority and invested the male sovereign with a supposed natural advantage over his
female counterpart; biblical and classical principles were interpreted to
assign to woman the domesticated position of the silent and enclosed
wife of a politically active and articulate husband. Gynocracy was thus a
rarity in the Europe of this period. Vives's treatise "Formación de la
mujer cristiana," written for Queen Catherine of Aragon concerning the
education of her daughter Mary, for instance, is exemplary in its reiteration of the notion that the familial structure with the male head of
household is the natural model for government as well. With reference
to "las leyes que la Naturaleza sancionó," he posits: "En el matrimonio,
como en el ser humano, el varón representa al alma; la mujer, al cuerpo;
a aquélla le compete mandar; a éste le toca servir. . . . Declaró esta misma
subordinación esencial la Naturaleza, que hizo al varón más apto para
el gobierno que la mujer." He continues with reference to Saint Paul's

injunction: "La cabeza del varón es Cristo; la cabeza de la mujer es el varón," to which he adds, "loca y temeraria es la mujer a quien no manda el marido" (1086). Later in the same work Vives cites the example of Queen Mary of Burgundy, who married Charles V's grandfather, Emperor Maximilian I:

A la reina doña María, mujer del emperador Maximiliano, habíale tocado en herencia de su padre Carlos esta tierra y condado de Flandes. Como tuviesen los flamencos en menguada opinión la llaneza y apacibilidad de Maximiliano y acudieran a doña María para todos los negocios de aquel dominio, jamás quiso ella determinar cosa alguna de poder absoluto sin consultarlo primero con su marido, cuya voluntad tuvo siempre por ley. . . . Y así fué que doña María, en muy breve tiempo, puso a su marido en la mayor autoridad, dándole las máximas atribuciones. [1104]

With this arrangement, Vives assures his female royal reader, "aquel Estado fué el más obdiente a sus príncipes, y a uno y otra prestaba reverencia igual, como si cada uno de los dos consortes sostuviese y sustentase la indivisa majestad de entrambos" (1104). Thus, as Jordan points out, "Vives's woman (like Erasmus's) is to live in two ways, presenting herself as one who is choosing and willing her destiny, and at the same time observing those immutable proprieties that attend her state of life" (118).

The relational model that the Renaissance feminists invoked in order to assert the equality of men and women and their harmonious and nonhierarchical pairing was instead used by male humanists such as Vives to reaffirm the inequality of the sexes, confirm male hegemony, and proclaim that national as well as familial stability depended upon the subordination of woman to man. Jordan further remarks that in his instructions to the Princess Mary Vives's

makes it clear that he does not think that she, a woman, can function as a monarch. For she cannot produce an heir to the throne without marrying, and she cannot marry and govern, since for a woman of any rank whatever not to be subordinate to her husband in all respects is to violate the laws of nature and thus to lose the . . . respect her rank entitles her to. . . . Far from assuming command, she was to be servile and self-effacing; in effect, to follow rules set for all wives and in some instances of exceptional rigor.[118]

Kelso's contention about the flattening out of different categories of women into the universalized Woman is thus evident in expectations for female monarchs. These limitations imposed upon women, whose gender cannot transcend social and political privilege, provide a context for the readings to follow. It is likewise helpful to consider authority and its exercise from the point of view of gender in Caro's *El conde Partinuplés* and Cueva's *La firmeza en la ausencia* and to ponder the concepts and terms that are often confused with it.[1] Authority suggests obedience through which subjects still retain their liberty; the obedience demanded of them does not result from the imposition of power or violence upon them (Arendt, 106, 92-93). Hannah Arendt contends that "authority precludes the use of external means of coercion; where force is used, authority itself has failed." Persuasion and authority, she explains, are likewise irreconcilable, since persuasion implies "equality and works through a process of argumentation. . . . [If] authority is to be defined at all, then, it must be in contradistinction to both coercion by force and persuasion through arguments." This view rests on an understanding of authority as "always hierarchical": "The authoritarian relation between the one who commands and the one who obeys rests neither on common reason nor on the power of the one who commands; what they have in common is the hierarchy itself, whose rightness and legitimacy both recognize and where both have their predetermined stable place" (93). The essentialism of gender ideology that invokes nature and the inherent capacity of the male to rule and of the female to serve are instrumental here in preserving a common recognition of the "rightness and legitimacy" of kingship as opposed to queenship.

Pondering such definitions of authority and the implications of the designation and institutionalization of social hierarchies, Kathleen B. Jones questions the resultant sociopolitical construction of "the separation of women qua women from the process of 'authorizing.'" She too recognizes that the traditional concepts of authority cast it as a form of male privilege that silences the female voice and the "forms of expression linked metaphorically and symbolically to 'female' speech" (120).

The Renaissance humanists invoke such standards through their insistence that "el callar era el más gracioso atavío femenino" and upon the connection between the closed mouth and a woman's chastity: "Puesto que el silencio sazona muy sabrosamente la castidad y la prudencia" (Vives, 1043).[2]

"It is my claim," Jones continues,

> that this discourse is constructed on the basis of a conceptual myopia that normalizes authority as a disciplinary, commanding gaze. Such a discourse secures authority by opposing it to emotive connectedness or compassion. Authority orders existence through rules. Actions and actors are defined by these rules. Compassion cuts through this orderly universe with feelings that connect us to the specificity and particularity of actions and actors. Authority's rules distance us from the person. Compassion pulls us into a face-to-face encounter with another person. [120-21]

The androcentric understanding of authority that seeks to order society and social behavior so as to make them manageable and predictable is thus based upon a system of rules and a discursive mode that give "expression to rank, order, definition, and distinction, and [hide] dimensions of human reality that disorient and disturb." This identification of authority with a hierarchical paradigm is construed by some feminist scholars as a "peculiarly male approach to decision making: the willingness to sacrifice relations to others in the face of established rules; or, to put it differently, to exchange the uncertainty of human relationship for the certainty of rules" (K. Jones, 122-23). The alternative emphasis on relationship over the abstract realm of regulations is for Jones the focus of what constitutes authority for women: that is, communal contexts of caring and connectedness that depend on interaction and mutual communication and understanding. Because being part of a community receives ontological privilege, "authority as a system of rules for securing private rights, structuring individual obligations, or protecting autonomy through reciprocal duties gives wayto authority as a communal connectedness. . . . In this female perspective, the quest for authority becomes the search for contexts of care that do not deteriorate into mechanisms of blind loyalty" (K. Jones, 127).

The much dramatized and depicted literary convention of the Spanish Golden Age honor code evinces such models of gendered responses as Gutierre, in Calderón's *El médico de su honra,* who arranges the bloody murder of the wife he still loves because the flimsiest of evidence leads him to suspect her of infidelity. Throughout this same body of literature, however, women characters work continuously both to restore broken relationships and to circumvent the honor code's rigidity by strategic moves embodying that circumvention through techniques such as cross-dressing.

Both views of authority are problematized in various ways in the female-authored plays of the Spanish Golden Age. Critiquing from a Renaissance feminist perspective the breakdown of a social and political system in which women suffer the oppression of "powerlessness and objectification . . . as the consequence of the moral perversion of men, who failed to live up to the challenge of being fully human" (Jordan, 9), the situations that Caro and Cueva dramatize deconstruct the depicted androcentric practice of authority. Caro's play reveals the difficulty, if not the impossibility, faced by a female monarch of ever occupying a legitimate place in the males' authorizing hierarchy. Cueva maps out a pattern in which the male participants in the hierarchy depend on its vertical structure of interactions, while the females excluded from its functions demonstrate the strength of their resistance to "mechanisms of blind loyalty" that lack compassion or emotional connection.

These *comedias* thus portray the breakdown of this rule-oriented system, a deterioration that consequently exposes the conflictive nature of the hierarchical paradigm, which can easily degenerate into violence, abusive power, and tyranny. These dramatizations question the androcentric system that bases its exclusion of women from regular participation in government on essentialist notions about women's inferior capacity for public activities and on the insistence that man is the head of family and state and woman his subject. Female rule challenges "the supposed ontological inferiority of woman, in theory a problem all women who participated in public life had to confront, and the political subordination of the wife, crucial to a married female magistrate" (Jordan, 116). Caro dramatizes this dilemma for a female monarch in *Partinuplés,* in which she reveals her overlapping of the Renaissance feminist individualist and relational models even as she critiques the patriarchal versions of essentialist and constructionist theory and praxis. Her disruption of the limited androcentric notion of Woman questions as it also promotes the more modern female model with its reliance on group connections as described by Kathleen Jones. Her female characters occupy emotionally and socially separate spaces from one another, however, as they seek to establish connections to the men of their choice and contend with their own exclusion from a comfortable exercise of authority—an exclusion due to the male characters' attitudes, which are conditioned by repeated confrontations of wills and the threat, if not the exercise, of power over women. Cueva's drama reveals that the emotive horizontal model of authoritative connections is sufficiently strong to withstand pressure from the patriarchal rule-dominated system, though the former does not necessarily replace the latter. The protofeminist positioning of the women writers of the seventeenth century does not involve a revolutionary approach to the dilemmas of gender that the depicted women confront. Rather, by means of the female characters' efforts, progress is made toward a goal of exposing the social and moral disorder—private and public—caused by the failure of the males to develop both the so-called male virtues (reason, bravery) and the female ones (temperance, mercy), and thus their failure to preserve stability in the hierarchical cultural system.

As Arendt and others demonstrate, the etymological derivation of the word authority is *augere*, whose meaning is "to augment" (K. Jones, 126). The Renaissance feminist vision that ponders the ways in which a woman can assume her proper place in the community is encoded in the depiction of an overlapping—however brief—of the male model of authority by the female one. In such a depiction, the playwrights affirm Kathleen Jones's contention that: "authority adds meaning to human action by connecting that action to a realm of value and to justifications for action beyond criteria of efficiency or feasibility. If we define authority as expressing and enabling political action in community—interaction among equals—then authority would be represented as a horizontal rather than a vertical relationship and as male/female rather than primarily male" (126). The horizontal relationship is inscribed in the Renaissance feminism that combines a relational and an individual perspective, because without negating the difference between the sexes and the assignment of spheres of gendered influence and activity, it emphasizes the equality and worth of both men and women.

The *comedias* examined in this chapter promote a new understanding of the value of women's interaction in the public arena of social and political life outside the domestic space, but they do not advance a notion of permanancy for this participation. As soon as a measure of order can be restored with regard to the males' handling of their authoritative hierarchy—via a reinvoking of their own adherence to femininized virtues such as compassion and a renewed acknowledgment of relationship and community—the women reenter the interior realm of family and the enclosure of marriage. The plays do not, however, necessarily accomplish closure. Instead, they suggest a potential for further disruption that implies the ongoing need for women to be alert to the shortcomings of the social organization based on male hegemony; thus they portend a dimension of agency in the female silence and invisibility that the life of the respectable *dama* imposes. If the women can emerge from behind the enclosed spaces they inhabited in the plays' prehistories, then they could presumably do so again, if necessary.

In addition, the female-authored plays about monarchical power and authority accomplish a tightening of the focus on gender in issues of rulership, while they also comment on the highly polemical questioning of the theory of rulership in general that prompted the composition of numerous Spanish treatises. These are often responses to extremes, ranging from Machiavellian pragmatism to the Protestant embrace of the divine right of a central authority figure. Dian Fox has traced the issues of the debate initiated in the climate of political and economic crisis of Counter Reformation Spain, when the "importance of a ruler's conscience and religious faith" took precedence over other concerns (12). Although the Spanish commentators agreed that the source of a monarch's authority was God, they offered different views on the sovereign's relationship to the community. From a perspective such as that of Alonso de Valdés, the community is first empowered by God to bestow authority on the monarch, a concept that invokes "the medieval contract of government" (Hamilton, 41). Theorists such as Juan de Mariana outlined the authoritative hierarchy within this constitutional context, holding the monarch accountable to the populace in a hierarchical pattern that followed a line from the monarch at the bottom to the community and then to God. As Fox explains, the Spanish commentators on rulership fall into three main categories with regard to the two poles of power: the throne's occupant and the populace with its threatened capacity for regicide. Citing Mariana as "the most liberal," Fox continues:

The more moderate [Francisco] Suárez, [Luis] de Soto, [Francisco de] Vitoria, and [Pedro de] Rivadeneira agreed with Mariana that the king receives his power from the people. They allowed protest when the ruler errs, but were exceedingly chary about when it is licit to remove a ruler from office. Only under the most extreme and specific circumstances was tyrannicide permitted. . . . [Francisco de] Quevedo was the most conspicuous advocate of a conservative position. Like his countrymen, he greatly stressed the ruler's religious duty [and] emphasized the Christlike quality of the king. In contrast to the other writers, however, Quevedo believed that a poor ruler must be suffered, not resisted. . . . The tyrant will get his just reward in hell. [13]

In these discussions, however, issues of queenship were not regularly raised, despite the Spanish rule of Isabel I, one of the most famous female monarchs of early modern Europe. The documents on monarchy reflect the male-dominated vision of rulership in Europe in general and in Spain in particular. Queen Isabel is the iconic representative of only one half of the partnership known as the Reyes Católicos. Lauded frequently in official documents as the wife/queen, her body politic and body natural are mutually inscribed one on the other. The royal chaplain Andrés Bernáldez, for example, wrote of the queen's impressive measures for justice: "Fue la más temida y acatada Reina que nunca fue en el mundo, ca todos los duques, maestres, condes, marqueses e grandes señores la temían y habían miedo della, durante el tiempo de su matrimonio: y el rey y ella fueron muy temidos e obedecidos" (quoted in Fernández Alvarés, 239). It is significant, however, that Bernáldez connected her reputed influence and ability to inspire fear and respect with "el tiempo de su matrimonio," emphasizing that she and "el rey" together were effective rulers. A passage from the writings of a German visitor to Spain at the end of the fifteenth century likewise noted: "Diríase que el Omnipotente, al ver languidecer a España, envió a esta mujer excepcional para que en unión de su marido, salvase a su patria de la ruina" (quoted in Fernández Alvarez, 238). Again, the queen in concert with her husband is the subject of praise. Isabel I thus did not enjoy the fame of the principal ruler in the same sense as her son and their heirs (no one scrutinizes the reigns of the wives of Charles V, Philip II, Philip III, or Philip IV, for example); rather, she was linked in deed, tradition, and chronicle to her spouse as one member of the Reyes

Católicos. It is certainly the case that Ferdinand likewise was not singled out for solitary recognition, but as a male ruler he risked less by sharing his monarchy with a woman than vice versa. One bit of evidence that indicates a tacit, if not overt, recognition of this situation is found in Isabel's marriage settlement with the Aragonese monarch Ferdinand, which ensured that her sovereign authority over her own realm of Castile remained intact, while he allowed their joint rule of his kingdom (Anderson and Zinsser, 323). Such a fact implies Queen Isabel's understanding of the risk of disempowerment for the female ruler as a result of marriage.

This Spanish queen in many ways fits the paradigm identified by Jankowski, in her survey of early modern European political theory, and its ramifications for women rulers: although "the political theorists in question sometimes discuss women, even as they relate to the political process and the nature of rule, no one proposes a real theory of rule for women" (58). Further consequences of marriage and its effects on the coincidence of the monarch's body natural and body politic, as is argued by Elizabethan scholars, profoundly affected the ways in which Elizabeth I of England "reconcile[d] her femaleness with her power" (Jankowski, 62).[3] Recent understanding of the English queen's negotiation of these issues shows her complicated resolution of the problem of conflating her two bodies:

> What she did was to make her body natural serve her body politic, by opting to remain a virgin and to forsake the roles of wife and mother. She made this decision part of her political theory by claiming either that she was married to her subjects, or that the English people were her children. Elizabeth's choice may not have been an ideal one, but it did have the virtue of allowing her to avoid the even greater difficulties she would have encountered had she tried to retain her sovereign power as a married queen. In that situation, Elizabeth's anomalous power as a woman sovereign would be necessarily threatened by the power her husband was entitled to exercise over his wife. [Jankowski, 62][4]

The discomfort that the monarchy of Elizabeth I and the regency of Catherine de' Medici caused among moralists was articulated by, for example, John Knox in England, who wrote in 1558: "It is more than

a monster in nature that a woman shall reign and have empire above
man . . . [for to] promote a woman to bear rule, above any realm,
nation, or city, is repugnant to nature, contumely to God, . . . and finally, it is the subversion of good order, of all equity and justice"
(quoted in M. King, 159).

Considering Ana Caro's play *El conde Partinuplés* within this context,
one notes that even though the playwright imagines for her cast of
characters a realm presided over by a female monarch, the drama is not
named for her but carries instead the title of the male protagonist. The
Empress Rosaura does not even enjoy the shared titular prominence ac-
corded the female half of the Reyes Católicos. From the initial scene it
is evident that Rosaura's reign is precarious because her subjects do not
recognize her singular authority. The dissenters among the citizenry and
courtiers are all depicted as male, and though she is the legitimate heir
to the throne, the empress struggles with the consequences of her problematical position as a female ruler not given the opportunity to make
the sort of choice that the rule of the English Elizabeth I represents—a
compromise that would have been uncalled for, as Jankowski points
out, if the royal had been a man: "The necessity of making such a
choice does not exist for male rulers" (72).

The desire and even the practical requirement for a royal heir—
"Sucesor pide el imperio" (1)[5]—is not a unique concern for a populace,
but the conditions imposed upon Rosaura bespeak the gendered norms
that put stringent limits on the unpartnered (and thus uncontrolled)
woman, be she political ruler or political subject.[6] Discussing her unmarried status in her absence, some of the courtiers articulate the choice
to be presented to Rosaura: "Cásese o pierda estos reinos" (5). Not only
does the retinue soon repeat these terms to her directly, but their insistence upon the need for speed in the matter reiterates the common
poetic convention of *carpe diem* and the emphasis on the woman's physical attributes as a criterion for success in the matchmaking process:

> Cásate pues, que no es justo
> que dejes pasar la aurora
> de tu edad tierna, aguardando
> a que de tu sol se ponga. [71-74]

She becomes the objectified courtly *dama,* gazed upon by the entire court and scrutinized as to her physical attractiveness from the male perspective. The terms her adviser Emilio presents to Rosaura are no different from those purported to be the threats from her subjects, that as a single woman she is unacceptable as monarch. The choice she hears is presented in terms of a loss, whatever she decides to do. On the one hand, if she does not marry, then "habías de ver tu corona / dividida en varios bandos / y arriesgada tu persona" (78-80). The threat of fragmentation of her political state and even her own body suggests the fragmented status the patriarchal society perceives in a monarchy presided over by a single woman. The threat of regicide implies as well a moral crisis based on her queenship, a crisis grave enough to permit what would otherwise be treason. On the other hand, marriage for Rosaura means losing her independent state: "Tú, emperatriz, mira ahora / si te importa el libre estado, / o si el casarte te importa" (88-90). Even royal office does not change the cultural demands upon woman for containment in the institution of marriage.

This play follows the conventional pattern of dramatizing the tensions of the transitional period between the virginity of youth and eventual wifehood when only limited options are available to the young woman; she must, under pressure from society's expectations, accept the choice made for her about how and with whom to spend the rest of her life. Rosaura, as woman, is physical body and cannot stand as royal body without a male counterpart. Unlike so many moral-political treatises and literary and dramatic representations concerning kings, Caro's play does not address the question of *how* Rosaura rules; the work's audience and readership are not asked to consider her governing abilities. She is never represented in administrative moments since what is at issue is not her execution of the royal office but her suggested natural incompleteness for rule as a female-gendered human being.

The demands made upon Rosaura are overtly grounded in the practical desire for a legitimate heir, something that urges marriage upon male monarchs as well, though usually without threat to life and occupation of the throne. Rosaura's royal office, however, does not assure her a place at the top of the authoritative hierarchy; her only hope of remaining in what amounts to a borrowed space of empowerment is to share it with a male. The focus of the court and the subjects on the woman ruler's natural rather than her political body presumes unsuitability of female rule and privileges the natural over the political identity of the woman monarch. In effect, the dilemma that Rosaura confronts means her subjects' rejection of her as ruler altogether, because if she does not marry she will lose everything; if she does marry, she will share the throne with a male ruler, becoming his wife and presumably mother of his children and thereby moving into the traditional female domestic roles with which society feels more comfortable.

The theater audience learns along with the portrayed courtly one that other concerns have motivated Rosaura's reticence to marry, another level of restraint that thwarts her authority and reaffirms her position as disempowered woman among the male members of a social network that does not recognize her as an equal participant. In her initial appearance this female monarch, surrounded by males who represent their own wishes, not hers, explains that her rejection of matrimony is predicated on her fear of the consequences announced in her horoscope, cast and interpreted by her father and his advisers in her infancy after the death of her mother in childbirth. Caro thus also demonstrates that motherhood in a double sense prescribes the mother's absence from the *comedia* stage, for this one potential and significant model of domesticated female monarch—Rosaura's mother and the queen consort—has died as a result of what is considered the more important of her roles. Another threat is thus imposed upon Rosaura by the demand that she marry.

According to the empress, her father's reading of the stars, in contradiction to the requirement put upon her by her subjects and courtiers, indicated "mil sucesos fatales" (174) and the destruction of her realm if she were to consider marriage:

> que un hombre ¡fiero daño!
> le trataría a mi verdad engaño,
> rompiéndome le fe por él jurada,
> y que si en este tiempo reparada
> no fuese por mi industria esta corona,
> riesgo corrían ella y mi persona;
> porque este hombre engañoso
> con palabra de esposo,

quebrantando después la fe debida,
el fin ocasionaba de mi vida. [177-86]

By these criteria her body natural must be denied in order to allow the
body politic to function as authoritative protector of the realm—yet her
subjects tell her that her body natural must be privileged at the expense
of her body politic. Thus, in Caro's dramatized version of the queen's
role, there is no easy way to allow the female monarch's two bodies to
function simultaneously with equal vigor. Her life and her empire are
threatened if she marries, as well as if she does not.

The male community of patriarchal figures—her father, advisers,
courtiers, populace—range from figures of familial and political authority to those who should consider themselves her subjects. The
entire realm operates against even the most liberal political theoretical
standard, which understands that the power of the ruler emanates from
the God-given power of the people, and removal from office and regicide are licit threats against only the most tyrannical monarch. But
Rosaura has committed no articulated act of abuse; she has only acted
with the desire to protect her realm from the peril foretold at her infancy. Her subjects nevertheless exercise their authority as males over
women to insist upon what they believe she must do. These contradictory mandates create for Rosaura an impossible situation in which she
cannot save herself or her realm.

The female monarch thus faces the specter of inefficacy—but she
does not surrender to it. Caro dramatizes Rosaura's use of the female
authoritative mechanism of negotiation, as the empress bargains with
her assembled courtiers for a year's time in which to consider the suitors
that the court and citizenry of Constantinople have picked for her. In
so doing, she also gains for herself the opportunity for guidance from
and connection to the only individual she trusts, her cousin Aldora,
whose magical powers are sufficient to help investigate more deeply
the characteristics of the empress's potential mates. Caro manipulates
the theatrical conventions of female characterization by including this
magical figure in the play, since the impossible dilemma Rosaura faces
demands an impossible resolution such as magic, a component that
offers both visual and verbal commentary upon the difficult alternatives
that woman and her performed mythic convention must face.

Caro's witch can be interpreted as a counterpoint to what feminist scholars have identified as "the systemic victimization and oppression of women . . . [during] the European witchcraze . . . [through] the conspiracy by powerful men to eliminate deviant and independent women in the interests of 'purifying the Body of Christ'" (McLuskie, 58-59). Mary Daly writes of this historical phenomenon and subsequent records of it: "Hags are re-membering and therefore understanding not only the intent of the Sado-State—the torture, dis-memberment, and murder of deviant women—but also the fact that this intent is justified and shared by scholars and other professional perpetrators of this State" (185). Caro validates both her female monarch and the depicted witch, making of their alliance an instrument to challenge societal notions of female deviance.

Because the female monarch's confrontation with the contradictory demands upon her weakens her ability to control and rule her realm, she needs the aid of magical force to contend with the conditions of uniting her two royal bodies and to avoid the disintegration of her society. Denied an easily occupied place in the vertical hierarchical paradigm of patriarchal authority, Rosaura invokes a means to strengthen a horizontal configuration of negotiation and unification.

Aldora, however, is not portrayed as a pagan practitioner of the black magic that threatens the souls of its victims. As she reminds Rosaura, ". . . es imposible intento / penetrar los corazones / y del alma los secretos" (290-92). She can only show her cousin a vision in which the *pretendientes* are made visible in characteristic poses; Rosaura must interpret for herself how suitable a marriage partner each might be:

> Lo más que hoy puedo hacer
> por ti, pues sabes mi ingenio
> en cuanto a la mágica arte,
> es enseñarte primero
> en aparentes personas
> estos príncipes propuestos.
> Y si es fuerza conocer
> las causas por los efectos,
> viendo en lo que se ejercitan,
> será fácil presupuesto
> saber cuál es entendido,

cuál arrogante o modesto,
cuál discreto y estudioso,
cuál amoroso o cuál tierno. [293-306]

There is no evidence of abilities to influence or enchant any of the
men proposed. What Aldora *is* able to do is reverse the pattern of the
male gaze and its female object. The men to be considered by Rosaura
are objects of her scrutiny and vision in the scene that Aldora summons
for her. Among the visions are the figures of Federico of Poland, who
looks at himself in a mirror; Eduardo from Scotland, with his books
and scholar's paraphernalia; Roberto of Transylvania, who appears as a
valiant warrior; and Partinuplés of France, seen staring intently at a portrait. Of them all, Aldora indicates that Partinuplés would be most
worthy of marrying Rosaura but for one impediment: his betrothal and
impending marriage to his countrywoman Lisbella. This one point in-
stantly and initially motivates Rosaura's desire for Partinuplés alone.
Although she rules out the others for more thoughtful reasons (Federico
is too vain and self-centered, Eduardo too studious, and Roberto too
bellicose), it is the existence of a rival for Partinuplés that makes him
more unattainable and thus more desirable: "Yo lo difícil intento; / lo
fácil es para todos" (420-21). In attempting to fulfill the demands
placed upon her, Rosaura moves away from an act that exclusively satisfies duty toward the personal fulfillment of picking a man for purely
emotional reasons.[7] At the same time, she enters into a contest with another woman—a struggle in this respect between two equals, unlike the
conflict between herself and the males who dominate her despite her
occupation of a high political status which, as dramatized, does not
transcend her gender. She will compete as royal woman with another
royal woman in a contest in which she, like all other women, exercises a
very limited range of agency.

Aldora's spells not only afford Rosaura a view of Partinuplés and his
competitors but provide the French count with Rosaura's portrait: "yo
haré que un retrato tuyo / sea brevemente objeto / de su vista . . . "
(425-27). What Aldora brings about is a reciprocity of desire's gaze:
Rosaura and Partinuplés each view the other's simulacrum and fall in
love with the image. Rosaura enjoys a greater advantage in this situation, however, since she knows who her beloved is, whereas Partinuplés

has no name or identity for the portrait he holds. That the match to which he is already pledged is merely a political convenience, moreover, constitutes a further critique of the marriage demands made upon Rosaura by her countrymen. In an early scene his uncle, the king of France, whose realm Partinuplés and Lisbella are to inherit, encourages the young count to speak words of love to his betrothed. Partinuplés declines on the grounds that such language would only embarrass Lisbella, and she concurs approvingly, agreeing that silence will be their medium of communication. Near the end of the play, Lisbella declares the truth of their situation, affirming "no le quiero / amante ya" (1993-94), explaining:

> no es amor, es conveniencia,
> pues es forzoso que vaya
> como legítimo rey,
> supuesto que murió en Francia
> mi tío. [1995-99]

When the count does get a brief glimpse of Rosaura, she appears, thanks to more intervention by Aldora, as a hunted animal that quickly changes into the image of the empress's portrait. The stage directions in the text evince Caro's implementation of stage machinery, the means of effecting the metamorphosis before the eyes of her theatrical audience. Partinuplés praises Rosaura's beauty and begs to know who she is; the only reply given before her image disappears is "Si me buscas, me hallarás" (633). The following scene is charged with satire and humor. When the count, aided by his servant Gaulín, literally searches the wooded area shown in his vision, the theatrical audience is aware that Aldora is hiding behind some trees. Just when Gaulín finds and tries to seize her, she transforms herself into a lion, which catches the *gracioso* but then quickly disappears, and with the sound of thunder and a building storm, Partinuplés and Gaulín find and enter a small boat in order to escape the dangers of the forest. That their adversaries are imaginary and conjured by a woman calls into question the stereotypical notion of male bravery and authority. The female manipulation of the situation, however, is depicted as dependent upon extraordinary means in the form of Aldora's benign but nevertheless effective sorcery, and the women's transformations into and from animal forms visually reinforce the conventional association between woman and animal nature, as well as her vulnerability to entrapment. But the metamorphoses reinforce the blurred categories of hunter/hunted, victimizer/victim, and empowered/disempowered, all of which parallel the ambiguous position of the female monarch who sits on the throne but must answer, in ways that male monarchs need not do, to those over whom she rules.

Transported in the magic boat to Rosaura's castle, Partinuplés remains under her control insofar as he is now in a space beyond his own jurisdiction. Rosaura maintains her dominion over him by refusing to allow the count to see her; when they meet, they speak in the darkness. Such a representation reverses the Cupid and Psyche myth, found in the romance cycle from which Caro borrows her story and characters. Yet this reversal of who is permitted to see whom adheres to gender constraints in that the female protagonist, in spite of royal status and the aid of magic, uses darkness as a form of enclosure that protects her from recognition in her transgression of woman's permissible expression of desire. The empress denies Partinuplés one of the male advantages by not allowing him to see (or scrutinize and critique) her, as the mythological Cupid is able to do to his beloved. Partinuplés thus loses his privilege as judge, and one of his questions evinces his sense of loss in this regard. Pondering her reasons for this visual secrecy, the count inquires, "¿No sois digna de mi amor?" (1017). The method of critiquing worthiness and the pattern of who can pick whom have been altered, and it is the woman, as Rosaura explains, who here tests the male's value: ". . . pero yo, / para acrisolar lo fino / del oro de vuestra fe" (1029-31). Rosaura, nevertheless, protects herself with the darkness and secrecy that hide her from public display in this apparent subversion of the norm that simultaneously reinscribes the dominant standard.[8]

Partinuplés is one of the four men Rosaura will interview as pretenders for her hand in marriage. Each aspires to be her husband and co-ruler and she, in consultation with her advisers, has the authority to choose. The royal male candidates are likewise bidders for the prize that she represents—a prize to be sponsored and auctioned off, in effect, by her subjects and court. Upon hearing three of them introduce themselves—Federico from Poland, Eduardo from Scotland, and Roberto from Transylvania—she reminds the group that it is her council of advisers that will decide among them—"La elección dejo / a los de mi consejo. / Esto se mirará con advertencia / de mi decoro y vuestra conveniencia" (1250-53)—though the audience knows she has already made up her mind that Partinuplés should be her mate. He, in the meantime, has surmised that the woman in the portrait, in the woods, and in the palace darkness are the same person. His assurances to Gaulín that he loves this enigmatic woman on other than material grounds are met with the *gracioso's* cynicism about his master's depth of amorous devotion, and in this same conversation the count renounces his union with Lisbella: "No hay Lisbella" (1296). The *comedia's enredos de amor*, which typically include a rejected woman, are incorporated in this dramatized tale about love among the members at the top of the sociopolitical hierarchy. For Lisbella, even a marriage of political convenience does not portend stability; the *comedia* female's conventional disadvantage remains.

Rosaura is still not ready to meet Partinuplés in the light, however, and the further condition she imposes reverses another aspect of the *comedia's* typical gendered portrayals, in which it is usually the woman whose honor and integrity must be tested and approved. In a conversation at the end of Act 2, Rosaura is portrayed as the more politically aware and strategically astute ruler with her advice to Partinuplés to return to France to defend his realm against the English:

> Francia está en grande peligro,
> el inglés cercada tiene
> a Paris, del rey, tu tío,
> famosa corte eminente. [1430-33]

She is willing to sacrifice his presence in her realm for the sake of protecting the integrity of his own. The second act ends with his departure, and the third begins with his return following a victory in France.

In their first conversation thereafter, Rosaura asks him to recount his exploits, but—subverting the usual arrangement of the courtly male reciter and female listener—falls asleep during his tale, which trivializes his feats and their description. In so doing, however, she cedes control of the conditions of their conversation to Partinuplés. Although his scruples make him reticent to betray her stipulation that he is not to view her face, Gaulín points out to his master the underlying physical advantage that the male enjoys in such a situation: "¿No es mujer y tú

eres hombre? / ¿Te ha de matar?" (1661-62). Again her natural body
does not secure her political authority. Obtaining a light, the two men
look at Rosaura and discover that she is indeed the woman they saw in
the forest. But his seeing her without her permission becomes the act of
treason that motivates Rosaura's rejection of Partinuplés. Caro dramatizes the ideological threat that being seen poses to a woman but insists
here on punishing the male observer rather than the observed woman.
The female sorcerer must now step in and save him from the Empress's
anger:

> ROS. . . . Presto, Aldora
> . . . .
>   Quítale ya de mis ojos.
>   . . . .
> ALD.   Ven, Conde, conmigo presto [1750-58]).

The female community of two does not maintain its coherent independence, and Aldora becomes from this point the active sponsor of
Partinuplés and the organizer of his means to win Rosaura by play's end.

Meanwhile, the count is portrayed as increasingly more passive and
out of control. In the next scene he is left wandering in the wilderness
as Lisbella enters with full military regalia and soldiers. She has come to
Constantinople to demand from Rosaura the return of Partinuplés. The
contest of exchange is now depicted between women, and the object of
exchange is the count. Caro creates a brief scene that insists upon the
strength of the female ruler and asserts the individualist feminist paradigm. At this moment, the two women face each other as political
bodies, both unmarried and capable of confronting adversaries without
male intervention.[9] Later in the same act Lisbella formally challenges
Rosaura and describes Partinuplés as the submissive and powerless prisoner of the empress:

> Yo he sabido, emperatriz,
> que usurpas, tienes y guardas
> al conde Partinuplés,
> mi primo, y que con él tratas
> casarte, no por los justos
> medios, sino por las falsas

> ilusiones de un encanto;
> y deslustrando su fama,
> le tiranizas y escondes,
> le rindes, prendes y guardas,
> contra tu real decoro.
> Yo pues, que me hallo obligada
> a redimir de este agravio
> la vejación o la infamia,
> te pido que me le des. [1977-91]

What happens soon afterward reinforces the Renaissance feminist vision of a balancing of the gendered values and entitlements. The contest arranged to test the worth of the suitors for Rosaura's hand takes place among Roberto, Eduardo, Federico, and a hooded individual whose identity remains concealed throughout the tournament. It is he, however, who wins the competition and then proceeds to reveal himself as Partinuplés. Rosaura quickly accepts him as her husband and consort to the protests of Lisbella: "Conde, mi primo y señor, / mira que te espera un reino" (2087-88). Because of his love for Rosaura, Partinuplés renounces his claim to the French throne in favor of Lisbella's queenship: "Gózale, Lisbella, hermana; / que sin Rosaura no quiero / bien ninguno" (2089-91). The contradictory moves of winning and relinquishing are reiterated in Lisbella's case, for as queen of France she retains her authority but within seconds is paired in a marriage arrangement designed by Partinuplés, who—no longer king or even pretender to the French throne—should have no more influence in matters pertaining to that nation's monarchy: "Prima, aquí no hay remedio; / Francia y Roberto son tuyos. / ¿Qué respondes?" (2092-94). Her answer, "Que obedezco" (2094), corresponds to Rosaura's "Yo soy tuya" (2091) to the count and to Aldora's "Tuya es mi mano"(2097) to *her* new partner, Eduardo—three similarly submissive responses from, respectively, a queen, an empress, and an enchantress. Thus, as the men regain control of the language that directs and organizes, the vertical hierarchy of patriarchal authority is reconfigured and reaffirmed. Partinuplés gives up a kingdom in order to marry Rosaura and live with her in Constantinople, a move that emphasizes his emotional devotion to her and supersedes his political duty to his native realm; he denies the responsibilities of the monarch's political body in favor of

the natural one. But he also accomplishes the deed that historical
female monarchs (such as Isabel I of Spain and Elizabeth I of England)
feared: that is, to become co-ruler over the empress's realm—in this
case, without even the reciprocating gift of his own throne to be shared
in a marriage contract, for Lisbella gives her body and realm to
Roberto.

The women monarchs throughout have acted out of a desire to preserve their realms and societies. By the end of the play Rosaura seems to
have done so, while fulfilling the conditions imposed by her court and
subjects. She will marry Partinuplés, the man of her choice, and he will
enter her empire rather than she moving her to his. The men she has
been allowed to consider, however, exhibit some of the characteristics
that make other *comedia galanes* undesirable lovers and husbands. The
narcissism of Federico, the self-absorbed scholarship of Eduardo, and
the intense warfaring nature of Roberto portended a less than happy
partnership for Rosaura. Nevertheless the last two are the partners
chosen for Aldora and Lisbella, respectively, and Roberto offers his
sister Rocisunda to Federico, sight unseen, a proposal the Transylvanian
monarch accepts. Partinuplés does return the love offered by Rosaura,
but at the expense of his earlier promise to marry Lisbella. It is the
women who compete to marry him; the fact that both are royal figures
does not preclude their trials of courtship. Caro represents in this
drama the double bind of a female monarch who, despite her openly
recognized and titled authority, is constrained by the participants in the
male-dominated hierarchy of authority around her to which she is ultimately subject. Guided for years by the words of her father, Rosaura has
tried to protect herself and her subjects by avoiding marriage. Her im-
petus has been the communal interest (just as Lisbella's is in her quest,
which brings her all the way to Constantinople from France in her
effort to preserve her country's legitimate monarchy). As the play
begins, Rosaura is threatened by other males with the destruction of her
empire if she does not marry. The contradictory demands from the
male hierarchy force her to abandon her strategy of control: that is, not
responding to marriage proposals in order to ensure the empire's safety
by her celibacy.

But discomfort over an unmarried—uncontrolled—female ruler is
unbearable for the populace. Rosaura can reign only as the wife of a

co-ruler, a dramatized situation that inscribes the dual feminist perspectives of the Renaissance: the partnership of the male and female couple is preserved at the end of the play, and it is accomplished through the exercise of reason and virtues—regardless of gender—by the principal characters in individualist feminist strategies. Yet the fulfillment of the demands upon the female monarch to marry in order to remain on the throne leaves the gendered roles essentially unchallenged, and, as Kaminsky points out, the foretold destruction of Rosaura's empire may still occur (92).

Caro's exploration of dramatized possibilities for agency during the limited period between virginal youth and marriage reiterates the transcendence of gender over class and social status, for even a *comedia* queen is vulnerable to the prohibitions against woman's life without husband or religious vocation. These are dramatized repeatedly in the Siglo de Oro. Inherent in the *comedias* under examination, however, is the element of resistance to patriarchal authority. The playwrights share with their characters explorations of woman's exercise of free will and conscience against abusive authority figures whose power relegates all subjects—both male and female—to an uncomfortable position relative to that authority. Leonor de la Cueva y Silva communicates an understanding of the usefulness for women of Renaissance male-authored apologies "based on a sympathetic identification with the 'female position,'" a perspective which, writes Jordan, "may distinguish Renaissance from later feminisms":

> The comments of such writers suggest that in the position of woman as the quintessential subject—that is, as politically subordinate, economically dependent, and legally incapacitated—many Renaissance men saw reflected aspects of their own social situations. For whatever his rank, a man of this period would have been obliged to contend with the effects of a social hierarchy. The more rigorous his experience of subordination and its consequent disempowerment, the more his "male position" would have resembled that of the "female." His maleness and masculinity were therefore susceptible to a degree of qualification quite alien to the experience of men in less stratified societies. . . . What is stressed overall, however, is the decisive part played by a common and essentially human experience—always seen in this period in a dialectical

tension with authority no matter what the subject—in testing and overcoming rigid categorizations of gender that are based on sexual difference. [20-21]

Cueva's *La firmeza en la ausencia* depicts the dilemma that two noble lovers face before their marriage when the king falls in love with the woman and exercises his power to remove his male rival by sending him to the military front, where the nobleman's death seems a certainty. Don Juan's submission to the sovereign's rule aligns his position with that of the disempowered female, but what takes place in this play likewise reinforces a Renaissance feminist rethinking of the theologically based notion of woman's inherent weakness and transgressive nature, passed on from Eve.[10] Cueva's female protagonist is the aristocratic *dama* Armesinda, who has been courted for six years by Juan while observing all proprieties to safeguard her reputation. When their difficulties ensue because of King Filiberto's passion, Armesinda is the only character depicted who can withstand the monarch's abusive manipulations.

Early in the first act Armesinda receives a letter from Juan in which he explains to her the royal orders that send him into battle as captain of troops in defense of the Italian borders against French invaders. Armesinda occupies the socially designated role of respectable and respectful woman, and she articulates her understanding of the consequences for that role with regard to a woman's use of language and public display. She explains to her maid Leonor, for instance, her surprise and distress over receiving Juan's missal:

> ¿qué puede escribirme aquí?
> A novedad lo he tenido,
> pues en seis años de amor
> es el primero, Leonor,
> que a mis manos ha venido;
> jamás confié a la pluma
> mis secretos; que en querer
> nunca en papel quise hacer
> de mis amores la suma,
> que suelen ser de una dama,
> por un descuido, la puerta

> que la deja siempre abierta
> para perder honra y fama.
> Don Juan, siguiendo mi gusto,
> tan de esta opinión ha sido,
> que jamás ha pretendido
> salir de lo que es tan justo.
> ¡Y al cabo de tantos años
> escribirme! ¡Extraña cosa!
> El alma está temerosa. [380-99]

To this initial instance of her suitor's infraction of their commitment to discretion, Armesinda's response is one of trepidation. In this play (as in the others considered) the task of the main female character is to negotiate problems that the male characters set in motion by their own failure to observe the standards of behavior which they profess to uphold and to which they hold women accountable. Also as in other women-authored plays, the female principal in *La firmeza en la ausencia* is assumed guilty of wrongdoing or inconstancy before the fact. Juan, for example, having no choice but to accept the commission given him by King Filiberto, assumes that the monarch's wealth and power will attract Armesinda in his absence—despite their longstanding devotion:

> porque viendo que me voy
> Armesinda, y que la quiere
> un rey de tanto valor,
> se rendirá a sus halagos,
> pues nunca menos se vio
> en una mujer ausente
> que apetecer lo mejor. [286-92]

Juan extracts a promise from his friend Don Carlos to watch over Armesinda and report to the absent lover what takes place in the palace between her and the king. Armesinda thus is surrounded by watchful males; she becomes the object of desire and suspicion, even though she has done nothing to attract either sort of scrutiny.

King Filiberto, occupying the position of authority, abuses his royal power by exercising the unscrupulous desires of his natural body while ignoring the obligations of his office. After sending Juan away to war he remains frustrated by Armesinda's refusal of his attention and continues his unethical attempts to win her affection, enlisting the nobleman Carlos as an aide in his suit. The participation of Carlos—Juan's friend—in this matter reinforces the male subject's powerlessness before hierarchical authority as well as the duplicitous nature of the depicted males. But his role as the king's spy also reveals that even the male monarch is powerless in the face of virtuous resistance; he needs the assistance of another male to carry out his seductive plot.

The monarch's next ploy redoubles his underhanded effort to eliminate Juan as a rival. By the beginning of Act 2, Filiberto still has not been successful with Armesinda, and so he vows to "hacer, con algún engaño, / que cese el desdén extraño" (842-43). The scheme involves a lie that Juan has married, preliminary to the king's intention of proclaiming falsely that Juan has died at the front. As the king's spokesperson about the fictitous marriage, Carlos accomplishes his task with much embellishment in a story about a captured Frenchman named Alberto who bargained for his liberty by promising Juan the hand of his daughter Clavela. Details of the wedding celebration accompany the explanation that Juan has forgotten about Armesinda because of his long absence from her.

Carlos is a dutiful participant in the male hierarchy that traps him, like other *comedia* noblemen, between the loyalty he feels to a friend and his obligation to serve and obey the king: "Yo soy amigo leal / y soy vasallo del rey," he says. " . . . ¿Hay pena igual?" (935-39). Carlos resolves his guilt over betraying Juan by assuring himself that Armesinda, feeling scorned and deserted, will accept the king's proposal. He is mistaken, however, for when he assures her that Juan is indeed happily married, the *dama* proclaims her resolution to remain true to the memory of the love she and Juan once shared. Even the temptations of queenship will not sway her:

> tan difícil olvidar
> jamás mi afición primera,
> aunque por ello ganare
> el ser de Nápoles reina. [1115-18]

Carlos then leaves open one possibility of reconciliation: contradicting his earlier insistence, he claims to be unsure whether Juan's wedding to the fictitious Clavela has taken place. But the king and his courtiers compound their lies with new ones, and Armesinda remains the only main character who adheres to the promises she has given.

In her next soliloquy Armesinda reexamines the injustice of the stereotype—so often invoked in the *comedia*—of woman's fickleness. Her words, delivered by the only figure untainted by lying or mistrust, communicate a woman-centered response to the societal double standard that blames women if they do or do not fall in love: they are accused of being heartless or faithless if they are not responsive to a lover, but deemed sexually permissive if they do respond positively. Reversing the components of the argument, she introduces a new field of complaint:

> Válgame Dios, lo que yerra
> la que fía de quien tiene
> tan varia naturaleza
> como en el hombre se ve;
> pues vuelve la espalda apenas
> de su dama, y en dos días
> no hay cosa que no apetezca.
> Mal ha dicho quien ha dicho
> que la mudanza se engendra
> solamente en las mujeres,
> por su femenil flaqueza;
> pues cuando alguna se rinde
> a amar y querer de veras,
> no hay amor, no, que se oponga
> con el suyo en competencia. [1162-76]

She goes on to list other famous historical examples of steadfast women from antiquity—Artemisa, Julia, Portia (1177-80)—and boasts, "y bien puedo yo contarme / por más constante que éstas" (1181-82), since she has no practical reason to remain true to Juan. Armesinda's argument reveals an essentialist paradigm, but she invokes such a standard in order to reverse the patriarchal recourse to clichés about female weakness of body and resolve. She confronts the constructionism of in-vocations of natural qualities and enacts the alternative to what is taken to be the norm.

Because, like her counterparts in the other *comedias,* she still has a brief period of opportunity to choose her course of action and her ulti-mate fate, Armesinda goes on to list her options. One possibility is to allow Filiberto to become her lover; she rules that out because of her own integrity. Or she could marry him, but she rejects this option be-cause she still has strong feelings for Juan and an emotional resistance to union with any other man. She eliminates the convent as a site of resolution because it does not afford her a means to relieve the amorous pain she feels. Finally, death seems to be the only solution," . . . que el morir / todas las cosas remedia" (1211-12). In the meantime, Juan cele-brates his military victories and is depicted as ever mindful of both his love for and suspicions of Armesinda. Upon receiving letters from her and from Carlos, describing Armesinda's unswerving devotion to him, he reiterates his uneasiness, since, "[s]iempre la desconfianza / a quien tiene amor alcanza" (1338-39).

In the palace, Armesinda endures the coercion not only of the king but also of her own maid, Leonor, and the king's sister, the Infanta Celidaura, all of whom urge her to forget Juan and consent to marry Fil-iberto. Armesinda's consistent rejection of the king results in his threat to have Juan killed if she does not acquiesce; even the other women—the infanta and the maid—deride her resistance, despite the king's unethical use of power. The male hierarchy over which the king presides holds her captive: she cannot dismantle the king's power over his subjects, nor can she alone meaningfully invoke the rules and codes of just behavior that the monarch has abandoned in favor of his self-interested comportment and attitudes. The rest of the society that he rules—symbolized by Celidaura and Leonor, representing the two ends of the class system—uphold the negative measures he takes to obtain what he wants. Thus, in Cueva's dramatized society as in Caro's, there is no female communal sol-idarity, no category of Woman into which all the depicted women can be collected. Even so, Armesinda's authority is a moral sort that reasserts her allegiance to the horizontal connections she will not abandon and also renders less than effective the king's vertical hierarchy.

As Filiberto continues to raise the stakes in his campaign of pressure, Armesinda's solitary dilemma is exacerbated by the other women's support of the king's demands. She is "enajenada en mi dolor esquivo, / sola entre tanta pena, / que estoy de alivio y de consuelo ajena" (1498-1500). Having obeyed all of society's rules for the unmarried woman, Armesinda believes that she has been forgotten by the man who pledged undying love to her; she is being blackmailed into a union with a man whom she does not love in order to save the reportedly unfaithful man; and she has no allies who agree with her adherence to her own principles. Cueva orchestrates a situation in which once again the young, unmarried woman cannot succeed on society's terms, even though she has followed the social tenets without deviation. As Armesinda herself complains at the end of Act 2, her predicament is not of her doing. Juan has left her "sola, triste y olvidada" (1595), and she feels herself "entre ahogos crueles / que a mi garganta aprietan los cordeles" (1597-98).

Act 3 reveals more of the duplicitous undertakings of the male characters. Carlos has been deceiving the king by writing encouraging letters to Juan, who nevertheless remains doubtful that Armesinda can withstand the suit of "tan fuerte competidor / como el rey" (1652-53). The king discloses that he has been routinely confiscating and destroying Juan's letters to Armesinda: "pues las cartas que la escribe, / tan buena maña me he dado / que ella ninguna recibe" (1692-94). He has denied her the opportunity to receive or read information from outside the palace walls. She is his resistant prisoner.

Filiberto eventually enters Armesinda's chambers and is on the point of raping her as she sleeps—an intention symbolic of the degeneration of his authority into tyrannical power, the only advantage he holds over her—when Carlos comes in with the news that Juan and his victorious army are returning to Naples. Juan has triumphed within the terms of the male hierarchy of authority that sent him into battle. His most important victory is in reality over the king, whom he has obeyed in all ways and to whom he has offered service and a military conquest. His return puts an end to the king's pursuit of Armesinda—but not before Filiberto tries his last method of coercion. He and Carlos decide to undertake a final deceit just before Juan arrives at the palace. They surrepitiously waken Armesinda and get out of sight. Then, Carlos comes in—as the stage directions indicate "fingiéndose muy triste"

(1966)—to give the young woman the false news of Juan's death in battle: "Disparáronle una bala / los enemigos franceses / en la postrera batalla" (1997-99). But his announcement does not accomplish what the king desires. Instead, Armesinda implores Filiberto to allow her to retire to a convent, thus reversing her earlier rejection of this option.

Cueva represents here an instance of the inadequacy of patriarchal authority and power once the unification of the monarch's two bodies is disrupted: Filiberto has proceeded in his devious schemes because of the desires of his physical body, abandoning the responsibilities of his political body. Completely unable to obtain what he wants at the personal level and faced with the failure of even his most inventive tricks, he perceives that physical force is all that is left and pursues this last line of action: "Dame aquesa mano, acaba, / o tomaréla por fuerza" (2129-30).

Cueva's representation of the limits of patriarchal authority that has been converted into abusive power through misuse of the highest political office suggests no means of escape for the resistant woman. Armesinda is enclosed, isolated, tricked, coerced, made victim of ultimatums, and finally threatened with physical violence because she is the object of desire of the male at the top of the power hierarchy. Yet ironically, she has been able to frustrate the monarch's schemes *because* she does not occupy an official position in the male chain of command. Her body natural is beyond the political control of the king. There is no acceptable way for Filiberto to demand that she give in to him. By contrast, he can send Juan to the front because the political system in which both males participate does not require force for its functioning. Juan therefore cannot refuse to do the king's bidding, because even though the command is given for base and personal reasons, it is couched in publicly licit terms. Armesinda exercises no public office, remaining throughout the play the lady-in-waiting to Princess Celidaura behind the palace walls, unseen and unheard by any who might recognize her plight. Reinforcing the fact that one can experience love with a basis in great conviction, she represents the many *comedia* women who do not change their minds about promises of love, even in the face of abandonment by the men to whom they have pledged their affection and by whom they have been wooed and left behind, hidden from public view.

One of Armesinda's monologues in the final act seems to summarize
not only what she has had to endure in this context but likewise the
conventional disparities that female characters must confront in the
dramatized myth of woman in Golden Age *comedias*. She considers the
resultant myth of *comedia* males:

No hay en los hombres verdad.
Miente, Leonor, quien dijere
que a la mujer se prefiere
en firmeza y en lealtad.
Pretende el galán la dama
que le ha parecido bien,
y conquista su desdén
bien a costa de su fama.
Paséala un mes la calle
en el caballo brioso,
con ostentación de airoso,
haciendo alarde del talle.
De noche, las rejas mira,
con músicas la enamora,
y a sus umbrales la aurora
le halla cuando rayos tira.
Ella, incauta y obligada
del amante cauteloso,
le hace dueño venturoso
de la prenda más preciada;
y apenas pues ha gozado
aquello que pretendía,
cuando porque esotro día
vio que la calle ha pasado
otro, y que por cortesía,
Leonor, la quitó el sombrero,
por encubrir su grosero
término y bellaquería,
dice que quien se rindió
tan presto a su amor primero,
que aquél no será el postrero,
pues a muchos puerta abrió.
Y fundando sobre nada
su maldad e injusta queja,

se va a otra parte, y la deja
para siempre deshonrada.
Como te pinto es el hombre. [1760-96]

Over and over again this sort of dilemma is dramatized in the *enredos de amor* of the seventeenth-century Spanish stage, and the gender issues reiterate the weight of consequence for the women characters after the male figures have proved fickle or unnecessarily suspicious. What the *comedias* dramatize finds echo in the moralists' diatribes against unchaste women. Vives, for example, comments as follows:

¡Loca de ti!, ¿nunca oíste decir que muchas mujeres seducidas pos estos amores prematuros rindieron su voluntad a quienes esperaban serían sus maridos? ¿Y que éstos, una vez que hubieron hartado sus deseos, las dejaron burladas y desdeñadas? Y esto con mucha razón, pues no merecen que las tomen por esposas aquellos hombres a quienes declararon ellas mismas poder ayuntarse con quien no era su marido legítimo, pues no habrán de faltarles arrestos para hacer una cosa semejante con otros galanes antes del casamiento, y después del casamiento con otros adúlteros. No amanece día sin que en cada lugar ocurran sucesos de éstos. [1069-70]

In Cueva's play, the issue throughout is whether or not Armesinda will remain faithful to Juan, even when she is told that he is married or dead. Carlos, the agent of such news, excuses his deceitful treatment of her by telling Armesinda in the last scene:

Cesen ya tantos enojos
y penas, bella Armesinda,
con saber que ha sido todo
probar la rara firmeza
de quien ejemplo glorioso
ha sido. Perdón te pido. [2397-2402]

A telling moment occurs also in the last scene. Juan recounts his exploits in battle and then reverses the dynamics of power briefly by relating to the king an exchange involved in the terms of surrender from the defeated French leader: the Infanta Celidaura will be given in marriage to the French monarch, whose sister Blanca will marry Filiberto. Never is Celidaura given dialogue to express her acceptance or rejection of such a trade; nor, of course, do we ever hear the voice of the absent Blanca. They occupy places in the hierarchy that Armesinda does not, since they are political pawns in the struggle for power between governments. But this play closes as the two men, Filiberto and Juan, in effect exchange the two women, Armesinda and Blanca, in an agreement that affirms not only peace between France and Italy but also between themselves.

Cueva has manipulated numerous dramatic conventions in crafting an emotional victory for her principal female character. The entire drama depends for its story and action on the sustained predicament of a rejected male lover, in this instance the king himself. Rather than serving as the means, or potential means, of resolution for romantic entanglements, the king himself is the center of the problem. Embracing fully the connection between woman and her emotions, Cueva develops her character Armesinda as an unwaveringly faithful individual whose moral strength derives from the depth of her affection for Juan. The playwright represents the vitality of the internal realm of emotion in which Armesinda's authority of virtue and chastity resides. The political power and force of monarchies and warriors is incapable of successful challenge to that inner dimension. The typical might, fortitude, and vigor of the knight, represented by Juan, are depicted in a somewhat questionable way through his overly long accounts of his exploits in tournament games (early in Act 1) and military conquests (late in Act 3). He and King Filiberto occupy two extremes of the male characterizations: the monarch enacts the unrequited lover; Juan, seemingly preoccupied with his knight's reputation and feats of military skill, courts Armesinda for six years without marrying her. Armesinda progresses through the play's action caught between the seductive lover and the warrior, each of whom enacts what could be by *comedia* standards the other's primary role.

Armesinda eventually obtains her goal of marriage to Juan and follows the pattern of female *comedia* protagonists, but she has done so in the face of conditions that test her convictions to that end. She has enacted the stipulations of the play's title by remaining firm in her emotional commitment despite the various dimensions of absence that Cueva writes into the drama. The absence of ethical royal authority is what causes the discomfort and predicament for all characters. Although it is not to be expected that a king have no personal feelings, it is necessarily incumbent upon the occupant of such an office to serve as model of morality. To pursue his love for Armesinda in the ways he does diminishes Filiberto's status as leader and relegates him to the position of a tyrant who resorts to underhanded abuses of power. The physical absence of Juan ironically does not change Armesinda or her feelings. Their longstanding courtship, in effect, has assured the absence of marriage vows, and she behaves when he is far away just as she did when he was at court. In addition, in the absence of any socially or politically recognizable authority of her own, Armesinda is able to thwart the designs of the most powerful male and to prove wrong the doubts of the man she has loved so well.[11]

Cueva's individualist feminism resonates in the characterization of Armesinda as a female who transcends the limitations attributed to her gender and who surmounts the shortcomings of the portrayed males. Nevertheless, the constructed qualities of Womanhood are depicted as strengths: Armesinda's emotional commitment and chastity celebrate a feminist essentialism that eventually helps reassert the relational model, which the men have subverted through suspicion, deception, and abuse of power. Order is restored in the end only because Armesinda remains beyond the king's rule.

3

MARRIAGE DILEMMAS

Dicha y desdicha del juego y devoción de la Virgen
and *La margarita del Tajo que dio nombre*
a Santarén (Azevedo)

La mujer debe gobernar la casa y el marido el arca.

—Proverb

Whoever takes a wife wants money.

—Alessandra Macinghi Strozzi (fifteenth century)

Porque no ay joya ni posesión tan preciada ni embiada como la buena muger.

—Fray Luis de León, *La perfecta casada*

Woman, insofar as she is a wife, is the glory of man

—Cornelius a Lapide

By 1647 the Spanish government had experienced its third royal bankruptcy (1607 during the reign of Philip III; both 1627 and 1647 under Philip IV). As J.H. Elliott explains, Spain's fiscal distress in this period had multiple causes, among them currency manipulations that fed inflation, alterations in revenue from the New World, the accumulation of royal debts, escalating costs and excessive taxation, and the high price of almost constant warfare.[1] Commenting on this last element in particular, Elliott contends: "Intense fiscal pressures were brought to bear on every group in Castilian society—privileged and unprivileged alike—with the result that some of the traditional social distinctions between the tax-payer and the tax-exempt began to be eroded. . . . But the erosion of old privileges was to some extent offset by the introduction of new ones [and] Castile fell prey to the profiteers" (129).

Changes in traditions and practices provoked many moralizing diatribes against the economic and moral *declinación* felt to be the result of
Spain's perceived loss of glory and power. Treatises known as *arbitrios*,
suggesting some means to rescue the state from its degenerate condition, were written and circulated by such figures as Sancho de
Moncada, Pedro Fernández de Navarrete, Pedro de Rivadeneyra, Jerónimo de Ceballos, Pedro de Guzmán, Fray Juan de Santa María, Luis
Valle de la Cerda, Miguel Caxa de Leruela. Citing sentiments articulated in the writing of Martín González de Cellorigo, and echoing those
in the *arbitrios* of many others, Elliott explains a major theme: "Things
had gone wrong because the social balance had been upset—all modera-
tion and just proportion had gone, as men aspired to a higher social
status than that of their fathers." He continues: "This was a commonplace of the times, repeated by the *arbitristas* and royal ministers and
echoed by playwrights. Once again, inevitably, it pointed to return—
return to an age when society was in balance. . . . They looked to the
past as a model, and therefore change took the form of restoration"
(256-57). This was but one of the models, however, for some social
critics addressed what they saw as backwardness in sociopolitical and
economic matters and prescribed solutions "provided not by an ideali-
zed version of the national past, but by the present practice of
contemporary states." These "two currents of reform competed for
attention—one pressing for a return to the ancient ways, the other for
innovating change" (Elliott, 257).

Among the issues central to the interests of Renaissance feminists
within such a context of disrupted economic conditions were abuses af-
fecting marriage practices and reflecting the discomfort of women who
functioned as commodities exchanged between fathers and husbands.
Jordan notes: "Works in which the status of women is the chief subject
also criticize the attitudes and practices of patriarchy, particularly paternal greed and marital brutality" (11). The tension between the relational feminist model and the individualist one suggests the dynamic
at work in the struggles for validation between the proponents of a
return to a better past and the supporters of a new mode, since for both
groups what was current practice was unacceptable and had to be re-
formed or redefined. In the dramatic depictions of untenable situations
for marriageable or married women examined in this chapter, the

playwright Angela de Azevedo concentrates on the disastrous situation for all concerned when hegemonical patriarchal essentialism is left unchecked. Her two plays *Dicha y desdicha del juego y devoción de la Virgen* and *La margarita del Tajo que dio nombre a Santarén* are pessimistic about the possibility of change in the prevailing system. Only supernatural means, they suggest, can rescue the women victimized by a nonegalitarian male hierarchy that allows men, whatever their shortcomings, to control the political, familial, and social dimensions of the portrayed societies.

In *Dicha y desdicha del juego,* chaotic conditions predominate when the male characters, representative of the degenerate nobility, turn their backs on the old values and rely on such current elements of desperation as gambling and fortune-hunting to settle their economic problems or satisfy their lust for extraordinary riches. Likewise, in *La margarita del Tajo* the institutions of secular and religious marriage—the two states considered legitimate for respectable women of the period—are portrayed as having been devalued in a moral dimension that parallels the economic one so deeply implicated in the other play. These two works reflect the dichotomous nature of the debates about restoration of the past or progress toward a renovated future and, like the plays by Caro and Cueva examined in Chapter 2, make a case for the feminist relational model, though it suffers because of moral deficiencies of the men. Azevedo's unrelentingly negative version of gendered imbalances permits her to urge attention to the injustices suffered by the disempowered women she portrays while validating both relational and individualist feminist models. Her female characters give every indication that they have internalized and upheld the contemporary notions about ideal womanhood, even with its demands for silence, chastity, and enclosure. Being the *perfecta casada* is an acceptable goal for these women; the disasters or near-disasters visited upon them are due to the deviation of the male characters from their "natural" hegemonic roles as leaders and caretakers. The normativeness of constructed gender positions is reinforced by the women's continual efforts to protect the threatened integrity of the social and spiritual institution of marriage. Yet in representing the impasse faced even by those women who embrace the social model of propriety, Azevedo offers a further complication to the pattern that Margaret King

identifies in her examination of myriad early and late Renaissance treatises on womanhood, marriage, and family matters: "Since women's
roles were defined by sexual and economic relationships to men, society made little place for the woman who was unattached to man or
God" (29). Azevedo creates dramatized societal situations in which
there is no comfortable place even for those women who are so
attached.

The birth of a daughter was understood in early modern Europe as
a burden, whereas the birth of a son was hailed as a benefit. As King
explains, "sons were preferred to daughters because the former could
increase, while the latter threatened, the patrimony" (25). While families from the peasantry and urban lower class struggled to subsist, even
the most affluent noble clans consistently faced the possibility of natural catastrophe or social disruption and reorganization; thus "children
offered the possibilities of survival on the one hand, and of ruin on the
other." In the case of a daughter, "from the instant of her birth, the
prospect of a dowry loomed large over the female; she represented potential loss rather than potential gain" (26).[2]

In *Dicha y desdicha del juego y devoción de la Virgen,* Azevedo emphasizes
the objectification and commodification of the female family member
by dramatizing an extreme case. It focuses on the social and economic
consequences for long-held cultural values of the inflationary effects
brought about by Spain's fiscal calamities and the growth of European
exchange relations. Azevedo incorporates these issues into a critique of
the male supervision of marriage arrangements, demonstrating that the
depicted family's father and son, who exercise control over the family
structure, are responsible for the group's economic ruin. Azevedo shows
how the dowry system—for centuries an established force in the provi-
sions for marriages among "all but the most destitute women" (Perry,
66)—was affected by the expanding importance of the marketplace "and
the increasing importance of money," which "disrupted traditional hierarchies of social status and privilege" (Beverley 221). With reference to
Jean-Christophe Agnew's study of early modern English theater, John
Beverley argues that this social situation in Spain also produced "a crisis
of representation that the emerging secular theater both reflected and
deepened" (221).

Azevedo's *Dicha y desdicha del juego* foregrounds these issues by depicting a pair of siblings whose poverty endangers their ability to maintain the privileged status their inherited nobility implies. Without their former wealth, Felisardo and María suffer a social devaluation, and their nobility counts for very little in the face of reduced assets. The family riches having been squandered by a now deceased father too much given to gambling, brother and sister must contend with the adverse results of penury in their plans for the future. Their individual and familial disempowerment is most heavily felt by the female sibling, yet the force for resolution is likewise female—the Virgin Mary. The male figures, who are able to participate in, if not control the economic and political factors, are shown to have completely disrupted the economic comfort of themselves and others. What economic strength is depicted, moreover, is often dependent upon fortune, chance, or greed rather than on the guidance and direction of a competent supervising agent or the structure of a stable social hierarchy.

Control over the family's wealth in Renaissance Europe remained with male heads of households, and women served as the medium of exchange. Upon marrying, a woman brought with her the fraction of the paternal assets designated to her; in Spain the dowry was her portion of the entire inheritance to be divided among all heirs, both male and female. The apportionment of the dowry removed all further claims by the daughter on the father's holdings, and "for the duration of her marriage, a woman retained title to her property. Husbands welcomed the wealth brought by wives into the marital household: it was theirs to use at the moment, and it would enrich their heirs in the future. . . . At all times, therefore, dowry wealth belonged perfectly to daughters, but remained ineluctably in male control" (M. King, 49).[3] This patriarchal relational system promoted harmony and provided for posterity, but relegated woman to a lowly place in the resultant hierarchy. Many of the humanists, for instance, urged the embrace of a family structure in which the husband in his public activity would provide for his family's economic well-being, while his enclosed wife would guard the wealth and see that it was spent wisely.[4]

Early in the first act of her drama, Azevedo allows the play's poverty-stricken nobleman to ponder his social quandary as the family member who controls the destiny of his female relative. What he can and must do about his sister María is described as Felisardo's problem, faced, as he is, with their ignoble poverty *and* the implied privilege their aristocratic bloodline still promises. There is no scene of joint contemplation of their mutual dilemma; the woman constitutes a problem that must be resolved before the brother can pursue his own desire to marry. To his servant's insistence that he could put an end to his fretting over the safety of a young and beautiful unmarried sister by "a tu hermana dar estado" (243), Felisardo laments:

> ¿Qué estado, di? ¿Tú estás necio?
> Si en toda aquesta ciudad
> no hay más pobre caballero
> que yo, aunque por la sangre
> a todos ventaja llevo,
> ¿dónde ha de venir el dote
> para mi hermana? [244-50]

Even Sombrero's suggestion that Felisardo arrange for his sister to enter a convent is met with the logical rebuttal that "siempre es preciso el dispendio / en la entrada y profesión" (275-76).[5]

The worth of María, like that of other women so discussed, is measured in family fortune, not in her many positive personal attributes that her brother also emphasizes. What emerges in the men's various discussions of her throughout the play is that she has fulfilled the conditions prescribed for her sex: both piety and chastity, through her absolute dedication to the Virgin Mary and her lack of experience with romantic love. María has remained aloof and enclosed, away from secular society, and is portrayed as a woman who has internalized the ideals of chastity, enclosure, and silence. But her portrayal also suggests a strength of conviction, demonstrated through her devotions and her adherence to the social rules, that her male relatives do not display. Chiding her maid Rosela, in fact, for revealing María's identity and residence in conversation with a nobleman's servant, the young woman reminds the *criada* that speaking "[e]n doncellas es prohibido" (1813). For *comedia* women, however, such careful observance of the requirements for respectability in a woman and prospective wife—which María embodies—seems not to matter except in its absence.

The devaluation of moral wealth and socially determined attributes and the inflationary appreciation of the material dimension are emphasized in Felisardo's initial conversation with Sombrero. The carnivalesque reversal of this scene focuses upon the inverse system of evaluation of a human being's worth in which only the material aspects are considered. The *gracioso* says:

> . . . Aquesto es desprecio
> para una moza bonita,
> discreta y noble; ¿este resto
> no vale nada? ¿Las gracias
> no es, señor, cosa de precio?
> ¿Las prendas ya no se estiman?
> ¿Puede haber mejor empleo
> para un hidalgo, si es rico,
> que el hallazgo de un sujeto
> con las partes de tu hermana? [251-60]

That it is the play's clown, the conventionally most materialistic character in a cast of *comedia* characters, who articulates a critique of this appraisal of María further reverses the hierarchical expectations. When told by his master that marriages of the sort he describes are no longer sought—"no quieren prendas los hombres" (262)—Sombrero continues in this transgressive pattern, offering himself to Felisardo as a prospective match for María: "¿No? Pues son unos jumentos; / dámela, señor, a mí, / que no reparo en dineros" (263-65). Regardless of the sentiments involved in either this side of the argument or the more materialistic side, Azevedo focuses on the fact that the woman is still the subject of discussion and decision-making by men, and that this takes place across social rank; neither class nor economic considerations supersede gender as a category of repression.

The play's action admits complications when a rival for the hand of Felisardo's beloved, Violante, arrives. Don Fadrique returns after a ten-year stay in the New World, where he went to seek his economic fortune. Coming home to Portugal with "quinientos mil ducados" (988), he has put an end to his own impoverished state. But he retains a spiritual and moral debt to the Virgin Mary, to whom he made a promise in exchange for her protection during a storm that almost shipwrecked his vessel:

> pues viéndome en el peligro
> de aquella tempestad brava,

has de saber que hice un voto
a la Virgen soberana,
de que si de aquel aprieto
con vida y caudal libraba,
en esta ciudad de Oporto
(noble empeño de la fama)
con la más pobre doncella,
siendo noble y siendo honrada,
casaría. [1020-30]

Seeing María in church, Fadrique learns through their servants that she is poor, honorable, and noble; she seems to represent the means to fulfill his promise to the Virgin. And Fadrique himself would seem the solution to the dilemma Felisardo has pondered about how to marry off his sister without a dowry.

Impediments to these ends arise, however, when the sudden death of Fadrique's father brings him into contact with Violante's father, Don Nuño Osorio. As one of Oporto's most noble and wealthiest citizens, Nuño contributed the majority of the funds to "disponer las exequias" (1226) for the funeral rites. According to Fadrique's servant Tijera, his own earlier conversation with Don Nuño has also dealt precisely with the marriage prospects of Violante, who is described in this subsequent judgmental discussion between the male adventurer and his servant as "la más noble y de más partes, / la más honrada y más rica" (1243-44). Fadrique's interest is immediately piqued, and his change of heart with regard to María prompts his servant to exclaim: "¡Jesús, no ha de haber mujer / que a ti, señor, no te agrade!" (1288). Since he has never seen her, Violante's attractiveness for Fadrique at this point rests primarily in the social ascension a marriage with her would afford him, since he is not of the same noble lineage as she. He comments directly upon "las desigualdades, / que hay de su sangre a la mía" (1297-98) and the fact that "el blasón de los Osorios" (1300) is a means to add social rank to his new-found wealth. Disregarding his vow to the Virgin, he decides to seize the opportunity that presents itself when Don Nuño seems not to worry about his lack of nobility: "mas ya que su padre quiere, / sin que en aquesto repare" (1302-3).

In fact, such disregard for social level was a danger warned against by some moralists, but usually in treatises that urged against allowing young people to choose their own spouses. In his seventeenth-century *Libro de la guía y de la virtud,* Alonso de Andrade claims: "Si se casase con menoscabo de su honra, y con persona de menor calidad, sería un pecado grave dar a sus padres tal afrenta, y causa de tanta amargura, con mancha de tanto deshonor."[6] Azevedo creates a reversal of certain elements in such a social configuration, for the young woman's father is the one who seeks her marriage with someone of lesser social rank than she and against his daughter's wishes—all in order to increase his own vast fortune. The men in this dramatized situation, even before meeting, are agreeable to an arranged marriage that is based on the noble's avarice and the newly rich adventurer's social ambition but that lacks any consent to or even awareness of the proceedings by the woman being exchanged. The weight of the moral debt to the Virgin is dismissed and made light of in a play on words: Fadrique wonders aloud to his servant, "Y el voto, que he hecho, di?" (1320), to which Tijera answers, "Ese voto es dispensable; / miren como está devoto" (1321-22).[7]

Through the portrayal of such a father as Nuño, Azevedo dramatizes a critique of the injustices that follow the breakdown of the virtues that are supposed to govern the social hierarchy. She focuses especially upon the woman commodified as merchandise to be haggled over by men. The playwright also suggests a negative appraisal of the handling of wealth from the New World, which by the seventeenth century had found its way into the coffers of other nations and had escaped Spain without sustained economic benefit to its treasury.[8] The greed that underlies Fadrique's attractiveness in Don Nuño's eyes, despite his illegitimacy—from the standpoint of traditional aristocratic standards—as an aspirant for Violante's hand, implies a deeper political commentary from someone like Azevedo. She, after all, lived at court and was exposed to much of the criticism from *arbitristas* and commentators of what they saw as evidence of Spain's decline in the "decay of manners and morals" as well as in matters "essentially economic and fiscal" (Elliott, 253). Azevedo's treatment of Nuño reveals the conservative element apparent in many of the works by the women writers of seventeenth-century Spain who depict the abandonment of traditional social structures and values having to do particularly with social class as a serious problem at the same time that they critique common gendered prejudices. As the senior member of the society portrayed, Nuño represents the top of the patriarchal familial hierarchy that the national monarchical structure symbolically replicates. As the source of the mounting crisis, Nuño's depiction implies an indirect critique of the national crisis that the *arbitristas* continued to write about more directly in their tracts.

Nuño articulates his calculated desire to augment his already sizable estate by marrying his daughter to a rich man, in spite of the feelings she shares with Felisardo. He comments to himself in Act 1:

> mis escrúpulos me están
> diciendo que a la nobleza
> atendiendo y gentileza
> de Felisardo, le elija
> por marido de mi hija,
> mas me embarga su pobreza.
> Con tan pobre casamiento
> ni dice riqueza tanta,
> pues ni caudal se adelanta,
> ni la casa va en aumento;
> yo pues que aumentarla intento. [904-14]

It is Nuño who seeks out Fadrique. He calls on the young adventurer at his home at a dramatically crucial point just after Fadrique's conversation with Tijera about abandoning the intended suit of María in favor of the match with the wealthier Violante. Nuño discusses the possibilities of this match and applies pressure of various sorts to elicit Fadrique's acceptance. Describing Violante as his only heir—"su dote es mi casa toda" (1396)—he also insists:

> dadme, señor, luego el sí,
> porque el tiempo es variable,
> y muchas veces sucede
> que en materias semejantes,
> lo que luego no se ajusta,
> sin logro se ve quedarse. [1402-7]

Such sentiments and behavior exemplify the practices that various Renaissance moralists urged against. Like his Spanish counterparts, the Italian humanist Francesco Barbaro, for instance, stressed the importance of virtue and nobility over monetary gain in the process of choosing a spouse: "Virtue, therefore, should be considered first, because its power, its dignity is such that if all other advantages are lacking, yet the marriage is desirable; and if they are present, they render it joyous." As if critiquing the very attitude portrayed by Don Nuño, Barbaro censures those who, "blinded by infamous and detestable avarice, only to acquire for themselves an abundance of gold, attached themselves at last to families of very low and sordid lineage" (quoted in M. King, 32). A century later, Vives also urged against the arrangement of marriages on unsound bases, and warned: "Ni conviene que el padre o los curadores de la doncella rueguen ni trafaguen . . . sino que debe ser el varón quien la pida en matrimonio. Así se haría si el dinero no lo midiese y gobernase todo. Ahora la mujer cásase con el dinero, y con el dinero se casa el hombre . . .Por eso es que tan a menudo vemos tan tristes e infelices casamientos" (1071).

Fadrique accepts Nuño's offer but admits to Tijera his surprise that so highborn a man with such wealth would be so anxious to have him for a son-in-law. The servant remarks: "No te espantes / ni te admires porque un rico / otro rico busca" (1435-37). The inversion of the traditional evaluation of honor and nobility leads to the ironic circular conclusion on Fadrique's part that there may be some hidden reason why Nuño would sacrifice his daughter to a marriage socially beneath her:

> ¿Sabes
> en lo que reparo sólo?
> En que así se apresurase,
> no sé si de algún secreto
> tanta diligencia sale. [1437-41]

The system of inflationary greed in which Nuño includes Fadrique has debased all the nonmaterial attributes that the woman in question embodies. Through no fault of her own, her honor and integrity now seem suspect because her father barters her as a market commodity to the highest bidder. One of the gravest abuses of patriarchal essentialism is represented in this inflationary objectification of Violante.[9]

Although Fadrique and Tijera now realize the power and prestige that the master's wealth affords them ("que han de venir a buscarte / más de dos mil casamientos; / y éstos, de los principales" [1449-51]),

Fadrique decides that he can make no better match. The scene ends
with the proposal of a poetry contest between the two: both master and
servant will compose verses to their ladies, Violante and her maid
Belisa. The possibility of exchanging the poems is proposed by Tijera,
who insists that the two women are in reality interchangeable: "pues
donde Belisa diga, / Violante puede encajarse" (1494-95). Azevedo thus
emphasizes the commonplace *comedia* pattern of replaceable partners,
which allows jilted lovers to be traded for others who seem more appealing for one reason or another; through the role-playing quality of
marriage matches, she also insinuates the breakdown of social stability.
This scene implies that all women are sexually accessible to all men because they are universalized regardless of social rank.

The negativity of the patriarchal essentializing, relentlessly depicted
in Azevedo's drama, reaches its most extreme point when Felisardo du-
plicates the sins of his father at the gambling table, committing the
further atrocity of using his sister as collateral for his debts. He can con-
ceive of no other way to overcome the impediments to his union with
Violante than to gamble with Fadrique in the hope of reversing their
economic fortunes. Here Azevedo makes a strong case against the inequities of materalistic marriage arrangements by reinforcing the
woman-as-commodity image and the lack of stability and integrity in
the men who control this system.

Ironically, on the basis of his scruples, Felisardo dismisses his servant's suggestion that he and Violante elope:

> ¿Yo a su padre dar disgustos,
>
> a Violante sobresaltos,
>
> a mi hermana turbaciones
>
> y a mí nombre de hombre bajo? [2227-30]

Instead, in admitted imitation of his father—who before the play's beginning gambled away all the family's assets—Felisardo follows the
advice of an astrologer whose prediction (". . . que afable el astro / me
promete por el juego / de ventura un grande hallazgo / en cierta
ocasión" [2264-67]) urges him to depend on chance. He thus takes
measures that render him completely out of control of his plan's outcome. He faces an adversary who himself has sought wealth through

the uncertainties of the colonial enterprise, and the playwright emphasizes the precariousness of a social system based on these arbitrary and extreme measures.

Azevedo's contribution here seems to match others, literary and non-literary, in its opposition to the governmental policies of Philip IV and his powerful minister the Count-Duke Olivares. Elliott, for instance, says of the latter's policies:

> It was [a] do-or-die mentality which kept Spain at war for decade after decade, even as the odds turned against it. It is a state of mind which needs explaining. The key to the relationship between foreign policy and domestic affairs in seventeenth-century Spain will ultimately be found to lie in the mentality of the imperial ruling class, and in its perception of the world around it. . . . Like gamblers with a dwindling pile of coins, they kept on hoping that one final throw would lead to a spectacular reversal of their fortunes. In this perhaps they were not totally misguided. The years of success—1625, 1634, 1636—suggested that shipwreck might yet be averted. And if God willed otherwise, then, in the Count-Duke's words, the most honourable response was to "die doing something." [135-36]

These suggestive phenomena find resonance in my reading of this play's portrayal of Fadrique, Felisardo, and Nuño. Azevedo's service as attendant to Queen Isabel de Borbón could have kept her at court at least until 1641, when the queen died, and so she can reasonably be assumed to have witnessed much of the disruption and intrigue evident in governmental affairs during the first half of Philip IV's reign.

Other dimensions of Azevedo's opposition to social conditions at the national level and their consequences at the more personal level seem also to be encoded in *Dicha y desdicha del juego*. As Elliott also remarks:

> Much of the aristocratic opposition inevitably took the form of palace intrigue. . . . To judge from the plays commissioned from Tirso de Molina by members of the Pimentel family, there may have been a theatre of opposition, but more serious for the regime was the posting of pasquinades and the circulation of clandestine pamphlets.[10] This covert opposition literature, circulating either in manuscript or in clandestine imprints, repeated certain standard themes: the disastrous consequences for Spain of the Count-Duke's economic and foreign policies; the arbi-

trary character of his government, and his usurpation of the powers of the king. [182]

Through her portrayal of unstable stewards of family wealth, Azevedo implies parallels between the consequences for the nation of unsound programs that included continuous warfare and uncontrolled spending, and the consequences for women of the rivalries generated between rich men who could bargain or gamble with the lives of their female relatives.[11]

Act 3 begins, in the aftermath of the game of chance between the two young men, with Felisardo's curse against idleness, gaming, and the inventor of gambling.[12] From his early lines we quickly learn that he initially won a great sum from Fadrique, only to lose the money once again and then to use his own sister as collateral for a further wager. His loss of this last round of cards and Fadrique's acceptance of the wager and expectation of collecting the debt dramatize a complicity on the part of the male characters with regard to women as means to an economic end. Both the man who has been driven to desperation by poverty and the one who is enjoying the comfort of monetary security display irresponsible attitudes toward their respective situations, and both demonstrate extreme disregard for the feelings and reputation of a woman whose importance to each of them is chiefly materialistic.

Even his hoped-for marriage to Violante likewise becomes a secondary concern to Felisardo at the gaming table, for although he laments his actions, his servant points out that greed and the male code of honor were overriding factors in his behavior. Sombrero surmises:

> que cuando ganado habías
> cuatrocientos mil ducados
> (que era bastanta mobilia)
> no quisiste levantarte;
> porque sin duda te hacían
> los ciento que le quedaban
> a don Fadrique cosquillas;
> y como todo lo pierde
> el que todo lo codicia,
> te ha dejado tu ambición
> en el estado que miras. [2493-1503]

At Felisardo's insistence that his motivation for persisting in the game was different, Sombrero suggests another reason: "el no querer cometer / aquella descortesía / de levantarte del juego" (2508-10). Felisardo's affirmative response reiterates the horrific system of inverted codes of honor and materialism that these male characters represent, showing that the standards of propriety at the gaming table take precedence over the rights of the female members of society. The women serve merely as physical bodies, objects to be exchanged or used as security in monetary dealings. The *gracioso* points out that not only has Fadrique won back all his money but, with regard to Violante and María, "que una ha de ser su mujer, / y otra su dama" (2538-39).

Felisardo shows himself completely incapable of handling the consequences of his disastrous actions. He realizes the magnitude of his error, but continuing to think primarily of himself, he decides to abandon both María and Violante and run away: "será vergüenza que viva / más en aquesta ciudad / . . . / Voyme por el mundo, adiós" (2555-58). Fadrique later admits his own base motivations for having participated in this agreement with Felisardo:

> ¿Ves cual me iba dejando
> Felisardo del juego en la contienda,
> que me iba ya ganando
> mi dinero a las pintas y mi hacienda,
> de que si no llegara
> otra vez a ganarle, reventara?
> Pero no has de creer,
> que sola aquesta pérdida lloraba;
> más lloraba el perder
> la mano de Violante a que aspiraba,
> que la riqueza mía
> (tan poderosa es) me concedía.
> Con esto, pues, quedé
> a Felisardo tan opuesto, amigo,
> que le aborreceré
> de hoy más cual mi contrario y mi enemigo;
> y es venganza tirana
> más que apetito el logro de su hermana. [3050-67]

As Felisardo prepares to flee, the reversal of the expected hierarchical relationships of master and buffoonlike servant, depicted numerous times during this play, is again enacted. Tijera points out the injustice done to María and says to Fadrique, "mira que no conviene / que ella pague la culpa que no tiene" (3072-73).

Azevedo insinuates through her characters that no solution can be found among the players of this dramatized situation, because the women lack empowerment and the men adhere to the materialistic values of a degenerated patriarchal system. Only through the intercession of external, divine forces can the ills of this society be remedied. Here too, however, gender issues continue to inform the representation. From the beginning of the play, María and Felisardo have referred to their shared devotion to the Virgin Mary, a devotion urged by their mother on her deathbed. María has respected this commitment more formally than her brother, but as the play proceeds there is evidence that it is also deeply meaningful to him.

Until late in the third act, the presence of the Virgin is evident only by her statue and devotional altar, which María faithfully attends in their home, and the rescue of Fadrique at sea. The Virgin Mary is counterposed by the Demonio, who appears physically once in each act. Through him, Azevedo turns upside down the traditional association between woman and Satan that traces its authority back to readings of Genesis and Eve's interaction with the serpent. In this play, it is only the men whom the devil can influence. He begins by inspiring the dream that Felisardo and Sombrero share in Act 1 when they believe that the house has been invaded by thieves. The devil's resentment of the Virgin and her strength and protection of the world are the focus of his desire for revenge; the devout and pious María, her brother, and his beloved Violante are the field of combat on which the Demonio proclaims "guerra contra devotos de María" (559).

While the male characters become the easily manipulated pawns of the devil, the women remain constant in their virtuous and faithful intentions. In Act 2, the Demonio laments his lack of success in influencing Violante's unfaltering love for Felisardo:

> Es verdad que a Violante,
> de Felisardo en el amor constante,

> obligar no he podido
> a que aquéste su amor ponga en olvido
> y a don Fadrique quiera,
> porque es al fin amante verdadera;
> y en llegando a querer,
> ni un demonio divierte la mujer. [1552-59]

Through this obvious reversal of the typical misogynous diatribe repeated in many *comedias* about the fickleness of women, this play, like
Cueva's, portrays the opposite situation. Violante, for instance, rejects
any notion that she might be able to adjust to a marriage with Fadrique
because, she protests, she will never stop loving Felisardo. This faith,
however, is not necessarily rewarded with appreciation from the men.
When Felisardo learns of the match that Don Nuño has contracted for
Violante, he assumes, in the absence of any concrete assurance to the
contrary from her, that she has willingly agreed to it: "Y del suceso Violante, / que avisarme no ha querido, / debe de ser de su gusto"
(1955-57).

Violante is the only character who devises a workable plan of resistance to the marriage for money that her father has prepared.
Instructing Belisa to gather together her jewels so that when her father
leaves the house, she can escape and go directly to Felisardo's home, Violante proves herself ready to risk her reputation and even her life in
order to marry him before Don Nuño comes in pursuit:

> No hay que advertir, mi amor busca
> mi marido, y tú responde
> de mi padre a la pregunta
> que me metí en un convento,
> porque mientras no se apura
> la verdad, tiempo se ofrezca
> para casarnos. [2719-25]

In the meantime, however, the cowardly Felisardo has retreated into
the woods in his journey to some place "donde a mi patria de mí /
jamás las noticias vengan / ni yo las tenga de mi patria" (2756-58). Furthermore, he has decided to deepen his separation from the traditional
beliefs and values of his culture by making a pact with the devil: "Pues
yo en mi pena tan fiera / el demonio he de invocar" (2779-80). Telling

the Demonio that "Está pronta mi obediencia / a la disposición tuya" (2815-16), and receiving the assurance that the figure from Hell can solve all his problems with regard to money and marriage, Felisardo hears the terms of the contract into which he is about to enter:

> Lo que importa, Felisardo,
> es que por lograr tu empresa,
> de Dios, de la fe cristiana
> y de los misterios que encierra
> reniegues. [2820-24]

Felisardo agrees—"yo estoy por lo que me dices" (2834)—but asks if there are any more conditions. When told that to finalize his bargain with the devil he must fulfill one more stipulation, to renounce the Virgin Mary ("con su lengua mesma / renegará de la Virgen" [2841-42]), he begins to resist. Stronger than his obedience and devotion to God the Father is his veneration of the Mother of God: "María en mi pecho reina, / y no he de hacerla ese agravio / . . . / Todo sin María es nada" (2853-60). Swept up into the air by the angry devil, he calls upon her for assistance.[13]

The floating male figures are thereupon joined by the figure of the Virgin Mary, who takes her place between the Demonio and Felisardo and assures the forgiveness of Felisardo through her intercession:

> y más con mi patrocinio,
> que tiene con Dios tal fuerza,
> que como le tenga el hombre
> de su parte, no experimenta
> de Dios el menor castigo. [2920-24]

She thus reiterates another instance of female authority and its basis in negotiation (see Chapter 1). She also resolves all facets of the personal dilemma Felisardo has been unable to remedy himself as she validates the personal connections he has disrupted:

> Y así, Felisardo, vete
> a tu casa norabuena,
> donde hallarás con Fadrique
> casada tu hermana bella,

y don Nuño te dará
a Violante . . . . [2934-39]

All of this comes to pass, and Azevedo assigns dialogue to the three
principal male characters in which each one publicly admits his errors
and his iniquities, thereby using the male prerogative of speech to reveal
his own shortcomings.

This play dramatizes the consequences of valuing persons on the
basis of their monetary worth. The negative quality of the gender ideology that makes of woman a commodity in the exchange market
between men is emphasized by the males' unseemly behavior and lack
of control over their economic status. The women's inability to exert
dominion over economic assets or choice of marriage partner is a state
of affairs then mirrored by the situation in which Azevedo places the
men in her play, for until the Virgin Mary comes to the rescue, Felisardo loses both women in his life, and Nuño does not really control his
daughter. Violante's curse on arranged marriages ("Mal haya el primero,
amén, / que haciendo al gusto violencia, / busca al casar conveniencia /
más que la del querer bien" [1600-1603]) is upheld by the Virgin herself, who in the end becomes the agent in arranging the marriages that
the women have been hoping for all along.

The image of the Virgin is significant as well for what she represents
within the multiple symbols of womanhood depicted in this work. As is
typical of the *comedia* in general, where weddings are announced in the
final moments, the marriages bargained for and planned do not take
place on stage. There are thus no mothers on stage, but Azevedo allows
the mother's influence to be felt in the counsel of dedication to the
Virgin that Felisardo's and María's dying mother is said to have given
her children. Unlike their vice-ridden father, who visits ruin upon his
family, their mother consigns them to the care of this heavenly representative of motherhood. The noblewoman emphasizes the strength of
her divine surrogate, who in the Christian tradition symbolizes the
highest degree of perfection for women and in this play supersedes all
male agents in her ability to match Violante and María with their preferred mates.

The Virgin's influence is such that Felisardo, though willing to renounce God and Christianity, cannot bring himself to renounce her. As

he recounts his experience with the devil, he quotes words uttered by the Virgin Mary when she saved him and sent the devil back to Hell: "porque no permite Dios / que mis devotos peligren" (3574-75). Reaffirming the position of ultimate authority that God the Father holds in the Christian tradition, the Virgin does not deviate from the theologically sound stance. But throughout the play other statements—such as Fadrique's "Todo lo rige / la Virgen" (3593-94)—indicate the dramatically symbolic importance Azevedo recognizes in this divine representative of womanhood.[14] Her inclusion of this extra-human agent of resolution echoes as well the sort of thinking and differing conclusions about national decline recorded in the *abitrios*. Although astrological and natural deterministic forces were often invoked, Elliott argues for the predominance of the more orthodox Christian viewpoint that "in every event, great or small, the hand of an omnipotent God whose judgements were inscrutable": thus there was "an escape clause: the miraculous could occur" (248). Azevedo transposes her miraculous resolution to an alternately gendered register.

The tension set up between the purely materialistic inflationary model followed by the males in charge of social relationships and the purely spiritual dimension that rewards nonmaterial virtues is sustained. It is through the men's handling, mishandling, and manipulation of factors beyond the control of the women that the latter are socially determined as appropriate candidates for marriage or even prostituted, as María is when her brother becomes in effect her pimp for a liaison she knows nothing about until after it is contracted. The validity of the depicted social roles of these women characters is questioned, given its arbitrariness. Simultaneously, the basis of evaluation that the men initially claim reveals itself to be a carnivalesque realm where the hierarchies of moral integrity, virtue, and honor have been supplanted by vices (gambling), dishonesty (reneging on vows), greed (choosing wealth over all other considerations), and the objectification of a human being (using female relatives as collateral for gaming debts).

That the champion of the women portrayed is the symbol of "chastity, industry, silence, compassion, and obedience" (Perry, 41) indicates the limited range of models available to Azevedo for a female of strength who can exercise agency in the system as it is portrayed. As argued in Chapter 2, independent female monarchs were not a readily accessible example for emulation. Furthermore, as Perry explains, "religious symbols functioned as a common language recognized by most people as representing widely held beliefs and attitudes. Moreover, they acted to shape reality, setting expectations and interpreting reality in terms of these expectations" (41). As a model of the qualities considered desirable in women, the Holy Virgin, a virgin mother, set a standard not readily attainable for mortal women, thereby reinforcing the imperfections of their sex and reiterating the limits of society's expectation for their behavior and attitudes (Perry, 41). Azevedo nevertheless invests the Virgin with the only strength of control, affirming her positive virtues and attributes and letting her stand as the counterweight to the negative qualities that all the portrayed men embody. In addition, the only other supernatural figure to appear in the play is the male devil, who must be defeated before order can be restored. In this play Azevedo's critique focuses dialectically upon traditional values and their degeneration, yet the new order—represented by the economic ruin of the once powerful in confrontation with the social power of economic opportunists—still operates on the basis of male public privilege and female enclosure.

Azevedo's play *La margarita del Tajo que dio nombre a Santarén* makes problematical certain aspects of secular and spiritual marriage for women, of woman's intellectual life, and of male desire in the face of female chastity. If, as Margaret King and others contend, the only legitimate social space for early modern women was wifehood—either secular or religious—then this play disrupts and finally closes that space too; in Azevedo's imagined society women are continually out of place.

The story she dramatizes becomes a version of a segment of Portuguese hagiography, emphasizing the different but interrelated predicaments of two women. One is Irene, a cloistered nun whose days are spent in devotional practices and scholarly pursuits but who nevertheless becomes the object of the illicit desires of both a nobleman and a cleric.[15] Irene embodies the model of female chastity and virtuous behavior at the same time that she piously exercises her mental faculties, which convent life—unlike the secular life of marriage and motherhood—allowed women to do.[16]

The other principal female character is Rosimunda. By marrying a nobleman with whom she professes mutual love, she fulfills the secular goal set for women in a way that seems to offer emotional fulfillment. But just after their marriage her husband, Britaldo, watches Irene in church and falls passionately in love with her. This substitution of one woman for another provides a further instance of the patriarchal conception of Woman as an undifferentiated category. In this play Azevedo also provides the somewhat less frequently seen dramatic portrayal of woman after marriage. What she depicts is unhappiness following the closing moments of traditional *comedia* plots, which end with announcements of forthcoming marriages.

The play begins with a conversation between Britaldo and his servant Etcétera about the nobleman's lovesickness. The *criado* remarks: "¡Tú triste recién casado! / En verdad que es caso extraño" (137-38). Describing his master's symptoms and the medical diagnosis in terms of irrationality and the passions, he tells Britaldo:

> ¿Qué es esto, señor, que ha dado
> tu pena, por peregrina,
> cuidado a la medicina,
> porque no la ha penetrado;
> y haciendo una junta fuerte
> los médicos contra ti,
> condenan tu frenesí
> a la sentencia de muerte?
> Aquél que tu mal procura
> curar, no habiendo podido,
> dice que locura ha sido,
> pues que ninguno lo cura. [145-56]

The terms *frenesí* and *locura* associate Britaldo with the unstable sort of melancholia that longstanding medical tradition characterized as typical of females, given their supposedly weaker mental and physical systems.[17]

Recounting the care he took to find the wife of his choice, operating within a special freedom his parents gave him to do so, Britaldo reiterates the attitude of wonder that Azevedo writes into the speeches of several characters about the nobleman's change of heart toward Rosimunda. (Azevedo does not depict Rosimunda as having been empowered in the same way Britaldo is to choose her life's trajectory. When her marriage proves to be unsettled and she unappreciated in spite of her conformity to the ideal of the "perfecta casada," however, she does eventually assume a position of active investigation.) Since he found himself "de mi esposa tan contento, / tan pagado de sus gracias, / de su amor tan satisfecho" (318-20), Britaldo ponders aloud how his happiness could have been so short-lived. In his explanation to Etcétera he relates the events of the day he saw Irene entering the "magnífico templo / de Pedro y Pablo" (332-33) with her religious sisters of the order of San Benito:

> Vila y quedé tan perdido
> que sentí abrasarse luego
> en las luces de sus ojos
> mariposa el pensamiento. [365-68]

Invoking thought, which was philosophically hailed as a male prerogative, Britaldo goes on to describe himself as beyond reason: "Yo estoy de razón desnudo, / y así a la razón no atiendo" (387-88). Azevedo thus reverses the commonplaces that privilege the male mind for its rationality.[18]

The consequences for Britaldo's marriage are that he now loves Irene ("que sólo a Irene idolatro" [391]) and despises his wife ("y a Rosimunda aborrezco" [392]). Etcétera poses a rather playful solution that nevertheless depends upon rational control of the mental faculties: that is, that Britaldo "haga entre lo ajeno y propio / tu imaginación un trueco" (467-68) in which he should imagine that Irene is his wife and that Rosimunda is the woman of his carnal desires. But even though Britaldo acknowledges the worth of such a suggestion, he is unable to fulfill its conditions: "ni imaginación poseo" (480). The *gracioso*'s suggestion, however, emphasizes the generalizing tendencies in the males' attitudes toward women, since for Etcétera, one of the women can easily substitute for the other. For Britaldo, the category of desired woman can be filled by at least these two women, but not simultaneously. He repeats the pattern dramatized in numerous *comedias* of the abandonment of the beloved once desire is satisfied.

There is, however, a difference between the women, which Azevedo examines, again dramatizing an impossible situation that her female characters suffer, even though they adhere to the prescribed categories of respectability dictated by social and literary conventions. One has chosen marriage and the other perpetual virginity, the two states within which a woman could be deemed acceptable in society. Rosimunda gives no evidence that she intends to exceed the limits set for her as wife; indeed, she lives in her husband's house with her father-in-law as confidant. But Irene exists in a space and a social and spiritual geography supposedly beyond male sexual control of her body. As Jankowski, among others, has pointed out, the celibate monastic life offered women avenues for their agency and escape from the physical and intellectual control exercised over them in secular life: "Women opted for virginity for many reasons, spiritual ones certainly primary among them. Yet it cannot be denied . . . that women often accepted a chaste life because it granted them complete autonomy over their own bodies. . . . Only celibacy could guarantee women such total control" (28).[19] Roman Catholic notions of virgins defined them "precisely by their isolation from men, by the fact that they were the property of no 'man' but God. The virgin, then, was the only woman who defined herself exclusively in relationship to her own body, to her own selfhood. Virginity is defined as a 'voluntary' choice of abstention from carnal relations." This dimension of autonomy challenged the "traditional definition of woman as a creature owned by either a father or a husband. In a society which denied women autonomy, a virgin existence explored the possibility of a female autonomy that could only be viewed as threatening" (Jankowski, 26). Some answered the threat by redefining the virgin woman as male because of her distancing from the sexualized life of a man's wife and mother of his children. Such notions were articulated by the church fathers, among them St. Jerome who said, for instance: "As long as woman is for birth and children, she is different from man as body is from soul. But when she wishes to serve Christ more than the world, then she ceases to be a woman and will be called a man."[20]

Beyond permitting nuns to escape life under the physical control of a man, then, the state of virginity allowed them to transcend gender. Since the early Christian era it had been accepted that men and women were both subject to martyrdom. Also accepted was the lack of gender distinction in Heaven, which, in conjunction with statements such as Jerome's, encouraged the belief that martyred women too became men.[21] Jankowski continues: "This notion spread to encompass everyday life, where it was argued that consecrated women virgins could be classified socially and legally as men. In fact,priests and bishops often objected to the fact thatwomen virgins *behaved* as though they were superior to other women, behaved, in fact, as though they were men. . . . Thus, from being a threat because of their anomaly, female virgins were now becoming a threat because they were trying to transcend their gender" (28).[22]

The voluntariness of the celibate life is important in the dramatization of conflictive notions about female virgins in Azevedo's play. According to the precepts of St. Augustine, the participation of the will is crucial to the definition of virginity, which could come into question in cases of rape. Jane T. Schulenburg points out: "In offering consolation to those women within the Christian fellowship who have been sexually assaulted, Augustine assures them that 'violation of chastity, without the will's consent, cannot pollute the character'" (35). In addition to stressing this division of body and soul, however, Augustine emphasizes their interconnectedness in the matter of sexual assault when the victim is blamed for a secret wish to be raped: "But there can be committed on another's body not only acts involving pain, but also acts involving lust. And so whenever any act of the latter kind has been committed, although it does not destroy a purity which has been maintained by the utmost resolution, still it does engender a sense of shame, because it may be believed that an act, which perhaps could not have-taken place without some physical pleasure, was accompanied by a consent of the mind" (quoted in Schulenberg, 35).[23]

In Azevedo's play the victim is blamed in just such a way, and her victimization is thus doubled. Irene symbolizes for Britaldo the voluntarily unreachable virgin who has chosen to live without expression of her sexuality and is thus beyond his influence and reach. Yet eventually even she is assumed guilty, on circumstantial evidence, of breaking her vows. Although she does not endure the ravages of a rape, her body becomes the field of contest between Britaldo and another male who desires her.

Neither entreaties nor expressions of concern from his wife and his father Castinaldo can effect a change in Britaldo's attitudes or elicit a clear explanation of his coldness toward Rosimunda and his stated wish to die. His wife becomes suspicious that his troubles result "de algún cuidado amoroso" (1025), and she enlists a family confidant, Banán, to spy on Britaldo. This reversal of the famous wife-murder plots, which depict jealous and suspicious husbands investigating the fidelity of their wives, emphasizes the wife's side of a dilemma of potential adultery.[24] In this dramatized family, the wife has followed the tenets of gender ideology by marrying well and willingly and demonstrating the qualities of ". . . lealtad, / recato y honestidad, / decoro, sangre y nobleza, / amor, constancia y firmeza" (628-31). In return, her husband exhibits the emotional reticence usually attributed to the female *esquiva* figure of literary convention, and Rosimunda's maid Lucinda remarks on " . . . la pena esquiva / de su esposo" (605-6). Azevedo subtly injects through such remarks the possibility of impotence on Britaldo's part and, by emphasizing his obsession with the sexuality of a celibate nun who in her sustained separation from heterosexuality would be culturally redefined as male, even a homoerotic suggestion. Nothing more than innuendo on such issues is present, yet Azevedo is relentless in her negative portrayal of heterosexual marriage or desire.

Repeating to Rosimunda the metaphor of the butterfly's destruction in the flame, which epitomizes Britaldo's thought before the attraction of Irene's beauty ("la mariposa la sigue / para en su luz abrasarse / por hallarla apetecible" [1263-65]), Banán reveals to the distressed woman the truth about where her husband goes when he leaves their house. Although he insists that his friend suffers "Amor sin aceptación" (1274), Rosimunda believes of Britaldo and the nun that "Los dos sin duda se quieren" (1286). She vows "al convento voy a reñirle" (1291). The response from the suspicious wife is far from the violence associated with the masculine response dramatized in numerous male-authored honor dramas.

Irene—the object of Britaldo's lust and Rosimunda's jealousy—has been raised in the Convent of San Benito "al amparo de unas tías" (359). There she has been the pupil of Remigio, a monk said to be "varón de virtud y ejemplo" (362) who, because of his wisdom and learning ("que por sus preceptos sabios" [363]), was Irene's choice as mentor and teacher ("tomó Irene por maestro" [364]). The young nun represents a dimension of experience both typical and atypical of women's opportunities. Enclosed and sheltered, she leads a life of pious devotion but in a place where regular study can take place.[25] She has even been able to choose her own tutor, who nevertheless still fits the model of *male* instructor for female students.[26] She likewise studies only scriptural lessons and seems to depend upon Remigio for their interpretation: "que es la lección sagrada, / que por Remigio me es bien explicada" (806-7). Irene thus stands as a well-defined example of what the humanists considered proper for the young female scholars. It is in Azevedo's development of what becomes of Irene that the tenets of gender ideology are revealed as the source of negative and ironic consequences for such a woman. From both outside and inside the convent walls come threats to her safety, reputation, and tranquillity, which according to the gendered precepts she lives by, should be preserved.

First, her serenity is threatened by a serenade that Britaldo arranges below her convent window. In this scene Azevedo introduces her most radical shift in representational conventions, for interference to Britaldo's courting comes from an angel disguised as sword-wielding gallant. The heavenly *galán* is able to drive off Britaldo and his entourage, but his presence and disguise only further complicate the situation, for now Britaldo understands that he has a rival for Irene's attention. Although the nobleman believes his antagonist to be another man like himself, he is literally competing with God for Irene's devotion. The playwright envisions a heterosexual paradigm of desire and violence overlying the divine realm which suggests the metaphorical role of marriage for nuns and their divine Spouse; there is thus no escape for a woman who does not wish to participate in intrigues of rivalry for her affection as long as the dimension of struggle is dominated by male figures— even the masculinized God; she is not left space or time to exercise her agency.

Britaldo begins to behave like a jilted lover: "los celos no disimulo; / pensamientos adelante, / que yo he de hacer vuestro gusto" (1227-29). It has, of course, been established that his thought processes are not balanced, so dependence upon his intellect can only provoke more problems. Although she is an innocent participant in the encounter be-

tween the man who wishes to court her and her divine defendant,
Irene presumes that she is somehow to blame: "Sin duda la causa soy /
desta moción; ¿mas qué dije?" (1336-37). Irene's dilemma is that of the
woman observed, watched, desired, and pursued against her will. In a
monologue early in Act 2, she wonders,

> si en este retiro santo,
> después que profesión hice,
> solamente a mi maestro
> permito que me visite,
> ¿puede haber quien obligado
> de persona tan humilde
> en aras de amor profano
> obsequios me sacrifique? [1342-49]

The "aras de amor" that Azevedo devises for her play and to which
Irene is seemingly both idol and sacrificial victim implicate not only the
profane devotee, Britaldo, but the supreme divine one as well. In her reversal of the already inverse "amor a lo divino," Azevedo portrays Irene's
figurative marriage to God as one in which the male Spouse responds
with jealousy, violence, and "capa y espada" intrigue in a relationship just as problematical as the secular one in which Rosimunda is sit-
uated. Using the caped angel as his proxy, God Himself sets in motion
a chain of misunderstandings that causes Britaldo to resort to violence
against Irene. He is described by the heavenly messenger as possessive in
worldly terms: "y de celoso tu Esposo / (que hasta en Dios celos se
admiten) / me encargó tu defensión" (1410-12). In his attempts to discourage Britaldo, the angel even serves as a kind of deputy for him,
urging Irene to ask permission to see the nobleman on the grounds that
she, like her religious sisters, fulfills charitable duty in ministering to
sick patients such as he.

Not long afterward, Rosimunda visits Irene, who kneels before her
accuser and thus secures the other's trust and realization that Britaldo is
the untrustworthy party. The two women make their peace, but even in
this accord Azevedo does not depict a true coalition of the women involved. Instead, what Irene and Rosimunda represent are the two
alternative life options for early modern women, and they pledge to do
their utmost to live as separately as possible in hopes of quelling

Britaldo's passion for Irene. She will strive to discourage him from his
suit, and Rosimunda will wait for him in their household.

Banán soon delivers a line that suggests what is to follow: "Nacieron
de un parto / amor y desconfianza" (1668-69). After Irene tells her teacher and confessor Remigio what has happened, he lingers, significantly,
to watch and observe her as she goes off to pray for divine protection
in "esta de amor pelea" (2122). Since God himself is implcated in the
courtly love struggles that threaten Irene, it is significant that one of his
supposed earthly representatives is the next man to hasten the course of
her difficulties. The stage directions state that she "vase andando despa-
cio" and about the monk that "y él queda mirándola" (2139). She cannot
escape the desiring male's gaze. Remigio's monologue, reveals the new
turn of events and emotions:

> ¡Qué bizarra es! ¡Qué airosa!
> ¡Qué gracia y donaire tiene!
> ¡Qué bien parece en Irene
> con ser bella el ser virtuosa!
> ¡No hay cosa más agradable
> que una honestidad compuesta,
> una gravedad honesta,
> y cómo que se hace amable! [2140-47]

But her "honestidad compuesta" and "gravedad honesta" do not inspire
in her admirer the appropriate feelings. Recognizing the nature of his
carnal desire for Irene, he continues to talk to himself:

> ¡Mas qué es esto, atención mía!
> ¿Parece que vuestro agrado
> los límites ha pasado,
> llegando a ser demasía?
> ¿Os alborotáis deseos?
> ¿Qué es aquesto? Reportaos,
> tened, tened, retiraos,
> parad, parad, deteneos.
> Mas ¡ay de mí, que parece
> que amor quiere cautivarme!
> ¡Ay que ya siento abrasarme!
> ¡Esto a Remigio acontece! [2148-59]

He ends his speech with references to love as a "contagio" and the hope that Irene will be shielded by God from Britaldo ("que de Britaldo te guarde") and that he himself will be saved from her ("y me defienda de ti" [2174-75]), as if she were the guilty seductive agent.

When Irene fulfills her mission of charity to the suffering Britaldo, she finds him a most enthusiastic recipient of her attention but resists all his overtures and rebuffs his attempts to take her hand. Insisting to him that his love of her is misplaced and wrong ("No queréis bien, queréis mucho, / . . . / son dos cosas muy contrarias" [2556-59]), she describes it in terms of selfishness:

> Querer mucho es apetito
> que de interés se acompaña,
> y en la posesión de un logro
> constituye la esperanza. [2572-75]

Exhorting him to join her in love of God ("Los dos en Dios nos amemos" [2624]), she also reminds him:

> Casados somos los dos,
> dos penas os amenazan;
> por Dios mi Esposo ofendido,
> por vuestra esposa agraviada.
> Si persistís en el yerro,
> mirad, que hay en el cielo espadas;
> mirad, que Dios tiene celos;
> mirad, que mi honor ampara. [2648-55]

After hearing from Irene the divine nature of his adversary in the struggle beneath her window, Britaldo has a change of heart; he agrees to cease his suit and to respect her vows of chastity. Nevertheless, he expresses a wish that amounts to a threat:

> Que ninguno otro lograra
> lo que yo no puedo, pues fuera
> de celos aquesta llaga
> peor que la del amor. [2717-20]

At the beginning of the third act Remigio articulates a disastrous state of mind with regard to his feelings for Irene. His interior monologue again depicts the male mind as overcome by the passions as he argues for and against his attraction. Finally, he surrenders to his emotions rather than rededicating himself to his obligation toward their respective vows of chastity:

> Pidamos al amor
> que en cautiverios tales
> nos quiera ser propicio,
> ya blando y favorable,
> influyendo en Irene,
> centro de las beldades,
> a las pasiones mías
> una atención afable. [2880-81]

When he next meets with Irene, Remigio acts on his intention to declare himself openly to her. She rejects him, and his desire turns from lust to revenge. His method of avenging his wounded pride involves his knowledge of herbal medicine, an ironic twist on the symbolism of motherhood and the virgin birth, and an inversion of the demonological associations between women and the casting of spells.[27] Remigio decides to administer secretly to Irene herbs that will induce the outward symptoms of pregnancy, with the result that "en los efectos publican / que perdió la castidad" (3134-35). Having consumed the herbs, Irene becomes the target of scorn among the members of her convent; the playwright thus dissolves the coherence of even this female community that had sheltered Irene.

The nun also loses her standing in the eyes of the world outside the convent walls when Banán brings news to Britaldo of her seeming dishonesty and abandonment of her vow of chastity. Britaldo's response carries with it the declaration of misogyny that the play dramatizes through representation of male efforts to possess the desired woman: "¡Viose nunca tal mudanza! / ¿Quién de mujeres se fía?" (3382-83). Angered most by the fact that she seems to have given her affection to another man, Britaldo devises his own method of revenge. The stakes are now revealed to be the struggle between men for possession of an objectified woman who should have remained outside their realm of physical control. Britaldo intends to ". . . quitar / la vida a Irene" (3464-65). At first bribing Banán with the promise of riches and then threatening him with bodily harm if he does not aid in this undertaking, Britaldo sets in motion the plan that now makes the three principal male figures cocontributors to the downfall of an innocent woman who has obeyed all the social and cultural caveats mandated for her sex by the patriarchal system.

As she sleeps, the angel again appears to Irene and reveals to her the truth of what she is experiencing. He likewise tells her of the death that awaits her and the "bello sepulcro" that "obra . . . de angeles es" (3701-2). When she awakens, Banán is standing over her. By his own admission he is "homicida / por fuerza del interés" (3743-44). Although she tries to escape by fleeing offstage (supposedly into the woods), he follows, only to return to the stage "con la espada ensangrentada" (3763).

Soon afterward, all the characters except Irene assemble for a scene in which the guilty men confess their wrongdoings. First Remigio discloses his betrayal of Irene, admitting that he not only administered the potion that made her look pregnant, but hastened the circuit of gossip "por el vulgo" (3946) that made her the target of derision from all strata of society. Now he proclaims his profound worry and fear for her safety because of Irene's unexplained absence from the convent. Appealing to Britaldo as "gobernador soberano" (3976), he has recourse to the male power structure of the region to organize a search party and to publicize the truth of his deed and her innocence. Remigio ends his confession by asking for his own death.

In spite of their shock, his companions do not carry out a death sentence on the monk. Instead, Britaldo acknowledges his desire to have Irene killed, but before he can recount all the details, Banán steps forward to disclose his part in the crime. He explains that he not only murdered her but threw her body in the Tagus River to hide the evidence of his deed. While the listeners marvel at what they hear, Irene's body appears, floating in the river, the fatal wound vividly apparent on her neck. Having permanently silenced her by slitting her throat, Banán has completed the cycle of offenses against Irene that disrupted her participation in all facets of worldly society—both secular and religious. Now her body appears surrounded by angels, who assure all present of her glorious place in the afterlife. Here Azevedo ironically lays bare a sense of the all-pervasive conventionalized male control: it is the highest male—God himself—who wins the contest and claims Irene for His own. The male/patriarchal hierarchy prevails, and the Rival against whom none other can win claims the victory.

The characters left behind begin to take their own vows of penitence. Remigio intends to wander the earth as a pilgrim, atoning for his sins and visiting "esos lugares / que la Tierra Santa encierra" (4161-62). Banán decides to accompany the monk, and Britaldo asks permission of his wife to do likewise. Rosimunda will retire to Irene's convent until her husband's return. These decisions situate the characters in places and relationships similar to those that precipitated the tragic happenings, for it has been demonstrated that a woman's safety and integrity are as threatened behind the cloistered walls of a convent as outside them, and the religious vows and practices of male clerics and lay nobles have not assured their strength to resist temptation or to devote themselves to good works. In Azevedo's portrayal, the only escape for the besieged woman is death, which silences her to the world and closes her off from the ills of the male-dominated secular and clerical realms of society, but delivers her to the spiritual parallel of a jealous spouse. The outcome suggests itself as a bizarre divine parallel to the Golden Age wife murder plays.

Azevedo's nun encounters numerous dichotomous issues in this dramatization of the conflict between exterior and interior—both of space and of the body/soul duality. It is through orifices of one kind or another that Irene is in all but one way violated. The windows of her convent are marginal spaces that open the interior of the cloister to the outer world and the apertures through which Britaldo brings his first messages of love to the nun in the musician's serenade. The convent doors that open to permit the nuns to perform their acts of charity become manipulated elements allowing Irene to talk face to face with Britaldo in order to persuade him to cease his suit. Although her plan seems to bring about the desired effect when Britaldo promises to honor her vows and return to his wife, it is with his warning that no other man may obtain what he has been denied. Apparently unable to cede to this woman's own will and to respect her voluntary chastity, he exerts external pressure meant to coerce her to abide by what he articulates now as his terms for her life's pattern: that is, instead of arguing against her celibacy, *he* now insists that she continue to live a sexless existence.

No man violates her sexually; with his poison, however, the monk penetrates her body by means of her mouth—the other orifice of female transgression, according to gender ideology. Azevedo challenges this tenet by means of the fictional nature of Irene's pregnancy. At the same time she allows this figure to embody the two extremes of womanhood invoked for centuries in the contradictory cultural conventions about women. The virginal Irene is, as the theatrical audience knows, innocent of any betrayal of her vows, yet her body outwardly belies this state of sexual purity by exhibiting the physical symptoms of pregnancy. Thus, she simultaneously calls to mind both a tragic version of the Virgin Mary and her sexless impregnation and the fallen woman who traces her lineage to Eve. She thus helps to dramatize the contradictory situation in which a woman is condemned for transgression even as she upholds the cultural tenets of female propriety. Neither Rosimunda's secular nor Irene's spiritual marriage is a solution; both bring disaster and difficulty for the women Azevedo portrays.

The feminist essentialism of the relational model is apparent in this dramatist's maintenance of the two categories of male and female figures who do not challenge either "what men and women say and do" or the well-established spheres in which God is also implicated. Although a possible step toward resolution of the dramatized predicament is suggested by the males' change of heart in the last scene, no new social space is created for the women. Rosimunda's only change is from husband's household to convent; Irene leaves the earthly life and her monastic setting to join her heavenly Husband in the afterlife. The male rivalry that has underridden so much of the play's action has been driven by male possessiveness over women's bodies. If the woman is not receptive to his sexual advances, then the man will destroy her; thus, Britaldo and Remigio contribute to Irene's death—with the help of Banán, another male figure, and likewise with the sanction of God himself through his angelic representative. The male characters are portrayed as overwhelmed by passions that the women have been able to conquer in themselves—yet as the humanistic treatises assure, the women are held more responsible for wrongdoing than the men.

Indeed, in this play, the women are the only principal characters who do not transgress their stations. Rosimunda is faithful to her marriage vows, and Irene is faithful to her vows of chastity. The men not only disregard these vows but conspire to murder an innocent victim, and do so with impunity. Nor is the relational harmony of male/female unity successfully restored at the end, when Rosimunda goes behind convent walls and Britaldo sets off to carry out his own mission of penance; the precariousness of his resolve and the potential for violation within the cloister remain as threats. Azevedo's seeming conservatism, in not providing in either of the plays considered here a model of gender transgression belies her strong challenge to the dominant system of gender relations and its construction of roles for men and women.

One sixteenth-century moralist who considered patriarchal rule as tyrannical, Claude de Taillemont, wrote in his *Discours des champs faez a l'honneur et exaltation de l'amour et des dames:* "However honest and perfect [wives] may be, their husbands esteem them as much as pigs do daisies" (qtd. in Jordan, 190). If this is true, then marriage, whether literal and secular or figurative and divine, offers no comfortable location of agency or existence to women. In this play, the daisy (*margarita*) of the title is disfavored and destroyed. That destruction makes of Irene an ironically mythic figure who found no social geography of her own but nevertheless gave her name to the place (Santarén) from which she was excluded.

4

CARNIVALESQUE IMPLICATIONS

Valor, agravio y mujer (Caro), *El muerto disimulado*
(Azevedo), and *La traición en la amistad* (Zayas)

> Porque hay mujeres Lisardos,
> y hay también Lisardas hombres.
> —Angela de Azevedo, *El muerto disimulado*

> [Men] know that, according to universal opinion, a loose life does not
> damage their reputations as it does women.
> —Baldassare Castiglione, *The Courtier*

> Los hombres empiezan amando, y acaban venciendo, y
> salen despreciando.
> —María de Zayas, *Desengaños amosoros*

The masquerading elements that become strategies for resolution of
the dilemmas portrayed in the *comedias* studied in this chapter transgress social and gender norms by suggesting the instability of roles and
categories. Literary scholars often associate such strategies with the temporary celebrations and artificial privileges that hierarchical society
incorporates during carnival, only to revoke them soon afterward. The
carnivalesque structure represented dramatically in these plays, however,
implies the seriousness of the challenge it offers society, for its suspension of expected behavior and relationships insinuates possible and
representable alternatives to hegemonical sociopolitical patterns that
disrupt the theoretical social harmony they purport to ensure. The subversion of accepted norms permits examination of the underlying
disarray of those norms and drives the depicted situation away from the
disorder that must, in effect, be overcome by the transgression.[1] The
process traced here in plays by Caro, Azevedo, and Zayas is thus akin to
what Jonathan Dollimore calls "transgressive reinscription" in Renais-

sance English drama: "a mode of transgression which finds expression through the inversion and perversion of just those preexisting categories and structures which humanist transgression seeks to transcend, to be liberated from, a mode of transgression which seeks not an escape from existing structures but rather a subversive reinscription within them—and in the process a dis-location of them" ("Subjectivity," 57).

The festivity associated historically with carnival hilarity and excess is not the basis of the reversals dramatized in *Valor, agravio y mujer, El muerto disimulado,* and *La traición en la amistad.* In the dramas by Azevedo and Caro, for instance, the gender reversals performed by their central female characters are undertaken for serious and threatening reasons and manifest aspects of the often depicted cross-dressed woman as *mujer varonil* in numerous Golden Age *comedias.* In his study "On the Carnivalesque," Robert Stamm defines both the positive, utopian aspect of carnival and its critical role. The first "suggests the joyful affirmation of becoming. It is ecstatic collectivity, the superseding of the individuating principle." The "negative, critical side" of the carnivalesque "suggests a demystificatory instrument for everything in the social formation which renders such collectivity difficult of access: class hierarchy, political manipulation, sexual repression, dogmatism and paranoia. Carnival in this sense implies an attitude of creative disrespect, a radical opposition to the illegitimately powerful, to the morose and monological" (55). Negative demystification of the tenets of gender ideology is evident in these three female-authored plays. Instead of the comically playful examples of blurred gender enacted in the Elizabethan and Jacobean theater, with female parts played by boys depicting cross-dressed women, the Spanish *comedia* incorporates a darker tone in the masquerading and carnival pretenses. In many instances the plot can move toward disaster and destruction if the carnivalesque ruse is not successful in bringing about a reconfiguration of pairings or a renewal of alliances.

With regard to similar issues in the "drag scenes for women" written by female English playwrights such as Susanna Centilivre, which "most critics have regarded . . . as imitations of Shakespeare," Sue Ellen Case notes:

> They differ a great deal from Shakespeare's. They are not happy, witty scenes set in forests such as Arden; rather, they are dark, desperate scenes

in which women cross-dress to gain the power or freedom to express
their wills. . . . Unlike Shakespeare, the use of drag in Centilivre does not
resolve social issues (as it does for Portia in *The Merchant of Venice*), but
demonstrates the anger and desperation of the female character. For
women, the necessity of male disguise caused privation and anxiety.
[*Feminism* 39]

Such is also true of the cross-dressed women in the plays by Azevedo
and Caro.[2]

Although my interrogation of the value of the carnivalesque in relation to gender impersonation in these Golden Age plays is not based
on a view of the theater as a site of polemics and struggle primarily between social classes, that argument certainly complements my own and
has been presented by various critics such as Michael Bristol with
regard to the English Renaissance stage.[3] What serves as a common
ground for me and scholars of other national theaters in this context is
the "controversy about the structure and the allocation of authority"
that the dramatic texts and the debates surrounding the plays of the
period suggest (Bristol, 110). Gender is one dimension of this controversy and becomes the starting point of the women playwrights' critical
and transgressive strategies. Social class is a secondary—but only
secondary—focus because the social abuses dramatized are portrayed
through upper-class men and responded to by their upper-class counterparts. Although such a configuration certainly critiques those
hegemonical figures of political authority, the issue problematized is
not class oppression but injustices residing in gender inequities and
subjugation.

In these three plays, then, the cultural assumptions of Renaissance
gender ideology transcend social class, since the authority of men over
women is taken to be the natural given in which the enacted problems
reside. Furthermore, as I argued in Chapter 1, the contentions of critics such as Laqueur and Orgel remind us that sexed identity was more
a political and social phenomenon than an ontological one in the sixteenth and seventeenth centuries:

There was no true, deep essential sex that differentiated cultural man
from woman. But neither were there two sexes juxtaposed in various
proportions: there was but one sex whose more perfect exemplars were

easily deemed males at birth and whose decidedly less perfect ones were labeled female. The modern question, about the "real" sex of a person, made no sense in this period, not because two sexes were mixed but because there was only one to pick from and it had to be shared by everyone, from the strongest warrior to the most effeminate courtier to the most aggressive virago to the gentlest maiden. Indeed, in the absence of a purportedly stable system of two sexes, strict sumptuary laws of the body attempted to stabilize gender—woman as woman and man as man—and punishments for transgression were quite severe. . . . [But] the body with its one elastic sex was far freer to express theatrical gender and the anxieties thereby produced than it would be when it came to be regarded as the foundation of gender. [Laqueur, 124-25]

In plays where cross-gendered performances are undertaken in an interior masquerade, the individualist feminist model is validated at the same time that the relational model is the basis for the performance. The female character is able to perform as a male in the male space of influence and privilege, but her performance validates that entitlement and reinstates the two socially constructed categories of masculine and feminine as her dimensions of enactment. In each case of such "transgressive reinscription," the woman must disappear so that another male figure can appear on stage. The theatrical visual effect is still one of male circles of communication and public interaction. But the shift of a human being from her usual social guise of womanhood into a realm of manhood does not require any great suspension of disbelief in the early modern era, since what the cross-dressed individual must ultimately do is decide which behavioral characteristics need to be emphasized in order to obtain a different set of privileges.

In response to questions posed by Linda Woodbridge in her book *Women and the English Renaissance*, Dollimore offers consideration of the Jacobean female transvestite which pertains as well to the similar *comedia* figures. For example Dollimore paraphrases Woodbridge's concerns: "Isn't it that . . . the transvestite seems to be a victim of false consciousness, and by switching gender roles rather than dissolving them, reinforces the very sexual divison which s/he finds oppressive?" (Dollimore, "Subjectivity," 68). Dollimore's answer suggests that to say

gender difference can be maintained through cross-dressing and inversion is still to maintain or imply the crucial claim: it is difference working in terms of custom and culture (and so contestable) rather than nature and divine law (and so immutable). Even with this conservative (ironic?) defense, then, sexual difference is sustained by the very inversion which divine law forbids, and the fact that it can be so sustained is simultaneously a repudiation of the claim that sexual difference is itself dictated by divine or natural law. ["Subjectivity," 70]

Such argumentation has points of convergence with the Renaissance feminism Jordan identifies through the period's many complaints about the consequences to women of "the moral perversion of men" (9). Renaissance feminists sought, among other things, to inspire reform of the "distorted humanity of men," but in this undertaking the males' weaknesses are often criticized as effeminacy, as opposed to femininity (Jordan, 9). The polemics of the debate in seventeenth-century England over women attired in men's clothing peaked with the 1620 publication of the pair of pamphlets entitled *Hic Mulier* and *Haec Vir* and whose writers, in particular, promote conclusions along these lines, as Jordan summarizes:

Man must resume his hegemony. . . . The writer of *Haec Vir* invokes the concept of a hierarchy of creation as the basis for reforming a society now corrupted by persons who share gender and obscure rank. . . . Because men have abandoned their masculinity (and ceased to control women) . . . the authority and power belonging to men have been (reluctantly) adopted by women lest distinctions of rank disappear. . . . Antifeminism here represents its opposition as caricature, the mannish woman who is desperately unhappy, anxious only to resume her former dependence, her only guarantee of economic security and social acceptance. [307]

The performative aspect of carnival celebrations incorporates role-playing and caricature through disguises, mimicry, and masking that blend the participants. The communal nature of the festivity produces a lack of clear distinction as well between those who play a part and those who observe. The appropriation of someone else's symbols of identity—whether of social class, political office, or gender—puts into question the stability of the political categories that the most powerful in society have every reason to want to preserve under the appearance of intrinsic and essential classifications. Scholars, in fact, often cite the sumptuary laws as evidence of class-based concern for preservation of

social distinctions between stations and societal categories.[4] And as
Loomba contends, cross-dressing is a principal Renaissance trope that
challenges such distinctions and very often is associated with women's
rebellion. She adds that the phenomenon "can hardly be attributed to
stage convention alone." Drawing on Lisa Jardine's study, Loomba
notes that "dress emerges as a crucial signifier of sexual and social identity in the prescription and enforcement of elaborate and precise codes
of dressing" (77).

In the sixteenth century, Vives's "Formación de la mujer cristiana"
was among those works that derided cross-dressing by women as an element of moral and social instability: "La diferencia del vestido
conserva el pudor, padre nutricio de la pureza . . . que también los vestidos lleven consigo las características de . . . diferencia, que menester es
que nosotros no confundamos aquella en que la Naturaleza puso distinción. Y por todo esto, quien torna el vestido promiscuo, con toda razón
es llamado por el Señor abominable, pues que intenta una cosa con-
traria a la ley natural, que introduciría en la convivencia social un
sinnúmero de peligros" (1026). In the following century, the *arbitristas*
who agitated for a return to "purity of morals and manners" urged passage of the sumptuary laws and also supported, among other measures,
the closing of theaters and the reaffirmation of class and professional
distinctions (Elliott, 252). In Spain as in other early modern European
nations, crossed-dressed women or female characters aroused societal
unease by displaying their so-called "extravagant and lustful natures"and
inciting attacks against "their appropriation of male prerogatives. . . .
The female transvestite is seen to transgress into male territory and
becomes a hermaphrodite, a monster who threatens sexual (and by implication all social) distinctions" (Loomba, 77-78).

Likewise, since the appropriation of someone else's words, demeanor,
and appearance is the basis of enacting a dramatic part, the speaking
and gesturing of female actors on the seventeenth-century Spanish stage
not only transgressed the patriarchal standard of silence and reclusion
for women but suggested an encroachment on and an appropriation of
the public domain of men. That female actors, generally regarded as
morally and spiritually suspect because of their relative freedom in the
theatrical groups to which they belonged could portray women of the
noble class also called into question the fixed quality of the social roles

within cultural hierarchies that bestow rank and wealth through the accident of birth.[5] This underlying challenge to the social and political status quo is evident in even the most ideologically conservative of the plays that include female parts to be enacted by women—not boys, as was the case in Renaissance England. The extreme rarity of a male cross-dressing as a female on the Spanish classical stage and the moralistic attacks against boys playing women in Spain (considered in Chapter 1) reveal as well the cultural anxiety over the fluidity of identity across lines of social construction. Whereas early modern feminists who promoted a positive androgyny—with the implications that "men and women shared common behaviors, attitudes, experiences" (Jordan, 137)—urged affirmation of the virtues accepted as feminine (mercy, compassion, patience, modesty) as appropriate for both sexes, they were careful to separate femininity from effeminacy.[6]

Seventeenth-century moralists and social critics such as Juan de Mariana, Jerónimo Pujades, and Fray Juan de Santa María, who catalogued the components they believed responsible for Spain's political and social decline, thus blamed what they considered the effeminate customs of the courtiers in service to Philip III and Philip IV for the nation's problems: "When a kingdom reaches such a point of moral corruption that men dress like women, . . . that the most exquisite delicacies are imported for its tables, and men go to sleep before they are tired, . . . then it can be regarded as lost, and its empire at an end" (quoted in Elliott, 251). In her second collection of short prose *novelas,* Zayas herself attacks males "llenos de galas y trajes femeniles" who have abandoned the active masculine virtues in favor of the effeminate practices of "estaros en la Corte, ajando galas y criando cabellos, hollando coches y paseando prados . . . todos efecto de la ociosidad en que gastáis el tiempo en ofensa de Dios y de vuestra nobleza" (*Desengaños,* 505-6). These are characteristics she derides in women as well. Much is also made by these critics of the foreign influence that contributed to these gender reversals—England and France being most frequently invoked as the sources of such corrupting models.[7] Although late Renaissance feminist writers like Zayas are careful to emphasize that the negative qualities of degenerate laziness and lethargic, courtly decadence are to be avoided by men and women, the message is still sounded that when men act like the stereotyped, universalized woman, the national

integrity and social morality are put at risk. Protection of the reconfigured universalized categories thus requires denunciation of any blurred
lines of demarcation.

In their study of the conceptual framework of Western societal hierarchies, Peter Stallybrass and Allon White interrogate such intersections
of limits and their subversions from a vantage point that begins with
Mikhail Bakhtin's notions about the carnivalesque but moves "beyond
[his] troublesome *folkloric* approach to a political anthropology of
binary extremism in class society." They continue: "This transposition
not only moves us beyond the rather unproductive debate over whether
carnivals are politically progressive or conservative, it reveals that the
underlying structural features of carnival operate far beyond the strict
confines of popular festivity and are intrinsic to the dialectics of social
classification as such" (26). For the purposes of this study, with its emphasis on interrogation of gendered "social classification" (which carried
more meaning than biological identity for the sexes at that time), these
notions and others such as Barbara Babcock's broad perspective on the
carnivalesque are informative. Babcock contends: "'Symbolic inversion'
may be broadly defined as any act of expressive behaviour which in-
verts, contradicts, abrogates, or in some fashion presents an alternative
to commonly held cultural codes, values and norms be they linguistic,
literary or artistic, religious, social and political" (14).

The theatrical experience, in the *comedias* under scrutiny, depends
upon acts of "expressive behavior" that challenge the cultural value
system precisely through the words and gestures displayed in the enactment of a story. That women in seventeenth-century Spain participate
or are textually represented as participating in this public display is part
of the "symbolic inversion" that immediately suggests alternative relationships to the organization of power and its exercise. But lest we
oversimplify such a process, it is helpful to repeat Dollimore's reminder
that inversion profoundly interrogates the dominant order: "Inversion
becomes a kind of transgressive mimesis; the subculture even as it imitates, reproducing itself in terms of its exclusion, also demystifies,
producing a knowledge of the dominant which excludes it, this being a
knowledge which the dominant has to suppress in order to dominate"
("Subjectivity," 61).

Presenting women on stage in a wide variety of *comedia* parts, from female heads of state or revered saints and martyrs to coquettish members of court or abused victims of social forces and violent mates, was a transgressive undertaking—not only because it involved women's public display but also because it defined the abuses of patriarchy, either directly or indirectly. In two of the plays discussed in this chapter (Azevedo's and Caro's), cross-dressing is a major element, and mimicry of masculine behavior without male costume is a strategy of the female principal in the third (Zayas's). In these plays, the critique of patriarchal essentialist/relational models finds expression through the moral and political injustices several women characters must strive to overcome while depending upon the Renaissance feminist individualist paradigm. The latter allows a female character to expose the gender construction operating in her depicted society by adopting masculine clothing or imitating male attitudes and comportment in order to acquire masculine privilege. Laqueur's arguments about the lack of ontological depth to sexual identity is nowhere better illustrated than in the Spanish *comedias* in which cross-dressing enhances a woman's relationship to the depicted sources of power. In Azevedo's play, moreover, a cross-dressed male figure adds a further dimension to the depicted potential fluidity of sexual/political identity. In Zayas's play it is precisely the lack of a masculine costume that complicates the female character's efforts to behave as males do in pursuit of numerous lovers.

The role reversals represented in these three plays depend not only on woman's usurpation of the privileged discursive space of the male speaker but also on her willingness to disappear. For a period of time, the cross-gendered female character must demonstrate her ability to occupy the masculine social space, but in so doing she must abandon the social geography assigned to her as woman. As the false male she does, however, approach the androgyne's convergence of the masculine and feminine, for she can enact the model of the morally feminized man or show herself capable of escaping the role of victim, even if it means adopting that of victimizer. If she is able to regain her earlier feminine space, however, there is usually no indication that the intersection of genders will continue to be accessible to her. Terry Eagleton's view of the carnivalesque as a "temporary retextualizing of the social formation that exposes its 'fictive' foundations" (149) can thus apply to the gender issues of the seventeenth-century theatrical experience. The performance of a drama and even the reading of the dramatic text through its representational suggestion show what is possible, and what subversion of gender roles threatens because "the *relation* between observer and observed is never fixed" (Stallybrass and White, 42). This destabilization is embodied by the cross-gendered and cross-dressed woman character whose appropriation of male privilege allows her to gaze without dissimulation, rather than to be only gazed upon as the focus of observation and critique.

Complaints made by moralists against the theater in Golden Age Spain and against the appearance of women on stage in male attire frequently center on the exhibition of the woman's body, which is outlined in more detail when she wears pants than when she appears in skirts. Countering the destablizing masculinization of such a figure, the moralists insist that her femaleness is too much foregrounded. Such a character thus does not escape objectification but, as Case has noted, continues to be accused of instigating men's lascivious thought and reaction (*Feminism,* 20) even as she embodies the notion of woman as a false—that is, imperfect—male. These patriarchal concerns and suspicions reveal societal discomfort over the ability to blur sociopolitical distinctions of all sorts. Vives, writing against gender indeterminacy, invoked the Old Testament caveats against a man or a woman who "hace este trueque" and is judged "[a]bominable . . . a los ojos del Señor" (1026). He went on to insist that differentiated clothing allowed individuals to represent their sexual identity, which, he implied, might fade before the eyes of the gazing public if not clearly marked through the conventions of outward decorations.

The plays in which a woman adopts male disguise, however, also problematize another version of the patriarchal efforts to silence and enclose women. The role-playing woman character's success in attaining her goal—usually defending her honor or reconciling with a neglectful lover—is directly related to her ability to abandon the gestures and language associated with femininity and to assume, temporarily, the appearance and demeanor accepted as masculine.[8] The plays reflect the closed quality of a social system that allows men to communicate among themselves and take action about life-altering elements (such as marriage contracts), whereas women may merely react, if even that. In these portrayed situations, the women characters who need to gain access to the male-controlled communication circles can do so only if they cease to represent themselves as women. The ironic result is that altering the superficial quality of the woman character does not disturb the facade of the social system; woman's speech and freedom from enclosure are not promoted but in fact negated by the very characters who become icons of that system's destabilization. At the same time, however, they examine in their theatrical pose the extent to which it is necessary to be or seem male in order to escape the enclosed spaces and the silence to which women are relegated and to become agents for justice. In their feminist individualist strategies, they demonstrate male and female equality in resolving dilemmas. But they also illustrate the performative dimension of gendered identity, putting into question the coherence of all socially defined groups, whether those of men and women or those based upon social class and national origin.

Case's observations about "drag scenes for women" pertain to the desperation of the so-called *mujer varonil* as cross-dressed woman in the *comedia* in general, the convention to which Azevedo and Caro contributed their dramatic versions. The common reason for dressing like and passing as a man in Golden Age plays is usually an honor problem that necessitates the woman's pursuit of the offender in order to confront him on terms of temporary social equality, to remain close enough to him to arrange a trick or coercion that will force fulfillment of a broken promise, or to take revenge for an as yet unpunished crime.

Caro's *Valor, agravio y mujer* depicts Leonor, an abandoned woman who appropriates male identity so that she can enter the male space of communication into which her former lover has been able to escape from her and from the promises of marriage that he now shirks. The freedom enjoyed by men in the standards of aristocratic courtship is dramatized in countless period plays in which the male characters move about with impunity during and after a love affair, while the woman is marked as property held in delicate balance and easily disparaged if not claimed by the original bidder.[9] This codified literary pattern is the focus of Caro's inquiry in a play that likewise interrogates the assumption of gendered identity and its constructed values and virtues. Accepted as the nobleman Leonardo at the Belgian court, Leonor displays behavior and attitudes that bespeak faithful adherence to promises and justice for the woman to whom a man pledges marriage. By portraying a masculine model of integrity and loyalty that the male characters do not live up to, Leonor invents a new role for males which challenges the social and literary double standard that devalues a once loved but abandoned woman.[10]

Presenting herself as her own suitor and thus a stand-in for her departed lover, Juan, Leonor's carnivalesque tactic promotes the inversion of identity and gender norms as means to resolve the discrepancies brought about when those in control of the social and political process abuse the norms they purport to uphold. Journeying from her home city of Seville to Brussels, where Juan has incorporated himself in the court society, Leonor introduces herself as Leonardo and gains immediate access to the inner circles of the aristocracy, a community that fosters other love intrigues and courtship rituals among the unmarried courtiers. Like Azevedo in *La margarita del Tajo* and *Dicha y desdicha*, Caro creates dramatic moments when her male characters incriminate themselves before the theatrical audience, even though the audience of male players with whom they share the stage do not reject them or insist upon a redressing of the grievances that can be leveled against them.

The representatives of the upper classes who control the prescriptive defining of female chastity and propriety are the violators of those same standards. Like her fictional sisters in other literary works, Leonor has lost her place among the members of her social milieu because she has moved unsuccessfully toward the culturally approved state of marriage with an appropriate mate. He himself has run no such risk of scandal by courting her and then reneging on his promise of marriage. The burden of punishment by exclusion from her social privilege is the woman's, once she accepts the man's active invitation and its professed grounding in promised faithfulness and union. The breaking of that faith and the disruption of that union are his offenses, but she is impugned for not resisting his advances.

This phenomenon has parallels in other aspects of the gender ideology that incorporates all aspects of the interaction of the sexes.
Margaret King's investigations of confessional manuals and marital
guidebooks reveal a Renaissance propensity toward such thinking with
regard to infractions by the male and the woman's subsequent burden
of expiation. She quotes Fra Cherubino da Siena, for example, concerning proper sexual conduct between spouses, which he suspects men of
violating but charges women with the responsibility to resist: "And if
because you do not wish to consent to such a horrible evil, your husband batters you, give yourself [to that punishment] with good will; for
you would die a martyr, and you would go surely to eternal life" (qtd.
in M. King, 41). King notes: "Clearly the act of the male, such a sin's
punishment and atonement was the female's burden. Although proper
sexual conduct was required of both men and women, compliance to
its unyielding strictures was disproportionately women's responsibility"
(41). Citing instances of support of such actions as wife beating, King
concludes: "The victims themselves were blamed for violence viewed as
just" (44). Vives likewise declared in the sixteenth century not only that
"nada queda a la mujer, perdida la pureza" (1010) but also that "el
mismo tormento pasan los hombres de mala vida; pero las mujeres lo
pasan mucho más agudo, por cuanto a los ojos de todos son más feas las
faltas de las mujeres y su natural es ser más vergonzosas" (1009).[11]

In Caro's play, Juan, for example, tells Don Fernando (royal equerry,
capitán of the royal guard, and, coincidentally, Leonor's brother) about
his experience of loving and then leaving a beautiful though unnamed
Sevillian woman who, the audience soon learns, is Leonor. Juan recounts the process of observing the woman for the first time in church),
(a location to which women could properly venture away from home,
admiring her, then investigating her social position and reputation
before courting her. As the critiqued object of Juan's gaze and desire,
she became the recipient of his seductive efforts:

> Vila, en efecto, y améla;
> supe su casa, su estado,
> partes, calidad y hacienda,
> y satisfecho de todo,

> persuadí sus enterezas,
> solicité sus descuidos,
> facilité mis promesas.
> Favoreció mis deseos
>
> . . . .
> Dila palabra de esposo; [377-88]

His report ends with his coldhearted "Cansado y arrepentido / la dejé" (402-3). The language he uses to explain his lack of ardor shifts to focus on external forces, and he rejects the responsibility he might otherwise assume:

> contra mi propio designio,
> cuanto los designios yerran,
> obligaciones tan justas,
> tan bien conocidas deudas,
> o su estrella o su desdicha
> desconocen o cancelan.
>
> . . . .
> . . . seguí la fuerza,
> si de mi fortuna no,
> de mis mudables estrellas.
> Sin despedirme ni hablarla,
> con resolución grosera,
> pasé a Lisboa. [396-408]

The unhonored secret marriage that victimizes so many *comedia* women traps Leonor in the dilemma of inaction that such a woman must face. The man against whom she could complain has left for distant places, and public accusations against him will only dishonor her openly. Trapped in the enclosed inarticulateness that society imposes upon her, she embraces woman's silence because of the further loss she would suffer if she articulated her complaint. The double bind involves the doubling of her silence: to be considered virtuous and proper she must not speak; victimized by the threat of dishonor she must also keep her mouth closed.

Juan, on the other hand, ready for further romantic involvements, takes great care not to speak of his experience in front of the Belgian Infanta Estela, who has become his newest object of desire. He does, however, tell all to Fernando, a member of the male aristocratic community who upholds the patriarchal male privileges. This conversation between men, from which Estela is excluded, reinforces through its physical positioning of the characters the separate communicative circles in which the depicted men and women operate. After listening to all the details of Juan's ignoble treatment of the Sevillian woman, Fernando praises him for his military exploits and travels throughout Europe; seeming to ignore the consequences of the past love affair, he says:

> Huélgome de conoceros,
> señor don Juan, y quisiera
> que a mi afecto se igualara
> el posible de mis fuerzas. [440-43]

Among the men depicted, no one holds Juan accountable for his actions or ostracizes him for his dishonorable treatment of Leonor. She, by contrast, can expect to be considered dishonored and cast out of the group of marriageable women of her social rank.

Leonor can confront her former lover only by reinstating her woman's silence and enclosure through the assumption of the surface identity of Leonardo, the male visitor to the court. By enacting her own absence, Leonor reiterates her exile from the social community that considers her dishonored, an exile symbolized as well by her journey away from her home to the distant court. The male disguise not only removes her from the position of observed object of male desire and critique but allows her to articulate, in the name of males, an alternative perspective on the treatment of women.[13] Leonor is able to invent different versions of Juan's account of the courtship of a beloved woman and to represent, in effect, a different performance of the role of male lover. In this way, she introduces into the hegemonic male community at court an alternative model for male behavior in the tensions and intrigues that lead to matrimonial pairings.

As her scheme to reunite with Juan progresses, she also eliminates for him all other possibilities but marrying her: not only does she become his rival for the affection of Estela, the only other principal female courtier in the depicted society, but she prepares to trap him into honoring his promise to her. Also revealed in this situation, however, is the need to sacrifice another woman's feelings. Caro does not build into her plot any overt homoerotic substructure for Estela and Leonor, but her indictment of the heterosexual dimension carries with it the attraction of one woman to another and their mutual recognition of what is truly appealing to them with regard to love and devotion. In a conversation between Estela and her companion Lisarda, the countess declares her newly recognized preference for Leonardo among the gallants, including Juan, who court her. Adopting the demeanor and words of the conventional *esquiva,* she tells Juan's spokesman Fernando to inform both Juan and her other suitor, the Príncipe de Pinoy, that "ni estoy enamorada, / ni me pretendo casar" (957-58). She has already declared her attraction to Leonardo, and in an ensuing conversation with this disguised figure she receives conventional praise for her beauty and statements of amorous devotion. Their exchange ends with the arrangement of a rendezvous in the garden later that night.

Leonor's ploy subverts as it interrupts the activities and intentions of the male community with its focus on men courting attractive women.[14] Her carnivalesque masquerade is unique among the players on stage, since no one but her servant Ribete knows of her pretense. This selective carnivalization, however, implicates what can be considered the charadelike practices—without costume—of the courting males, who use false words and promises and the conventions of flattery and wooing to deceive the women targeted for such attention. The courtship deception leads to the masquerade of redress and cross-dress. Leonor's lengthy speech of traditional courtly adoration to Estela in fact heightens Caro's emphasis on the falsity of the language of courtship, which women believe but men offer without sincerity. Leonor /Leonardo's initial statement to Estela reiterates the true basis of their mutual dilemma: "Mi silencio, hermosa Estela, / mucho os dice sin hablar" (959-60).

As Don Leonardo, however, Leonor is able to speak in behalf of women, whose plight otherwise silences her, and thus to dramatize the political dimension of late Renaissance gendered identity. Through her character's performance as a male courtier, Caro investigates various possibilities for this feminist individualist position. For example, Leonor proclaims herself capable of physical confrontation with her adversary if that becomes necessary to accomplish her goal of reconciliation with him. Further, since only she and Ribete know she is not a man, they represent a partnership of two figures outside the hegemonic category of male courtier and become co-conspirators in a plot that effects a blurring of social and gender identities. The carnivalesque relationship of these two characters is enhanced by Ribete's focus on the metatheatrical value of his dramatic type and the class-based devaluation of his social worth:

> Estoy mal con enfadosos
> que introducen los graciosos
> muertos de hambre y gallinas.
> El que ha nacido alentado
> ¿no lo ha de ser si no es noble?
> ¿Que no podrá serlo al doble
> del caballero el criado? [529-35]

Ribete also becomes Caro's mouthpiece in responding to the misogynistic scorn that his fellow *gracioso* Tomillo expresses about the report that there are now women in Madrid writing poetry: "¡Válgame Dios! Pues ¿no fuera / mejor coser e hilar? / ¿Mujeres poetas?" (1171-73). Ribete counters with the justification:

> Sí;
> mas no es nuevo, pues están
> Argentaria, Sofoareta,
> Blesilla y más de un millar
> de modernas que hoy a Italia
> lustre soberano dan. [1173-78][15]

His defense is qualified, however, when he adds, "disculpando la osadía / de su nueva vanidad" (1179-80). Nevertheless, Ribete is Leonor's confidant and assistant in her quest to reestablish her social identity, and their ruse allies the upper-class woman with the lower-class man against the dominant aristocratic males who exclude them both from circles of influence.[16]

Leonor's masquerade sets in motion conspiracies and liaisons among all the male courtiers in competition for the love of Estela, who responds with consistent favor only to "Leonardo." In effect, Leonor displaces them all from the position of primary suitor for the hand of the only eligible female courtier, and the different model of masculinity she enacts counterposes the weaknesses in the discourse and demeanor of the males around her who serve as the standard against which she transgresses. But because Leonor is not male and undertakes her cross-dressing in pursuit of her goal of marriage with the man of her choice, she will also reenact the disappearance of the preferred but deceptive man: when she changes back to her woman's attire, "Leonardo" disappears.

Leonor is able to match her male clothes with a performance of male discourse and behavior that indicates the skill with which the female courtier learns the courtly games of decorum and courtship, in which her part is that of listener. She is taken by Juan to be his rival when, in fact, her interruption of his suit of Estela results from her as yet undisclosed rivalry with the countess for Juan's affection. This playing with the gendered identities of courting pairs points up the game-playing quality that informs the wooing of the aristocrats. In a series of nighttime trysts that Leonor arranges, Juan comes to believe that Estela knows of his previous deceitful treatment of the Sevillian woman, and Estela speaks with Prince Ludovico believing him to be Juan. Such scenes of unwitting confusion are commonplace in *comedia* practice, but Caro's version emphasizes that the substitutions of partners and blurred gender distinctions that are possible in the dark only parallel those that occur in the light, thanks to the universalization of woman in the patriarchal system.

Leonor's performance as her own suitor serves as a measure of Juan's fulfillment of the same role. As the play progresses, it becomes obvious that no man pleases either of the two principal women. Juan, for example, has left Leonor but is admired and praised for his military career and his physical valor in the play's first scene when he saves Estela and her companions from bandits. Such a scene, however, is a more violent manifestation of what has happened to Leonor, at the hands of Juan, who has left her socially violated. A further irony is apparent only later in the drama when it is revealed that Fernando is Leonor's brother. In this early scene it is he who almost mistakes Juan for a brigand and is on the point of attacking him when Estela speaks up and identifies him as her rescuer. In these moments it is clear that the body of the woman is the territory that must be protected by certain men from the assaults of other men, but this territory is constantly redefined as defensible or not according to the political, economic, or relational stake a male may have in the woman in question. Fernando, for instance, does not know initially that the woman in Juan's earlier love affair is his own sister.

The playing of social roles becomes the motivating force among the characters, although Caro's depiction of these roles reveals their hollowness. Each is representable by any one of several figures, even across gender lines. As Leonor makes clear, if a woman delivers the right dialogue and dons the proper apparel, she can fulfill the part of a man within the stereotypical courtship conventions, even attracting a female lover. What Estela and Leonor (as Leonardo) enact is the possibility of eliminating men altogether from a politically self-sufficient female universe. Such a universe, however, is still populated by representatives of both genders and is a refashioning rather than a transcendence of the patriarchal discursive order.

The highest-ranking among the courtiers is the Príncipe de Pinoy, whose egotistical and dandyish attitudes repulse Estela. At one point she declares: "No hay disgusto / para mí como su nombre" (899-900). She continues: "¡Jesús, líbrenme los cielos / de su ambición! / . . . /¡Qué bárbaro hombre!" (901-3). The prince exposes his self-centered qualities at various moments during the play. After learning that Estela does not love him, he expresses not sorrow at having lost the woman he adores but irritation over being embarrassed: "desaire que me ha enfadado, / por ser tan pública ya / mi pretensión" (1114-16). In the last scene when the couples are matched for marriage, he turns to Estela's companion Lisarda, in whom he has shown no interest up to this point, and says: "Ganar quiero tu belleza, / Lisarda hermosa; pues pierdo / a Estela, dame tu mano" (2736-38).

When finally Leonor reaches a point in her scheme at which she is ready to resume her female identity, it is impossible for Juan to refuse to honor his commitment to her. And she has effected this without having to resort to the physical violence that the males argue must be the basis of the honor dilemma they finally come to recognize. While enacting the role of devoted lover, Leonor does reiterate the males' system of violence:

> mas yo, amante verdadero,
> la prometí de vengar
> su agravio, y dando al silencio
> con la muerte de don Juan
> la ley forzosa del duelo,
> ser su esposo. [2625-30]

Nevertheless, the solution she prepares is based instead on an intellectual trap. Upon hearing from "Leonardo" his supposed commitment to Leonor, both Fernando and Juan blame the abandoned woman for lack of faith. At one point Juan cries "¡En qué de afrentas me has puesto, / Leonor!" (2547-48). When contemplating the need to fight a duel with Leonardo, he also makes clear that he considers Leonor damaged and unworthy for consideration as a wife: "pues aunque muráis, no acorta / en mí esta afrenta pesada, / este infame deshonor" (2500-2502). Not only does he complain about "habiendo sido Leonor / fácil después de ser mía" (2505-6), but her brother likewise reiterates, "¡Hoy la vida y honor pierdo! / ¡Ah, hermana fácil!" (2641-42). The only resolution to the rivalry for honor's restoration that the men involved can envision is violence. Fernando declares, "todos hemos de matarnos, / yo no hallo otro remedio," to which Ludovico responds, "Ni yo le miro, ¡por Dios! / y ése es bárbaro y sangriento" (2662-65).

Leonor, however, provides an alternative. When Juan proclaims, "¡Ah, si hubiera sido honrada!" (2656), Leonardo soon asks, "¿la quisieras?" (2670). Upon receiving Juan's answer, "La adorara" (2670), she quickly exits to change her clothing and resume her female identity; in so doing she becomes the voluntary peace offering between the warring males. Returning as Leonor, she speaks before an assembled body of courtiers presided over by the prince, her brother, and Juan. Once the truth of her identity is revealed and Juan's connection to her is explained, he can do nothing but restate his devotion to her and affirm their marriage. The hostilities cease once Fernando can deliver his sister to Juan, and although Caro does not dismantle this basic pattern of woman's commodification, she does give Leonor the satisfaction of obtaining her personal goal by manipulating the imposed contract.

Estela now occupies the role of the woman disappointed in matters of love and is left without any means of redress. She even complains, "Leonardo, ¿así me engañabas?" (2730). There is no Leonardo, of course, and Leonor summarily excuses her deception with the words: "Fue fuerza, Estela" (2731). The two women promise sisterly love between them as Caro allows Estela to make her own match: "Fernando, ¿de esposo y dueño / me dad la mano?" (2733-34). The play thus closes with restoration of the social configuration that predominated before its beginning. The pairings of Juan and Leonor, Fernando and Estela are reinstated, and the carnivalesque displacements are revoked.

In *El muerto disimulado,* Azevedo expands the cross-dressing possibilities to include not only the woman masquerading as a man but also her infrequently portrayed counterpart, a man dressed as a woman. By dramatizing the possibility that there is a social reason for a man's wanting to be taken for a woman, the playwright reverses the typical carnivalesque gender crossing, but her male figure Clarindo undertakes his masquerade for less than the desperate reasons his female peer must confront. The motivation for the young woman Lisarda's disguise is the reported murder of her brother, Clarindo, by an unnamed assassin. The very much alive Clarindo, however, helps perpetuate the belief in his death by all those close to him—including his sister, his beloved Jacinta, her father, and his would-be murderer, Don Alvaro—by not sending word of his recovery. Lisarda's carnivalesque ruse is thus one of female desperation, for it is in response not only to a crime but also to the fact that after the death of her father she is the only family member left to pursue the wrongdoer. Azevedo's depiction of Lisarda reiterates the woman's need to appropriate male identity in order to act with impunity in public matters. Even when all her male reltives are dead or believed to be so, Lisarda does not feel empowered to exercise the social freedom the male figures enjoy. The daughter/sister of a noble family, she is nevertheless depicted as just as capable of undertaking this quest as her brother, and their equality is enhanced and emphasized by the cross-gendered appearance they both adopt.

Although both Lisarda and Clarindo work toward the same goal, achieving personal justice in the matter of his reported death, her disguise is indispensable for her attempts:

> De aqueste traje me valgo
> para la venganza mía,
> con más libertad buscando
> de mi hermano el homicida. [738-41]

Clarindo's disguise, on the other hand, is merely a convenience that affords him both the opportunity to observe and ensnare his attacker Alvaro and to spy on his beloved Jacinta in order to test her promise to love only him, be he dead or alive. He thinks she may betray him, however, since he is believed dead and she is "por casar" (1397). Jacinta is thus held responsible for keeping promises to a dead man and, in the absence of any evidence to support such a presumption, suspected of faithlessness.

El muerto disimulado also depicts complications in the marriage arrangements made between Jacinta's wealthy father, Don Rodrigo de Aguilar, and the homicidal nobleman Don Alvaro de Gamboa. Don Alvaro is the older man's choice of husband for his daughter, even though she pledged her undying love to Clarindo before his departure to join the Spanish troops fighting in Italy. Again, the play's theatrical and textual audiences observe a world without mothers in which young women, coerced by fathers and male overseers, are moved toward marriages that are at odds with their own preferences. The issue of filial cooperation in the matter of marriage arrangements is confronted in a way that emphasizes the daughter's untenable position. Believing that her beloved is forever lost to her, Jacinta would prefer to enter a convent—a socially acceptable alternative to secular marriage but one that does not afford the parental household the economic benefits of a wealthy match or the dynastic advantage of future heirs. Thus, Rodrigo forbids Jacinta to enter the convent and offers as a sort of bribe the freedom to pick her husband without his intervention. Insisting upon his own largesse ("Privilegio no pequeño, / que muchos padres prolijos / nunca fían de los hijos [109-11]), he nevertheless gives her an ultimatum. Soliciting her maid Dorotea's help in persuading Jacinta to acquiesce to his demands, he threatens:

> Dila, si quiere vivir,
> que mi gusto ha de observar,
> que o Jacinta ha de casar
> o Jacinta ha de morir. [141-44]

The practical servant urges her to accept her father's offer with regard to choosing a marriage partner in order to avoid the more negative alternative:

> Cuando no es el casamiento
> al gusto de la mujer,
> no hay duda que viene a ser
> el casar grande tormento.
> Mas si en su mano se deja
> la elección, de aquesta suerte
> es vida lo que era muerte,
> lisonja que era queja. [153-60]

Dorotea's sympathies are with Jacinta in the loss of her beloved Clarindo ("El primer amor, no hay duda / que es del alma impresión fuerte" [433-44]), but she encourages her mistress to consider Don Alvaro, now that a union with the reportedly dead lover is impossible. But Jacinta not only has rejected Alvaro's attentions to this point ("Su porfía de amor, ciega, / prolija, importuna y vana / me enfada" [457-59]) but she receives a letter from him that contains circumstantial but incriminating evidence that he is the murderer of her beloved Clarindo. Hence, she meets his proposal to replace Clarindo in her affection and favor with renewed rejection and fresh disapproval, based on her suspicion of his criminal deed: "¿Y quién le habrá dicho a él / que era Clarindo mi amante? (489-90). She concludes, "Don Alvaro fue sin duda / de Clarindo el homicida" (497-98).

When Lisarda arrives in Lisbon in the hope of avenging her brother's death, she enters in male clothing and calls herself Lisardo. Her plan depends initially on the legal means available to a petitioner to the king in such a matter: she seeks a royal decree offering twelve thousand ducats as reward for information about the murder. Relying on the greed that may motivate informants, she hopes thus to learn the identity of Clarindo's assailant:

> Ir determino
> a hablar al rey a palacio
> y requerirle un decreto
> en que doce mil ducados
> prometa a quien descubriere
> quien dio la muerte a mi hermano. [655-60]

Her ability to exercise control over family wealth is crucial at this point, and she reiterates money's importance in this endeavor:" . . . y aun más daré, / amigo, por alcanzarlo, / pues no me faltan dineros / como sabes . . . " (661-64). Her financial agency is imaginary, however, since her brother is not really dead, and she must pretend to be a man in order to access the political avenues of resolution. She vows, furthermore, that she herself will be the executioner of her brother's murderer:

> no pienses que por justicia,
> Papagayo, he de llevarlo,
> aguardando a que el verdugo
> deje en su muerte vengado
> a mi enojo; porque yo misma,
> cogiéndole con mis brazos,
> le he de hacer víctima horrible
> para ejemplo de tiranos. [677-84]

She exemplifies the agency that women characters in her position exercise once no male relatives are left to take action, but like Leonor in Caro's play she relies on the male disguise for the freedom to act on her capabilities. She no longer has to hide her potential for public accomplishments, but she must hide her female identity in order to open doors that remain traditionally closed to women's political bodies.

Don Alvaro himself is the protector of his sister Beatriz and bitterly opposes *her* favored suitor, their cousin Don Alberto, whom he has found talking with the young woman in their house. It is precisely during Alvaro's confrontation at sword point with Alberto that Lisarda/Lisardo makes his aquaintance. She enacts a reversal of gender roles by interrupting the fight and, upon Alberto's escape, defeating Alvaro. Here Azevedo dramatizes the presumed effects of invoking the feminist individualist model, for what the men usually do in *capa y espada* altercations, her female character also accomplishes. Soon, however, the combatants make their peace, and Alvaro explains his anger over his cousin's presence in the family home and the disappearance of his sister. Lisarda in her male clothing then delivers a short speech in which she explains to Alvaro the woman's point of view that may have motivated Beatriz to flee:

De ausentarse esa señora,
es presunción temeraria
inferirse en ella culpa,
pues del recelo obligada
de los excrúpulos vuestros,
temiendo alguna venganza,
que de la inocencia suya
en esta ocasión tomara
vuestra presunción celosa,
de alguna vecina a casa
se acogería. [913-23]

As in Caro's depiction of Leonor/Leonardo, the speech delivered by a female character dressed in male clothing enhances the infraction of gendered boundaries while simultaneously suggesting what a male might say and do when his potential for the so-called feminine virtues is realized.

As in the other Azevedo plays, it is a principal male character in *El muerto disimulado* who displays irrational reactions to events. Alvaro's response to his sister's relationship with Alberto and his own highly complicated plan to deceive everyone about his attempted murder of Clarindo are what drive many of the plot's further complications. Clarindo also shares the responsibility, for he allows the difficulties to proceed longer than might have been necessary had he merely come forward to tell the truth. Of his two motivations for pretending to be dead and feigning female identity—finding his assailant and testing Jacinta's loyalty—the first does not require the ruse he undertakes, and the second is based not on a desire for justice but on his vanity and curiosity.

Jacinta is the most reliable character in the play, given her unchanged feelings and efforts to abide by the norms of the gender ideology that underlies the play's social critique. Her commitment to Clarindo and to their mutual promise is not swayed by threats from her father or the urgings of her maid to get on with her life. Following the patterns of acceptability open to women like her in the portrayed or the actual society, Jacinta proposes to enter a convent, since she cannot marry the man she loves. But pressured by her father and courted fervently by Alvaro, whom she suspects of the treachery against Clarindo, Jacinta executes her own careful plan to wrest the truth from her lover's assailant. Like Leonor in Caro's play, she sets an intellectual trap. She writes Alvaro a letter that places him in an impossible position: she agrees to consider his proposal of marriage if he will help find out who attacked her brother. Thus, he can win her only by uttering words that will lose her, ending his courtship and putting him in jeopardy with his male peers in the hierarchized patriarchal system of honor and public justice.

The cross-gendering that Azevedo openly depicts through costuming is paralleled by the situations of the male characters: Alvaro must confront the double bind of a conflict between dual demands upon him and his goals; Clarindo is the victim of male violence and betrayal and, in his metatheatrical role as Clarinda, will eventually be the only character to speak the part of the traditional abandoned female in this play. Alvaro continues to reveal his unstable nature as well. Without realizing the familial ties between the individual before him and Clarindo, he admits to Lisarda/Lisardo his guilt in the earlier incident. His explanation reveals that jealousy and uncontrolled resentment motivated his attack on Clarindo, who, unaware of Alvaro's unrequited affection for Jacinta, told of his own budding love affair with the young woman. As in all the *comedias* considered so far, the pursuit of justice and the fulfillment of promises are the basis of the women characters' struggles, whereas rivalry over possession of the desired female is the locus of tensions between males.[17]

When Lisarda intervenes in the sword fight between Alvaro and Alberto, the scene foregrounds the individualist feminist model. It is at her insistence that the two men cease their combat, resulting in Alberto's relief that the two male opponents do not have to come to mortal blows: "A muy buen tiempo ha venido / este hombre para excusarnos / a los dos una desdicha" (793-95). Alvaro's reaction is not so reasoned, though, and he turns on "Lisardo": "Pues que me habéis estorbado / mi venganza, contra vos / se han de volver mis enfados"

(802-4), a challenge that is met with the other's willingness to continue the duel. When Lisardo knocks Alvaro's sword from his hand, the latter claims to be so impressed with his adversary's skill that he urges a truce. Thus, the choice of diplomatic over physical means of resolution shifts from Lisardo to Alvaro, just as the role of triumphant aggressor previously shifted from Alvaro (with Alberto) to Lisardo (with Alvaro). Azevedo's presentation supports Zayas's arguments about the gendered roles men and women are asked to play and her insistence that women are fully capable of taking up arms.[18]

In these early scenes of *El muerto disimulado,* the characters are depicted as capable of the physical and emotional reaction supposedly typical of the other sex, but this episode of a disguised though literal battle of the sexes ends with the reinvocation of the heterosexual universe. In spite of Alvaro's confession that he is her brother's attacker, Lisarda has fallen in love with him: "que el amor por él me obliga / a que mil finezas haga" (1084-85). Thus, her desire for revenge is rechanneled into amorous desire for Alvaro, which leads her as well into deeper dimensions of metatheatricality. Not only is she feigning her male role, but she also agrees to Alvaro's proposition that she (as Lisardo) be named Clarindo's assassin:

> Vos me habéis de dar licencia
> y permitir que me valga
> de una mentira, diciendo
> que aquesta muerte fue obrada
> por vos [1098-1102]

In an aside, Lisarda acknowledges: "Sólo aquesto me faltaba; / ¡ser yo mi enemigo mismo, / y en amores de otra dama!" (1107-9).

The confrontation with Alvaro takes place against a background of commentary provided by Papagayo, the only other character besides Lisarda herself who knows that she is a woman. He notes specifically the lack of distinction between the genders in a speech answering his mistress's warning that he must remember to call her Lisardo:

> . . . no está el punto
> en el nombre, yo me declaro;
> no hace el nombre macho o hembra,

>pues entre los papagayos
>hay papagayas también,
>y en las golondrinas damos
>con golondrinos, y vemos
>que éstos son apellidados
>con el nombre femenino,
>y aquéllas también nombramos
>con la masculina voz;
>lo mismo en ti estoy pensando
>que aunque mi voz te apellide
>Lisarda, ¿quién te ha quitado
>el ser Lisardo, señora,
>porque hay mujeres Lisardos,
>y hay también Lisardas hombres? [721-37]

This insistence upon the unstable discursive formation of men and women underlies the structure and plot of this play. Not only do the men and women exhibit tendencies toward the virtues or faults conventionally associated with the other gender, but two of the principal characters spend the majority of the play cross-dressed. Clarindo's disguise is a particularly subversive component, since Spanish dramaturgy was generally opposed to cross-dressed males. Azevedo challenges this caveat by presenting a nobleman dressed as a woman.

When Clarindo first appears on stage, he does so as himself before the startled and frightened Papagayo, who takes him for a "Sombra, fantasma o ilusión" (1222). Through their conversation, the two men and the audience learn what has happened since Clarindo's supposed demise. Emphasizing as well the transgressive nature of Lisarda's undertaking, Papagayo explains in an aside to the audience that he lies about the young woman's presence in Lisbon in order not to add to his master's discomfort and grief concerning the death of their father. To Clarindo he declares: "Tu hermana se metió fraile" (1302). His claim again reiterates the insufficiency of discursive limits upon gendered identity:

>Monja decir quiero,
>que esto de frailes y monjas
>todo viene a ser lo mesmo,
>pues tienen hábitos todos
>y viven en monasterios. [1303-07]

Still fearing that Clarindo is a ghost, the *gracioso* flees, and the nobleman is left to ponder his next move. He learned while lodged in the
house of a French noble in Nice during his convalescence that the news
of his death was publicized because, coincidentally, another soldier by
the same name did expire. Now, depending upon this circumstantial interchangeability and the general assumption that he has died, he organizes his plan of revenge against Alvaro ("un ingrato / que la amistad
ofendiendo / me quiso sacar la vida" [1376-78]), as well as his test of
Jacinta's faithfulness:

> saber ahora pretendo
> (pues ya sé que está Jacinta
> por casar) si los deseos
> de don Alvaro conquistan
> la belleza por qué muero,
> y si Jacinta rebate
> sus amantes galanteos
> con la constancia debida,
> que de su fineza espero. [1395-1403]

Ironically, in order to assure himself of her virtue, Clarindo decides to
transgress the enclosed boundary he and the other men in Jacinta's life
have instituted. In woman's disguise he will incorporate himself into his
beloved's household—a violation of sorts, since he will do so surrep-
tiously.

By the midpoint of Act 2, Clarindo has settled upon a ploy to
pretend to be a female vendor of cosmetics—a blurring of both gender
and class boundaries and a role that crosses the intertextual boundaries
between this drama and the early sixteenth-century *novela dialogada
La Celestina*. At this juncture, Clarindo dramatizes one dimension
of the social conventions imposed on women, for the only way to gain
free access to a stranger's home is to present himself initially as a public
woman. The role of street vendor with her Celestinesque taint of
promiscuity allows him open movement as a female figure. Entering
the stage in a dress and with a basket on his head, "Clarinda" hawks
baubles and ornaments to Jacinta, Beatriz, and their respective servants,
Dorotea and Hipólita. In an aside, Jacinta ponders the stranger's re-
semblance to Clarindo, and the disguised young man comments to

himself that his masquerade is aided by the fact that he does not yet have a beard: "a que en tal traje me anima / mi edad, que aun le faltan señas / por do el hombre se divisa" (1700-1702). His role breaks down across class lines, however, when everyone realizes that this individual knows nothing about selling ribbons and trinkets. Confessing to the assembled women, "bien muestro que ha poco tiempo / aqueste oficio ejercita / quien tan mal sabe vender" (1755-57),Clarindo declares, "Soy una mujer perdida" (1754). He embellishes the charade with a story about the dishonor "she" suffered because of the deceit of a nobleman from the Portuguese court who left after promising marriage:

> Con promesa al fin de esposo
> (¡o promesa fementida!)
> me robó amante la joya
> que en el mundo más se estima.
> Con la armada en fin partióse,
> diciendo a la despedida
> que iba a disponer sus cosas,
> y que entonces volvería
> para ponerse en efecto
> la palabra prometida.
> Viendo pues que de la vuelta
> el plazo pasado había
> que me dio, por engañada
> me di luego en su malicia. [1783-96]

The tale also incorporates an account of how the fictitious Clarinda was compelled by circumstance to steal her father's jewelry and money in order to go in search of her betrayer.

As in Caro's *Valor, agravio y mujer,* the playwright calls attention to the individualist position through a superficial regendering of the character who articulates the abandoned woman's dilemma. In Caro's play, Leonor disguised as Leonardo delivers a version of her own story and represents a potential response on the part of her own male lover. Azevedo complicates the blurring of genders even further by assigning to one of her male protagonists the abandoned woman's speech of complaint. In neither instance, however, are the gender conventions thoroughly subverted, since the emotionally abused figure is still embodied or described as female in the Renaissance feminists' straddling of the relational and individualist paradigms.

Clarinda's narration is further strengthened through the explanation of her motivation for taking the disguise of street vendor:

> Y viendo que una mujer
> de aqueste trato tenía
> libertad para correr
> las calles y de esta guisa
> entrarse en cualquiera casa,
> me ha animado a que le siga
> por si topo su persona
> ingrata y desconocida. [1815-22]

Clarindo's ruse is thus manipulated as he exchanges the performance of street vendor for that of dishonored noblewoman, a transition that further dramatizes the contemporary gender ideology's social conventions. Social class must repeatedly be redefined in the female role in order to make practical use of the cross-gendered performance. The enclosure of the respectable noblewoman must first be transcended by playing the bawd. Once Clarindo's position, both physically and socially, as a woman with access to solitary movement in the streets accomplishes his entry into Jacinta's house, then Clarinda the vendor becomes Clarinda the abandoned noblewoman who, with a portion of her family's male-dominated fortune ("y hurtando a mi padre joyas / y dineros" [1797-98]), claims to have set out first dressed as a man: "de hombre el hábito tomando" (1801). As the explanation continues ("Y viendo que una mujer / de aqueste trato tenía / libertad para correr / las calles" [1815-17]), Clarindo affirms the multiplicity of his role-playing, which has actually included dead nobleman, purported man dressed as woman dressed as man, crossed-dressed man as noblewoman dressed as street vendor, and finally nobleman dressed as noblewoman.

Azevedo's reworking of theatrical conventions destabilizes the fixed quality of assigned roles by reassigning them to improbable figures. In *El muerto disimulado* there is no depicted woman who suffers because of a fickle lover. The playwright does write this role into the play, but it is a counterfeit woman who articulates the speech, familiar to regular theater-goers, about the trials of the many betrayed *damas* of the seventeenth-century Spanish *comedia*. Through the depiction of Clarindo/Clarinda, Azevedo also accomplishes a critique of the socially constructed roles with which Renaissance gender ideology threatens women if they do not abide within its narrow limitations for their behavior and speech. Once she is considered dishonored, there is no place for such a woman in the social ambiance in which she once lived. Clarinda enacts the alternative of sexual openness that leads to being out on the street, an icon for the ostensible fate of the unchaste woman. Azevedo nevertheless allows for Clarinda's reincorporation into the ranks of noblewomen, for Jacinta admits her into her upper-class household. Whereas cross-dressing permits a woman character like Lisarda to move around more freely in public with access to the discourse of authority, the male cross-dresses in this play in order to move inside.

Jealousy or potential jealousy, however, is a large part of the motivation for Clarindo's masquerade, for he wants to carry out his secret investigation of Jacinta's honesty and devotion. It is ironic that it is she who must undergo this scrutiny, for she has remained true to him even after believing him dead. In addition to her wish to enter a convent, in Act 2 she gives direct evidence of her care to remain unseen, abiding scrupulously by society's expectations for a respectable young woman. When Beatriz's suitor Alberto calls upon Jacinta's father, and Beatriz asks her friend to remain with her so she can speak with her suitor, Jacinta answers: "Yo no tengo de ser vista" (1858). Clarindo/Clarinda is still with the women and remarks in an aside: "Aqueso es lo que me agrada" (1859). The critique follows the traditional trajectory from male observer toward female object of scrutiny, but Clarindo's female disguise places a filter before the gaze, thus suggesting what the play dramatizes: that the abusive patriarchal system is vulnerable to scrutiny. The disguised male character helps symbolize this watchful stance, even though it is directed toward himself as well as his male peers.

Alberto does speak with Beatriz and hears her tale of escape from the wrath of her brother Alvaro. She has taken refuge in Jacinta's home and depends on Jacinta's father, Don Rodrigo, to mollify Alvaro and help her come to an agreement with him. Azevedo's dramatization does not radicalize the practice of negotiations between men in social and political matters; Alberto listens to Beatriz's account and approves of Rodrigo as a mediator. Like the other males in the drama, however, he is depicted as overly jealous, for he articulates his suspicious uneasiness about the identity of the man (Lisarda in disguise) who appeared at Beatriz's house to interrupt his fight with Alvaro:

> ¿Y qué hombres (pregunto yo)
> serían, Beatriz, aquéllos
> que subieron y uno de ellos
> a los dos nos apartó? [1915-18]

Alvaro himself is greatly angered over his sister's flight from their home, but he acknowledges that her choice of havens is respectable because of the honor and reputation of Don Rodrigo and his family: "ha tomado buen puerto su flaqueza" (1972). Alvaro nevertheless exhibits the typical angst of the conventional male relative over the threat that a woman's love for the man of *her* choice poses to family honor. Unlike Rodrigo, who refuses to allow his daughter to join a religious order, Alvaro's solution for the challenge to his authority over Beatriz is to place her in a convent forcefully: "que una celda / de un convento la oculte determino. / . . . si la muerte / no le doy, la sepulto de esta suerte" (1975-78).

These concerns for integrity and honor seem remarkably out of place in a man who is no more than a traitorous murderer. Further irony emerges when Rodrigo—who himself not only denied his daughter's wish to enter the convent but threatened her with death—warns that the plan to send Beatriz to a religious house will cause suspicion of her virtue:

> Eso es dar ocasión,
> para que de Beatriz, contra el decoro,
> alguna presunción
> se atreva a concebir algún desdoro. [1979-82]

The men who oversee the lives of their female relatives in this play openly reject the women's wishes, and Rodrigo's expressed opinion reveals just how little control over their own lives Azevedo envisions for her female characters. Beatriz, like Jacinta, is mindful of the proprieties, but her efforts to observe them are seemingly futile, given the social suspicion routinely directed at women. The control by males of what females can do and how their actions are evaluated is examined in the play, but not disrupted.

Like carnival celebrations, the temporary changes that Clarindo's and Lisarda's cross-gendered disguises represent only interrupt the usual procedures and events. Through Lisarda, Azevedo reiterates the limitations on woman's public intervention as well as on the female agency that allows a character like her to negotiate the difficulties and gendered boundaries she confronts. Through Clarindo, the playwright scrutinizes in a new way the woman's plight, assigning to a male figure the abandoned woman's complaints against an irresponsible male lover. Like Caro's Leonardo, Lisardo and Clarinda disappear, and the social relationships reorganize to bring about, in one case, the original pairing that precipitated the dramatized social and emotional disorganization. Since Jacinta cannot be claimed by two men, Azevedo continues to the end of the play to write against convention by allowing Alvaro and Clarindo to follow the suggestions of the counterfeit male character Lisardo: that is, to end their dispute peacefully. Forgiveness settles the criminal charges against Alvaro, who accepts Lisarda as his new spouse. This pairing accomplishes a reestablishment of the gender norms and yet another exchange of a woman between male relative and future spouse. Yet, this union suggests further reversals, since it links a woman with a man she has proved capable of defeating physically in their earlier sword duel—something that Alberto and, even earlier, her brother were unable to do.

The play likewise dramatizes a dispersion of authority not only among the pretenders to its exercise but also among the transgressors against its order. The misrule represented by Alvaro's crime motivates an erasure of discriminations of gender, producing the performances of the two siblings as Lisardo and Clarinda. Clarindo's performance has many levels, the principal one his pretense to being dead. This ruse extends the disorder and hampers the smooth carriage of justice against the crime that Alvaro intended to commit. Coming forward to reveal that he is alive and to accuse his attacker would have precluded any further action—but it would have also precluded Azevedo's depiction of the questionable integrity and ethics of males who exercise authority while exempting themselves from accountability.

By the last scene the carnivalesque deviation from the recognizable order is brought to an end, and the patriarchal figures regain their ability to direct events and influence their outcome. As Alvaro kneels before Lisarda to ask her forgiveness ("pidiendo humilde y postrado / perdón de la culpa mía" [3745-46]), it is Clarindo who first speaks words of pardon and authorizes the other's union with his sister: "quiero constante mostraros / que soy para vos amigo / y vos para mí cuñado" (3751-53). Clarindo and Jacinta pledge mutual love before all with a cursory acknowledgment of the need to acquire her father's blessing. The elderly Don Rodrigo grants them permission to marry— "Mi agrado / y mi gusto apruebo" (3765-66)—but the dispersion of the authority that the oldest male usually claims is also revealed when he demands the right to make at least one match, that of Alberto and Beatriz. Pointing out that he was unsuccessful in arranging the marriage he preferred for his daughter, he says to Alvaro:

> señor don Alvaro, hacedme
> una merced de barato,
> pues la suerte me impidió
> el haber en vos logrado
> el yerno que deseé. [3773-77]

In this male negotiation over the matching of couples, the women raise no voice except to agree to the terms specified. The younger man acquiesces to the older man's authority, and Alvaro says: "Siempre soy vuestro criado, / y en todo he de obedeceros" (3778-79). To this Rodrigo commands:

> Pues salid de aquese cuarto,
> señor Alberto, salid
> señora Beatriz; tomado
> he por mi cuenta este empeño,
> y vos habéis de otorgarlo;
> este casamiento es mío. [3780-85]

Jacinta and Beatriz are fortunate in Azevedo's depiction of them, for they do gain the partners of their choosing. The *criados* are matched in the final moments, and the *gracioso* Papagayo delivers the last speech:

> Tal caso no ha sucedido;
> pero como casos raros
> suceden, también supongo
> que ha sucedido este caso. [3805-08]

The termination of the carnivalesque deviation from expected order on stage now opens the possibility of the transgression of boundaries with the suggestion that there is no distinction between the representation and its spectators. Azevedo has included in her representation of the solution of a criminal mystery the combination of the noble male victim with his role as the male in drag, so generally censured in seventeenth-century Spanish theater. The character who has moved another male figure to jealous irrationality and has inspired the faithful dedication of his beloved even beyond the grave spends most of two acts of the play dressed as a woman, thus questioning the efficacy of the assigned gender conventions. Azevedo creates a means to show that gendered behavior is a role to play but recognizes that the departure from the accepted norm can be successful only as long as it is an unrecognized one. Thus, the playwright's theatrical audience becomes implicated in the carnivalesque appropriation of cross-gendered attributes, since the interior audience of the representation does not understand that Lisardo and Clarinda are not who they seem to be.

The strategy of the cross-dressed woman invokes the individualist feminism of the Renaissance by demonstrating the fluidity of gendered identity; at the same time it reinforces the patriarchal relational model through evidence that masculine political identity carries privileges which feminine identity does not. Plays in which women characters dress as men do not revolutionize the patriarchal assumptions that endow men with the opportunity to confront problems and negotiate solutions. Although such a system is questioned by a woman's participation, she must appear as a man in order to participate. The relational model is thus preserved, even as the individualist model is enacted.

The symbolic inversion that Caro and Azevedo accomplish through carnivalesque cross-dressing is achieved by Zayas without such disguises. Instead, her one extant play, *La traición en la amistad,* critiques the courtship rituals of the aristocratic class and its premarital gendered codes of behavior through the actions and attitudes particularly of a carnivalesque female principal named Fenisa. Markedly very similar to both her men and women friends at court, Fenisa becomes the center of disorder and general disapproval as she consciously enacts a challenge to the privileges enjoyed by the male courtiers. Zayas stages a counter-poise to the role of Caro's Leonor in *Valor, agravio y mujer* in that Fenisa represents the negative side of a woman's appropriation of the male norm instead of the male's potential for more just behavior. Fenisa is also a more radical figure, for she crosses the gender boundaries without cross-dressing. She finds far less success in her undertaking, however, than the characters previously discussed in this chapter.

When Fenisa, enjoying the attention of multiple suitors, refuses to choose one among them, she becomes the target of condemnation from all the other characters, men and women.[19] Their society cannot accommodate a woman who insists on claiming the social privileges culturally assigned to men. Fenisa's disruption of their community, moreover, prolongs the courtship rituals and thus extends the period of time when pairings are not yet fixed and the women remain just outside the control of the men with whom they will eventually live as wives. In this play it is the female characters who more actively manipulate the situations depicted and who finally arrange or ratify the marriages with which the play ends, a dramatization that suggests alternatives to the male-dominated marriage market that so many *comedias* promote.[20]

Throughout the play Fenisa resists the passage into the fixed categories of chosen or choosing partner, preferring instead to maintain the freedom that not choosing or being chosen affords her. Although she does privilege one man in the list of her suitors, she consistently avows her reluctance to marry or settle on one:

> Diez amantes me adoran, y yo a todos
> los adoro, los quiero, los estimo,
> y todos juntos en mi alma caben,
> aunque Liseo como rey preside. [1518-21]

Zayas has thus created a character who seems to conflate the theatrical and dramatic dimensions, since Fenisa, though part of the represented society, embodies the perceived promiscuity of seventeenth-century actors, who were accused of leading unsettled lives and indulging in indiscriminate sexual practices in their constant travels from town to town.[21]

The *comedia*'s male-identified values with regard to courtship, which Fenisa has appropriated, are made apparent by the comments and attitudes of her favorite suitor, Liseo. Having courted several of the women in the drama, he ranks them according to his intentions toward and feelings for each:

> Es Marcia de mi amor prenda querida
> y Fenisa adorada en tal manera
> que está mi voluntad loca y perdida.
> Laura ya no es mujer, es una fiera;
> Marcia es un ángel; mi Fenisa diosa;
> éstas vivan, León, y Laura muera. [1278-83]

Zayas questions the theatrical conventions and social standards through these two parallel characters, who, by virtue of their respective genders, coincide in very different ways with the hierarchical assumptions of the opposition order/disorder. The playwright eliminates from this representation all governing figures, for there are no fathers or monarchs to impose their wills upon the young nobles with regard to marriage arrangements. Fenisa's enactment of misrule puts into question the so-called privilege of male infidelity and deception, which Liseo represents, and so again a carnivalesque dimension reveals that its disorder is not any more chaotic than the apparent order it subverts. Zayas's critique of the social construction of gender, in her play as in her *novelas,* expresses the late Renaissance feminist apologies, which are a mixture of individualist and relational strategies. Her characters demonstrate that men and women are capable of the same behavior—in her version, within a negative register.

Like the other female dramatists considered, Zayas is consistent in disrupting the women's potential for community. Early in Act 1, Fenisa herself remarks upon her competition with her friend Marcia for Liseo's affection: "¿Dónde, voluntad, caminas / contra Marcia, tras Liseo?" (168-69). Soon, however, she proclaims, "cayó el amistad en tierra / y amor victoria apellida" (173-74). Although the other women characters reject Fenisa and work to defeat her in her amorous pursuit of all the available males, they are motivated not by a wish to build cohesion among themselves but by their desire to win back their respective suitors and establish unions with them. Among these women, Laura stands as this play's representative of the dishonored beloved. She is the victim of Liseo's earlier promises of love and marriage and then callous change of attitude toward her.

The play reveals that no one woman is capable of redressing such a grievance; therefore, Marcia and Belisa join with Laura to trick Liseo into honoring his promises to the latter. They also pledge to defeat Fenisa in her pursuit of all their potential suitors, a decision that replicates the patriarchal tendency to blame women for the fickleness or lasciviousness of men. Belisa says, for example,

> . . . que si puedo
> le he de quitar a don Juan,
> mi antiguo y querido dueño,
> que también le persuadió
> a que no me viese. [1068-72]

The banding together of these women in this undertaking is enhanced by the suggestion of a brief erotic attraction among them, evinced in Belisa's comments about Laura:

> No hay más bien
> que ver cuando viendo estoy
> tal belleza; el cielo os dé
> la ventura cual la cara;
> si hombre fuera, yo empleara
> en vuestra afición mi fe. [915-20]

Although there is no repetition of this homoerotic possibility, it symbolizes another untenable dimension of the amorous life of these women in that they, not their male suitors, must make sacrifices so that social stability can be maintained. Thus, Marcia renounces her interest in Liseo, proclaiming, "desde aquí de amarle dejo" (1002), and decides to accept Gerardo, the man who has unsuccessfully courted her for seven years. She rationalizes her choice as follows:

> Porque viendo, Belisa, los engaños
> de los hombres de ahora y conociendo
> que ha siete años que este mozo noble

> me quiera sin que fuerza de desdenes
> hayan quitado su afición tan firme,
> ya como amor su lance había hecho
> en mi alma en Liseo transformada,
> conociendo su engaño, en lugar suyo
> aposento a Gerardo. [1637-45]

She opts for security rather than love, but her attitude and that of her companions reveal that all characters in this drama depend on gendered universalizations—of and about both men and women—that result in questionable pairings. Marcia will marry a man she has long rejected; Belisa and Laura will marry men who have proved unfaithful to them.

Fenisa's comportment is based on her resentment of the advantage men enjoy in the social double standard. The darker tone to her carnivalesque performance is revealed when she vows:

> Hombres, así vuestros engaños vengo;
> guárdenos [de las] necias que no saben,
> aunque más su firmeza menoscaben,
> entretenerse como me entretengo. [1467-70]

The seriousness with which the other characters interpret Fenisa's reversals is evident in the men's anger toward her, which builds in proportion to their sense of betrayal because she does not make a choice among them. Their rivalry parallels their jealousy. Juan, for instance, tells Fenisa, as she teases him about their affair, "tú pagas mal / mi amor" (202-3). It is also Juan who late in Act 2 reveals to Belisa that, summoned to a garden tryst with Fenisa, he went merely to spy on her and indeed witnessed first her amorous conversation with Lauro, a young friend of Liseo, and then her revelry with the latter. Angered by her conduct—a reaction which he self-righteously promises "no son celos, / mi Belisa" (1708)—he followed Fenisa back to her house and was on the point of killing her with his knife ("Yo entonces la mano puesta / en la daga, quise darle" [1733-34]) when his fear of public reprisal stopped him. He did slap her, however, and now imputes to her all the blame for the amorous adventures in which she has participated with the various men, including himself:

> Dejé sangrientas venganzas,
> y para mayor afrenta
> con la mano de su cara
> saqué por fuerza vergüenza,
> diciendo: "Así se castigan
> a las mujeres que intentan
> desatinos semejantes
> y que a los hombres enredan." [1744-51]

Her body is beyond the bounds of possession of a single man and so becomes the site of castigation for her resistance to tradition. The male community closes ranks on Fenisa, for, as Juan narrates, he next followed Liseo and explained to him the multiple love affairs Fenisa had organized for herself. From this point on, Fenisa is abandoned by all the noblemen with whom she has been involved, the certainty of which Lauro comes to tell her, adding that "yo, que te amaba, / no te aborrezco, mas al fin te dejo" (2448-49).

There is no conventional social space for Fenisa to occupy; she has been excluded by both the female and male members of her depicted society. Yet even though she both fails in her attempt to prolong indefinitely her amorous games and also loses Liseo, she does maintain her freedom after all the other women are matched with their respective husbands. She thus escapes patriarchal control and enclosure, and the play's final speech, delivered by the *gracioso* León, articulates the tension Zayas seems to recognize as a product of such behavior as Fenisa's. León turns to the theatrical audience and declares:

> Señores míos, Fenisa,
> cual ven, sin amantes queda;
> si alguno la quiere, avise
> para que su casa sepa. [2911-14]

The space that Fenisa has created for herself is untraditional but beyond the bounds of the closed world of female enclosure—symbolized here by the theatrical stage, which can be configured as open (as is finally implied) to the space beyond the curtain. Zayas does not destroy Fenisa but allows her to perpetuate her carnival disruption, implying dramatic material for future carnivalesque parodies of well-known honor dramas in which wives, such as Marcia and Belisa, might punish unfaithful husbands.

5

Locales of Dramaturgy

Tragicomedia los jardines y campos sabeos
(Enríquez)

Everything is calm, and time is very much pregnant with novelties that they say will soon be born.
> —José Pellicer, *Avisos*

All newness is dangerous.
> —Gabriel del Corral, *La Cintia de Aranjuez*

Republics meet their end and are carried away (as are all natural things) by the stream of time and by change.
> —Eugenio de Narbona, *Doctrina política y civil*

> sólo en esto de poetas
> hay notable novedad
> por innumerables tanto
> que aun quieren poetizar
> las mujeres y se atreven
> a hacer comedias ya.
> —Ana Caro, *Valor, agravio y mujer*

The unique composition of two separate but connected plays, *Primera parte* and *Segunda parte de la Tragicomedia los jardines y campos sabeos,* with their accompanying choruses and interludes constitute the contribution of Feliciana Enríquez de Guzmán to the dramatic output of Spain's Golden Age. Further, her short theoretical proclamations about the plays add to her efforts to situate herself as a woman author in the theatrical milieu. Identifying herself as a female crusader for classical precepts, Enríquez touts her adherence to ancient authority at the same time that her works question authoritative figures and their political offices and openly demonstrate the poetic license she takes with the classical artistic paradigms. Calling attention to the fact that she is a woman writing among the male dramatists who have promoted the Spanish popular theater, she challenges the Lopean *comedia nueva* while claiming that the popular dramatists disparage her classically based *Tragicomedia* "por novela impertinente y a la autora della por autora de novedades y dislates" (p. 268). Her theoretical de-fense describes these complaints against her by "los poetas cómicos de España" before an imagined "Consejo Real de Poesía," presided over by a panoply of Olympian figures, including "la serenísima princesa de las ciencias, Pallas Minerva": "por la cual se querellaron de ella y le pusieron demanda, diciendo que siendo mujer y no pudiendo hablar entre poetas, había tenido atrevimiento de componer la dicha tragicomedia, y dejádose decir en ella que había sido la primera que con toda propiedad y rigor había imitado a los cómicos antiguos, y guardado su arte poética y preceptos" (p. 268).

These words sound an anticipatory echo of what today French feminists celebrate in their various calls to practice *l'écriture féminine*. Enríquez does not urge or even suggest a move to write through the body, as do theorists such as Hélène Cixous and Luce Irigaray, but her search for a different kind of dramatic writing is a project that shares a speculative dimension with some of their notions. Cixous claims in her famous essay "The Laugh of the Medusa," for example:

> I mean it when I speak of male writing. I maintain unequivocally that there is such a thing as *marked* writing; that, until now, far more extensively and repressively than is ever suspected or admitted, writing has been run by a libidinal and cultural—hence political, typically masculine—economy; that this is a locus where the repression of women has been perpetuated, over and over, more or less consciously, and in a manner that's frightening since it's often hidden or adorned with the mystifying charms of fiction; that this locus has grossly exaggerated all the signs of sexual opposition (and not sexual difference), where woman has never *her* turn to speak—this being all the more serious and unpardonable in that writing is precisely *the very possibility of change,* the space that can serve as a springboard for subversive thought, the precursory movement of a transformation of social and cultural structures. [311]

The location of the metaphorical space in which to write or speak is important in Cixous's project to break women's silence: "by taking up the challenge of speech which has been governed by the phallus . . . women will confirm women in a place other than that which is reserved in and by the symbolic, that is, in a place other than silence." Such a risk nevertheless suggests a double bind, as Cixous indicates in describing the woman who dares speech: "A double distress, for even if she transgresses, her words fall almost always upon the deaf male ear, which hears in language only that which speaks in the masculine" (312).

Enríquez negotiates such a "double distress" through the process that Ann Jones finds in the French feminists efforts at "inventing new kinds of writing": "It takes a thoroughgoing familiarity with *male* figureheads of Western culture to recognize the intertextual games played by all these writers; their work shows that a resistance to culture is always built, at first, of bits and pieces of that culture, however they are disassembled, criticized, and transcended. . . . Women's writing will be more accessible to writers and readers alike if we recognize it as a conscious response to socioliterary realities" ("Writing the Body," 374). Such an undertaking is represented in the Renaissance relational dimension within which Enríquez writes as a female writing differently yet within the Renaissance individualist context which challenges the construction of the cultural, linguistic, and artistic conventions that leave for women only the negative space of silence or the category of curiosity or novelty as a writer.[1]

The multiple levels of *novedades* that Enríquez accomplishes are addressed in her theoretical passages. She not only presents herself among the ranks of male writers of plays but also confronts the polemical theater debate between those advocating Lope's native drama and those deriding it as commercial pap for the unlettered *vulgo*. Renouncing the *comedia nueva*, she aligns her works with the ancient dramatic form yet paradoxically extols her theater as *novedad*, the same term her detractors in the debate use to taunt her.

The word *novedad* is charged with social and political import, as Maravall demonstrates in his examination of baroque culture. Discussing the paradoxical nature of the concept of novelty, he argues that in seventeenth-century Spain it was invoked approvingly when linked to consolidation of an established system, driving its force in two directions: "O bien desviando el impulso a favor de lo nuevo hacia esferas de la vida colectiva en las que una innovación no sea peligrosa para el futuro, O bien aceptando presentar bajo aspectos nuevos la tradición heredada" (269). Thus, contradictory exhortations were sounded by those *arbitristas*, such as Fernando Carrillo and Angel Manrique, urging action against national decline: "Novelties (*novedades*) are absolutely bad when they run counter to the established forms of state and government" and "Novelties have always brought great difficulties and inconveniences in their train;" but also "New needs and new situations demand a search for new remedies" (quoted in Elliott, 258). The latter motivation would seem to undergird Enríquez's desire to challenge through innovation, but at the same time her challenge overlaps facets of the seventeenth-century suspicion of *novedades*. Maravall writes, for example:

> La novedad en la vida social se rechaza. De ahí la tendencia a atribuir el gusto por la misma a ciertos grupos que, en una sociedad dada—en este caso, la de la época barroca—, soportan una cierta nota adversa, una mayor o menor descalificación (por ejemplo: a los ignorantes, a los pobres, a los jóvenes, a las mujeres, o a ciertos grupos extraños, como puede ser el de los indios u otros pueblos, etc.). Lope achaca reiteradamente ese gusto a la masa de no distinguidos que se hace oír por todas partes: ". . . El vulgo siente / con baja condición las novedades." [270]

Reiterating that novelty meant change, destabilization, and disturbance, Maravall contends that hegemonic interests were best served by those deriding such a force (270-71).[2] Enríquez's invocation of novelty in connection to her dramatic output encodes her redefinition of these debates in the artistic dimension. As a woman, she finds no place either in the pre-Lope theatrical world or in that of his *comedia nueva,* in both of which men dominate. She thus dismantles as she reassembles the traditional and non-traditional dramatic forms through transgression of the very precepts she purports to uphold.[3]

Acknowledging the classical principles that promoted the unities of time, space, and action, in dramatic composition, she claims on the one hand to have preserved these but, on the other, to have done so with "la licencia poética usada discretamente" (p. 269). The plaintiffs in the case, who include "poetas y no poetas," argue before her mythological judges that the national dramatic art form supersedes any other, which is denounced as "novedad y cosa de risa" (p. 270). Insisting on the contradictory notions of the newness *and* classical basis of her theatrical pieces, Enríquez's "Carta" promotes the dichotomous notion that the modern *comedias nuevas* of her attackers are actually old and traditional. And so declare the Muses and company:

Declaramos la *Tragicomedia los jardines y campos sabeos* haber ganado nuestra corona de laurel en la arte y preceptos de los cómicos antiguos a todas las comedias y tragedias españolas compuestas hasta los tiempos del Magno Felipe Cuarto de las Españas. Y mandamos a nuestros poetas españoles que en las comedias, que de aquí adelante se hicieren, guarden las leyes y preceptos de su *Primera* y *Segunda parte,* so pena de no ser tenidos de nos por cómicos ni trágicos; y que los mandaremos borrar y tildar del catálogo de nuestros poetas y de los libros de nuestras mercedes y situados con destierro a nuestra voluntad, de las altas cumbres de nuestro Parnaso. Y mandamos se lea en todas nuestras academias por arte de buenas comedias, ley y pragmática sanción hecha en nuestras cortes la dicha *Tragicomedia* y sus reglas y preceptos.[4] [p. 270]

Enríquez's rejection of the national theater thus includes both its structural features and its site of performance. Her *Tragicomedia* is to be read in salons ("se lea en todas nuestras academias"), a requirement enhanced by her theoretical tract "A los lectores," in which she says of her play "que puede salir en público, a ver no los teatros y coliseos, en los cuales no he querido ni quiero que parezca; mas los palacios y salas de los príncipes y grandes señores y sus regocijos públicos y de sus ciudades y reinos; y asímismo, con menos ruido, visitar en sus casas a los aficionados a buenas letras" (p. 271). The courtly context for the presentation of her work validates a world of learning and erudition of which she purports to be a part, in opposition to the popular theaters where the *vulgo* dominates and influences the productions.

Such arguments against the propriety of the atmosphere of the *corrales* were fodder for the moralists' denunciations of women's participation and even attendance in the theater, which they considered a corrupting influence. There is thus a sidestepping maneuver on Enríquez's part, an avoidance of the site of contention and public display in favor of the site of patronage and class privilege, the courtly circles

where women's educated minds might have a somewhat more appreciative audience. She reasserts the conditions that women should perform
and exhibit their talents behind closed doors, an intellectual enclaustra-
tion that satisfies the desire for expression but does so within the
limitations that seventeenth-century gender ideology imposes. Enríquez's Renaissance feminism is not revolutionary; like her female peers
she challenges the males merely to redress the excesses and abuses of the
social system in order to preserve its order. The author's insistence upon
the injustice of judgments against her because of her gender therefore
rest on the support of the ancient authorities, who are male, and upon
the contemporary patriarchal figures of political authority and patronage. Yet it is these groups and their power that her dramatic works
nevertheless proceed to question and even ridicule.

Enríquez begins her *Primera parte* with a "Prólogo" in which she an-
nounces the subject to be dramatized and its complications:

> De dos Amantes, que en sus tiernos años
> Se amaron, y adoraron con invidia,
> Y emulacion de muchos enemigos,
> Desde el primero instante, en que se vieron,
> Y en el mismo en sus almas dulcemente
> Con reciproco amor se transformaron;
> Aunque ella se mudo, y a el que fue firme,
> Remuneró el muy Alto con ventajas. [2r]

The story is contemporary with the playwright and her audience ("en
nuestros tiempos sucedida") although distant from them (". . . que en
Arabia, / Finge aver sucedido en los Sabeos, / Campos, y sus jardines"
[2r]). The prologue devotes much critical attention to those dramatists
who ignore the classical unities. First the limits of space are stretched so
that, for instance:

> Unas vezes Borbon da assalto a Roma;
> Y en Bolonia el Pontifice Clemente
> Corona a Carlos Maximo; y Florencia
> Contra su Duque, y Medicis conjura;
> . . . .
> Y el auditorio a todas estas partes

> Por Malgesi es llevado; o qual Perseo
> por las velozes alas de Mercurio;
> o el roxo Apolo por su carro ardiente.
> Dexo, que muchas vezes el Teatro
> ya es sala, ya jardín, ya plaza, y calle;
> ya ciudad, ya desierto, ya recámara;
> ya templo, ya oratorio, ya floresta;
> ya navio, ya mar, ya el propio cielo. [2v-3r]

Admitting that "Esto es quanto al lugar" Enríquez goes on to "quanto al tiempo" in which occurs, among other abuses, the practice in which "junta sin poetica licencia / unos siglos con otros" (3r). With continued emphasis on the propriety of representation that includes the number of acts, the proper way to change scenes, the mixture of characters, and so on, Enríquez disputes Lope's "Arte nuevo" with one of her own.[5]

She also proclaims her editing of the first version of her plays, published in 1624, by exchanging the term *jornada* for *acto* to indicate the drama's divisions. Claiming preference for the "uso español" in this, she further reports her elimination of such classical terminology as "protasis," "epitasis," and "catástrofe" ("A los lectores," p. 271), insisting, through her inclusion of the division title "Protasis" in the 1627 *Primera parte* (3v), that she observes the classical precepts at the same time that she breaks with them.[6]

What Enríquez confronts and represents in her drama and in her theoretical treatises is the hybrid world in which the female dramatist must function, since the space created and dominated by the male playwrights is not readily accessible to their female colleagues. Enríquez rejects the public space of the *corrales,* in which the males as authors and actors overshadow their female counterparts through sheer numbers. She opts instead for the courtly space of palace and salon, suggesting that her dramas are more appropriate for discussion than for action-filled performance. Enríquez promotes her plays and *entreactos* as models for critique and emulation by the most intellectual participants in the theatrical experience, patrons who can open opportunities for artists and writers.[7] But the hybridity of this geography of dramatization—which Enríquez fills with characters and scenes purported to reinscribe the classical precepts of order and elite values—in reality mixes ancient tenets and some popularized *comedia* ingredients. Her two-part play itself grafts or combines parts into a whole that broadens the spectrum of possibilities for portrayals on stage, combining love stories, mortal characters and mythological deities, large expanses of time and location, and all aspects of performance typical of seventeenth-century Spain's *staged* drama, plus *entremeses,* songs, dances, choruses, and *loas.*[8] Enríquez's contribution to the world of Siglo de Oro theater stands as a recognition of its myriad possibilities at the same time that it manifests the problematical identity of a woman and the limitations on her composed work.

Primera parte of her two-part *Tragicomedia* dramatizes the story of a pair of princesses, Belidiana and Clarinda, and their struggles against parental opposition to their marriage contracts with the two royal figures they love, the Greek prince Clarisel and the Macedonian king Beloribo. Set in Arabia, this play contains many of the most conventional features of the *comedia de enredo:* each of the principal *galanes* is disguised as a common gardener in order to remain close to his royal beloved through trysts in the palace grounds; a *privado* to the Arabian king who, in his desire for revenge against Belidiana, (for having caused, he claims, the death of his sister) becomes the agent of treason in the love affairs; a rival for the hand of Belidiana in the person of Adonis, who is aided in his suit by none other than the goddess Venus; a dishonorable sword fight before the king that results in the imprisonment of the two foreign men; clandestine communication between the women and the imprisoned men; and finally the reluctant paternal acceptance of the marriage match proposed by the young royals. This play, like the others examined, focuses on the upper and royal classes but nevertheless reveals the transcendence of gender over class identity.

The love matches between the royal women of Arabia (Belidiana) and Cyprus (Clarinda) and the foreign princes from Greece (Clarisel) and Macedonia (Beloribo) have been interrupted by the men's absence, a condition that ends as the play opens and the royal suitors enter the kingdom of Belidiana's father Belerante. Much of the dramatic space and time is devoted to talking about the love affairs. In Act 1, for instance, Clarisel and his servant Birano discuss the master's feelings for Belidiana and her "beldad soberana" (4r). Comic moments ensue as well when, for example, Birano forgets to address Clarisel by the name he uses in disguise, Cryselo. In this early act there is also a recital of Clarisel's dreams of impending disasters in the love affairs, visions in

which the women themselves announce their alliances with other men.
The imagined Belidiana says:

> Ay Clarisel, Clarisel,
> perdona mi grave culpa,
> que mi padre me disculpa,
> de averte sido cruel.
> Pudiste esperar presente;
> mas fue error necio, y demencia
> sobre tres años de ausencia,
> que aun el sol no alumbra ausente. [5v]

In another visionary moment, Clarinda proclaims:

> Ay Rey de Macedon, no fue
> en mi mano, no negarte;
> Ni ya puedo no olvidarte;
> que a otro devo la fee. [5v]

These words become more significant when their import is dramatized
in *Segunda parte* of the bipartite play.

Primera parte emphasizes the period of intrigue and seemingly un-
necessary delay between the return to Arabia of Clarisel and Beloribo
and the Arabian court's enthusiastic celebration of their matches with
Belidiana and Clarinda at play's end. The pretense of gardener's clothing and hidden identity is not a significant part in the plot, which is
almost devoid of action. Although Clarisel is in disfavor with King Belerante, the monarch's attitude is easily changed in the last scene within
moments of finding out who the disguised prince really is:

> Cryselo, es Clarisel? o grande yerro;
> y Lisdanso su amigo Beloribo?
> . . . .
> Rey, y Principe ilustres, el destierro,
> y furor mio ciego, quanto esquivo,
> en amor se conviertan, y hospedaje,
> que en nuestra casa enmienda nuestro ultraje.
> . . . .
> Los braços gozaran de essos favores. [26v]

Much of the struggle during the preceding five acts has been given over to commentary on what is or was happening and what the other characters are like, descriptions of reactions and dreams, and dialogue among the mythological figures on their interests in the situations of the mortal characters depicted.

One unconventional discussion, among Clarisel, Beloribo, and Yleda, an aristocratic woman of the court, about the beauty of Belidiana and Clarinda, for example, consists of contradictory discourse on a point of dramatic representation that is usually taken for granted: that is, whether or not the woman being courted is physically appealing. Curiously, it is the man who professes to love Belidiana who asks about her appearance: "dicen que es hermosa." Yleda responds, "No mucho; mas es briosa, / grave, y arrogante," adding, "Cerca estoy de parecer / Ninfa, y Dea soberana, / si es hermosa Belidiana." About Clarinda she says: "Bella, y hermosa / Clarinda? no sé tal cosa" (6r). The two men refuse to accept such opinions, attributing her disparaging remarks to jealousy ("una poquilla de embidia") or insanity ("Que seays loca me pesa" [6r]).

Elsewhere, Belidiana's age is questioned. Clarisel attributes her father's recalcitrant attitude toward their marriage to her tender years:

> que se escusa de casalla,
> y darle tan presto estado;
> Alegando ser muy niña
> de catorze solamente. [4v]

The monarch's servant disputes this: "Pues ya yo è oído en palacio" that the Princess "o corre en los quince apriessa, / o en ellos anda de espacio" (4v). In a subsequent scene Birano and Yleda continue to argue over Belidiana's age, now fixing it between seventeen and eighteen years. Enríquez thus comments on the dramatic and poetic conventions of amorous discourse in which female beauty is objectified and scrutinized. She raises these issues, however, through characters and speeches that are not typical in *comedia* love matches; instead, they problematize, scrutinize, and critique the conventional poetics to the exclusion of acting to accomplish the goal of uniting the young lovers.

The major obstacles to the marriages of Clarisel to Belidiana and Beloribo to Clarinda are the vengeful plotting of the *privado* Sinamber and King Belerante's tendency to use expedient cruelty to rid himself of inconveniences. For instance, after Sinamber reveals to the king that his own earlier account of Clarisel/Cryselo's communication with Belidiana was an embellished one to make the monarch think that his honor had been violated, the deceitful courtier throws himself on his own sword. Belerante orders that the body be thrown in a well and that Clarisel be charged with the murder, taking advantage of his knowledge about a wound inflicted during the prince's altercation at sword point with Sinamber. The males are depicted either as duplicitous, as in these two cases, or as relatively passive, as when Clarisel and Beloribo hide behind disguises or are immobilized through incarceration in the Arabian king's tower prison. Only through the intercession of the queen, Belidiana's mother, does the king soften his attitude and agree to abide by his daughter's wishes.

Other influential figures are also thwarted in their efforts to marry Belidiana to a different mate. The goddess Venus, for example, is represented as an advocate for the match that her beloved Adonis seeks with Belidiana. Because he is one of her most faithful devotees, she is willing to put aside her own feelings for him ("Preferir quiero a mi gusto / el tuyo" [11r]), an attitude that mirrors what is expected of marriageable daughters, such as Belidiana, who must contemplate arranged marriages or sacrifice emotional attachments under familial, political, or economic pressures. Venus promises Adonis:

> Que si yo hija de Júpiter
> soy en la espuma formada
> del Occeano arrogante,
> tuya sera Belidiana. (11v)

Adonis's parentage—which is confusing and scandalous, according to the mythological versions of Enríquez's other characters—adds to the play's complications. Venus alludes to "la insania" (11r) of Adonis's mother Mirra, whose incestuous love for her father, Ciniras, inspired her trickery so that she could sleep with him. The result was the pregnancy that produced Adonis. Thus, the princess Clarinda, represented as a legitimate offspring of Ciniras, continues the problematical familial pattern of forbidden desire when she tries to further her half-brother's suit of Belidiana and tells her cousin:

> Quisieran (prima) los Dioses,
> que el no fuera hijo, y nieto
> de mi padre, y de mi hermana
> hermano, y hijo, que el lecho
> de Clarinda (que no fuera
> su hermana, y tia) y sus Reynos
> el posseyera, y conmigo
> diera leyes a Citero. [13r]

Belidiana proceeds to map out the complications of such a union:

> Mirra vuestra hermana, prima,
> os disculparà de yerro,
> que por nietos, y sobrinos
> vos le deys los hijos vuestros.
> Y suya será la culpa,
> que vengan a ser bisnietos
> de vuestro padre Ciniras,
> padre de Adonis y abuelo. [13r]

The ingredients of this play emphasize the necessity of complications for dramatized entertainment, the clash of *lo justo* and *el gusto* upon which the popular *comedia* thrives. As her drama unfolds, the playwright manipulates this tension to suggest the disruption of the social fabric, its order, and its structure by the privileging of the realm of diversion that the theater represents. She accomplishes a blurring of the division between popular and elite forms of entertainment by denouncing the *corrales* in favor of the academic salons and palaces but layering her components in a dense composite of many familiar dramatic elements flourishing in the professional theaters.

Although the majority of the characters in this play are unsympathetic figures, the exception, significantly, is Belidiana's mother, the queen. Not relegated in this drama to the victimhood of childbirth, she is included instead as a minor character but one with deep compassion for her daughter's desire to marry the man she loves. The queen is actually present in two scenes (unlike so many *comedia* mothers, who are merely described after their deaths), and she is the only figure, divine or mortal, able to bring about the matches the young royals want.

Enríquez's queen thus suggests the potential for interaction that such maternal figures could add to *comedia* plots, but her presence is nevertheless marginalized, for she appears and says less than anyone else and is the only one without a name either in the list of dramatic personae or in the text. Like Caro's empress in *El conde Partinuplés,* this royal woman is denied easy access to social or dramatic space of her own.

Primera parte ends with a joyful celebration of the impending marriages and with a sense that the mortals have triumphed over at least some of the mythological deities—Venus and Adonis, for instance. Venus pronounces a curse against the newly paired lovers and protests against her own Olympian superior Juno, who has sponsored the mortals' union:

> Bien ultrajada, Juno, de ti quedo:
> yo me darè satisfacion, si puedo.
> Yo juro por el padre omnipotente,
> que me engendrò de la salada espuma,
> que sus bodas no me an de ver presente,
> aunque juntallos Hymeneo presuma;
> primero frio de muerte, y fiebre ardiente,
> de mi Adonis el humido consuma,
> y un javali me le desgarre fiero,
> que en su talamo alumbre mi luzero. [25v]

While other mythological figures such as Aglaya, Hymeneo, Amor, and Juno herself dance, the stage directions indicate that "Quedanse pasmados mirandose uno a otro Venus, y Adonis" [26r]. The dimensions of interaction are not intermingled peacefully as the drama ends. The closure suggested by the marriage announcements proves to be as cheated of actual closure as are many of the endings of traditional *comedia* plots, in which disruption and unhappiness are implied for the future of the matched couples.

Segunda parte of the *Tragicomedia los jardines y campos sabeos* proceeds to negate completely all that has been accomplished in *Primera parte.* This work begins after a three-year interlude since the betrothals of Clarisel to Belidiana and Beloribo to Clarinda. In the first scene, songs sung by the now vindicated mythological figures Venus and Adonis and a sonnet delivered by Clarisel reveal to the audience that Belidiana has changed her mind and is currently in love with another. Clarisel refers to his (now moderated) anger and to the injustice that he believes his "deseo casto y puro" (120) and his "amor honesto" (121) have suffered because Belidiana's "fe y palabra vana / se llevó el viento" (122-23).

Much of the dialogue of the first act is dedicated to reviewing what happened in the three-year interval. In Clarisel's absence Belidiana's father has arranged her marriage to Rogerio, a fact communicated in writing to Clarisel and prompting his renunciation of all interest in the Arabian princess. But the inconstancy of all characters is made a problematical element in what this drama depicts. Belidiana's father, in particular, is blamed for reneging on the marriage agreement with which the first play closes. Belidiana herself complains, for example:

> Los dioses te perdonen, padre fiero,
> que sabiendo mi gusto, así quisiste
> que faltase la fe y amor primero
> para siempre vivir llorosa y triste.
> No fuiste padre, mas cruel y austero,
> capital enemigo, que pusiste
> duro cuchillo al cuello de tu hija,
> que a todas horas, noche y día, la aflija.
> Padre protervo, duro y porfiado. [386-94]

During one conversation with her cousin Clarinda, Belidiana attributes her misfortune in love to the death of her mother: "Si viviera, / Clarisel mi esposo fuera; / somos mortales, murió" (275-77). Clarinda, however, imputes culpability to the deceased queen—"Vuestra madre culpo yo / mudarse así" (274-75)—and Belidiana herself in the diatribe against her father declares about both her parents and their treatment of Rogerio

> que dentro de tu casa lo hospedastes,
> ¡y ya por yerno e hijo regalado,
> tú y la reina mi madre lo tratastes!
> ¡Leístes la canción con el dechado

que me envió; y tú y ella os admirastes!
Un mes entero y más de noche y día
comió a tu mesa con presencia mía. [395-401]

It is as if Enríquez uses the disjunction from one play to the other to
emphasize the problematical nature of *comedia* endings with their multiple weddings, which nevertheless often portend difficulties if not
disasters.

Clarisel's protestations of constant but unappreciated love for Belidiana is also questioned in *Segunda parte*. In the fifth scene of Act 1,
Venus functions as the source of historical information, recounting to
Apollo and Adonis a version of how Rogerio replaced Clarisel at Belidiana's side. Apollo reminds her that despite the intervention of her son
Cupid in Clarisel's emotional life, the Greek prince reacted to the news
of Belidiana's marriage "con tanta serenidad, / que mayor no la percibo"
(320-21). A new union between Clarisel and the Spanish princess Maya
is easily effected, although it is given very little dramatic space or time.

Much of the drama is taken up with the mythological figures, the
majority of whose numerous activities have nothing to do with the
royal mortals toward whose marriages the play's action indirectly progresses. Act 2, for example, is entirely given over to interaction first
between Venus and Adonis and then between Vulcan and three Cupid
figures. Venus initially dominates the dialogue by recounting the story
of Atalanta and Hippomenes, concerning a beautiful young woman
who valued her independence more than anything else and thus re-
fused to marry. As so many *comedia* plots reiterate, this is an attitude
not well tolerated by the staged society. Thus the mythological context
mirrors the more frequently depicted secular realm, and Atalanta becomes the "amoroso trofeo" (660) to which many suitors aspire: "el
premio era tan supremo, / que no faltaron amantes, / que se tenían por
cuerdos" (668-70). Hippomenes himself is at first reluctant to participate in the dangerous races that Atalanta demands of her admirers, but
when he sees her beauty, he changes his mind: "Fue la causa de mi
culpa / no haber visto el digno premio" (691-92). The well-known tale
ends with the victory of Hippomenes in the race, not because he can
outdistance Atalanta physically but because he tricks her with the

golden apples dropped on the racetrack. A victory for one carries with it a defeat for the other—"Quedó Atalanta vencida"—although Venus quickly adds, "sin pena del vencimiento" (851-52). The goddess of love is, of course, an interested narrator in that she promotes the unions of lovers, but her story is also self-interested: it ends with the account of the metamorphosis of Atalanta and Hippomenes, because of their sacrilegious lovemaking in her temple, into lions that pull the sun's chariot. The complications of love affairs and marriage matches are constantly reiterated throughout the play, which models the standard *comedia* components in multi-layered fashion.

The last section of this act is devoted to a parodic conversation between Vulcan, Venus's cuckolded husband, and a group of Cupids who remind him that although he is the husband of their mother Venus, he is not their father. When the primary Cupid himself enters with the news that Adonis has been killed by a wild boar (in adherence to the myth about him), Vulcan rejoices over the "nuevas tan agradables" (1100). But the act ends with the younger Cupids singing "Y todavía tú con ojos tiernos, / llora por Marte más ramosos cuernos" (1108-9), emphasizing the continued unfaithfulness of Venus to her husband and the replacement of one lover by another.

This sort of replacement is accentuated in Enríquez's two-part play, with great stress on the ease with which such an exchange is made. Belidiana and Clarisel are portrayed in *Primera parte* as the most devoted of lovers, as are also Beloribo and Clarinda. In *Segunda parte* these love affairs have been superseded by new ones, but there is no dramatization of the subsequent process of falling in love or the progress of devotion. These characters do not even appear in Act 2, for instance, and Act 4 is taken up with a comic situation that challenges gender identity and carries out the consequences for Birano of washing his face in a certain enchanted fountain at the end of Act 3 ("Si me transformó en Birana" [1619]). Also in Act 4, Beloribo is invited by Yleda to wash in these same waters, and the effect is the same, affording the vain Yleda revenge against the two men who have not recognized her as the most beautiful woman among all those in the play. As Act 4 progresses, three mythological deities—Pan, god of the shepherds: Vertuno, god of the gardens; and Guasorapo, god of hunters—plot to seduce the "women," urging the supposed females to pick two of them as amorous partners.

In this satiric scene the discomfort of the two transformed men carries with it the disorganization of the multitude of elements combined in Enríquez's play, which merely exaggerates the dramatic potpourri found in popular *comedia*. Beloribo appeals to the three gods to be left alone on the grounds that the mixture of mortal and divine is inappropriate: "Porque dioses a las diosas / deben amar, no a nosotras" (1948-49). The three male deities end the act with a surprised rejection of the two mortals when they realize that they must flee from "de estos falsos" (1970), a term that in this context connotes the facade of identity, whereas elsewhere it applies to the ethical character of unfaithful lovers. In both situations, the end of a love match is the outcome of the falsehood depicted.

In the beginning of Act 5 the theme of revenge is continued. Cries from offstage are explained as the screams of Belidiana and Clarinda and their husbands Rogerio and Ercilio, attacked by the vindictive Sinamber. While Vulcan rushes off to the rescue, in an important scene presided over by Cupid and Himeneo, the deity of weddings, those now determined to constitute appropriate matches are approved. Maya and Clarisel for the first time in the play pledge their mutual love:

> CLARISEL.　　　Yo os recibo
> 　　　　　　　por mi esposa, mi señora.
> MAYA.　　　　Yo a vos por dueño y esposo. [2041-43].

The union of Hesperia and Beloribo, though effected, is made more problematical because of his feminine appearance:

> HESPERIA.　Vuestra soy, rey Beloribo,
> 　　　　　　con condición que seáis hombre.
> 　　　　. . . . .
> BELORIBO.　Yo soy vuestro. [2036-39]

Divine assistance is instrumental in bringing about the happy ending the young lovers desire, for in the last moments when the women's fathers are about to marry them to their two cousins—the kings' choices—Apollo intervenes:

> Ya las manos, reyes, dadas
> estaban, ya no hay remedio;
> Himeneo de por medio
> entró y las tiene enlazadas. [2156-59]

Other divinely inspired events reported are the transformation of Rogerio and Ercilio into peacocks, Belidiana and Clarinda into doves, and Sinamber and Ermila into worms:

> En pavones transformó
> Juno a Ercilio y a Rogerio,
> y Venus, no sin misterio,
> en palomas convirtió
> a Clarinda y Belidiana,
> y a sus carros los unieron,
> y con ellos discurrieron
> a la corte soberana.
> A Ermila y su Sinamber
> Vulcano cuquillos hizo,
> porque su nombre postizo
> quiso estas postas tener. [2052-63]

The communal approval of the Olympians suggests the appropriateness of the new matches, while the metamorphoses of the other mortals reflects their inappropriateness in the social scheme Enríquez portrays.

Apollo's song ends the play. In it he celebrates the conflation of the figure Maya with the playwright Feliciana Enríquez, a theatrical move that erases the generally accepted boundaries separating the staged world from the world beyond the platform. Praising her verses and invoking her presence among the Muses, Apollo enhances the overlapping space of the dramatist as artist among myriad male contemporaries and that of her play and its challenges to the popularized conventions, claiming for her the right to manipulate those conventions.

That Enríquez chooses the courtly, elite space of salon and palace for her plays' presentation does not exempt those spheres from her critique of the society and the art that imitates it, for example, in the interludes that separate the acts of her dramas. There, mythological monarchs and deities mirror the actions and attitudes in the main plays. In the first two, meant for representation respectively between Acts 2 and 3 and between Acts 3 and 4 of *Primera parte*, characters with broken bodies and deformities carry on a tale of love or lust in which the god Baco Poltrón, described as "viejo ridiculo" (4v), entertains the proposals for the hands of his daughters offered by six male figures: Sabà ("Tuerto . . . con una cuchillada de oreja a oreja, y una pierna sobre una media muleta, y un baculo" [2v]); Pancaya ("con otra cuchillada, y otra pierna sobre otra media muleta, y otro baculo, y un perrillo de una cadenilla" [2v]); Nisa ("un corcobado . . . con una pierna en una media muleta, y un baculo" [2v]); Anga ("un Contrecho . . . las rodillas un una espuerta, las manos por el suelo en unos chapines" [2v-3r]); Orfeo ("ciego" [4r]); and Anfión ("tuerto con instrumentos musicos, con sus cuchilladas, como Sabà y Pancaya; y sendas piernas en muletas" [4r]). The daughters of Baco Poltrón are the "Gracias mohosas": "Aglaya tuerta, Talia, y Eurfosina ciegas, con tres muletas, y muchos harapos" (5r). The problem of who to match with whom in the arithmetical disequilibrium is resolved when Baco Poltrón accepts the declaration of his daughters that each loves all six of the suitors and Orfeo's recommendation that "sean esposas, y mujeres, y matronas, y madres de familias de todos seys, renunciadas todas las leyes de la division" (6v-7r). The tone of hilarity and incredibility dominates the scenes of these two *entremeses* as the characters who enact the situation find their resolution a natural and acceptable one. Enríquez thus suggests the preposterous quality of many mainstream *comedia* plots in which the actions lead, if not to such exaggerated consequences, at least to questionable liasons and outlandish and coincidental settlements.

The interludes within *Segunda parte* again depict flawed mythological characters. In a version of an episode from the life of the cursed monarch Midas, he and a group of characters that includes Bacchus, Apollo, and Sileno all gather to participate in a drinking contest, which will last several days. The props of the first piece in this pair include "mesas con vasos, picheles, frascos y cantimploras" (1), thus emphasizing the excesses that are to be portrayed. Midas presides over the contest, unable to participate because of the famous curse that prevents him from going beyond the boundaries of his own touch. After Bacchus, not surprisingly, wins the drinking bout, a musical contest is proposed in which Pan and Apollo compete. Though the general consensus is that Apollo is the winner, Midas favors Pan and becomes the victim of the other god's retaliation. Apollo demands that Bacchus remove from Midas the curse of the golden touch, but he himself inflicts a new curse by force of which the king sprouts donkey ears.

Wearing these new appendages, Midas enacts his part in the second interlude of the second play. In this short piece the ridiculed monarch converses with his servant Licas, who sports a donkey tail. Reiterating the absence of boundaries between figures, classes, and realms of fiction and reality, Enríquez makes of these two the components of a larger whole. They serve merely as audience to the chases and comings and goings of other mythological characters until the final conversation, when Midas, Timolo, Cupid, and Licas consider the theatrical trope of life and its roles. Midas, the donkey king, serves as a central focus. Licas asserts: "la verdad es que toda nuestra vida, no es otra cosa sino una comedia" (p. 266). The role of King Midas becomes complicated and problematized by his hybrid identity, but he symbolizes the quality among the nobility that Enríquez most appeals to for appreciation of her plays: that is, their ability to listen to readings of her works. Midas himself insists on the need to listen and hear when, in his last speech, he exhorts the assembled elite to beware of the self-interested advisers around them: "No deis oídos a lisonjeros, músicos y bufones, que si los diéredes, no os faltarán orejas de las mías" (p. 267). Enríquez's audience has, of course, just listened to such characters, and the implication of such a warning to popular playwrights in the *corrales* is not to be missed.

The conflation of the character Maya with Feliciana Enríquez in the textual space of the play's final moments reasserts the emphasis placed throughout the double drama and its ancillary parts upon the importance of including as subjects of her dramatic endeavor the intellectual and artistic legitimacy of the author herself and her act of composing. Enríquez thus positions herself in such a way that she can be understood to represent all the female dramatists examined here in that her presence in the theatrical circles is the novelty to be accommodated first. Women writers of the early modern period—among them the literary sisters Azevedo, Caro, Cueva, Enríquez, and Zayas—become their own subjects of depiction by representing the difficulty of being recognized as publicly legitimate.

Appealing to her persona as the invocation of Spain itself, Enríquez overlaps the legitimacy of her undertaking with the strength of the national interests. Participating in the novelty of her undertaking, she enters the novel dramatic text of her play ("y diré que Feliciana / es de España hoy Maya viva" [2324-25]) while invoking as a basis of her endeavor both national ("Celebren de hoy más las damas / de las béticas orillas / vuestras canciones suaves" [2318-20]) and Christian symbols: the Immaculate Conception and its resonance of female perfection and sexual autonomy ("y a la que en su Concepción / y nacimiento fue limpia" [2328-29]) as well as the Cross ("Repártanlo las liberales manos, / que del Arbol pendieron exaltado" [2356-57]). Having departed from the realm of tradition in order to write as a woman through disruption of the conventional representational model, Enríquez finally invokes the stabilizing poles of religion and patriotism in order to assure her audience of the suitability of recognizing her, her work, and her claimed space among the celebrated dramatists.

In the last section of her *Segunda parte,* Enríquez acknowledges the connection between invented characters inhabiting the textual/performative spaces and the women, like her, who create them while straining against the limits of expression considered appropriate for females. Through Apollo's song, the playwright reminds the audience of the retinue of mythological female agents of inspiration and artistic creation who converge, the song insists, in the figure of Feliciana: Urania, Polymnia, Caliope, Clío, Euterpe, Melpómene, Talía, Tersicore, Aglaya, Eurfosina, Ninfas, Rétorica. Enríquez takes pains to overcome what Nancy Cotton has termed "the Salic law of wit," a figurative instrument by which "literary critics who disliked women playwrights" in the seventeenth and eighteenth centuries imagined the law's imposition and its "operation in various 'sessions' of the poets. . . . [It was a] genre of literary criticism and lampoon, originated by Trajano Boccalini in Italy in 1612, [that] found numerous translators, adaptors and imitators" (181). Such a reference brings us full circle to Enriquez's "Carta executoria," which follows the final act in the 1627 edition of her double play. She turns the tables on this misogynist ploy and refutes "the Salic

law of wit" by assigning victory to herself in this judgment taken
on Mount Parnassus. This move nevertheless evinces what Ann Jones
recognizes in the French feminists' inventions of new kinds of writing:
that is, "a conscious response to socioliterary realities" ("Writing the
Body," 374). In Enríquez's representation, it is the writer herself who
embodies novelty. With recourse again to conventions of her age, she
calls attention to her uniqueness as symbolized by the phoenix—an al-
lusion that calls to mind her declared victory over Lope de Vega, also
popularly and admiringly associated with the epithet *fénix*. This allu-
sion comes in the last tercet of a sonnet—said to have been written by
her sister Carlota Enríquez de Guzmán—addressed to the "Tragicomedia los jardines, y campos sabeos," which the playwright chooses as the
closing words of her text. These last lines are also a fitting tribute to the
other women dramatists considered in this study, all of whom share
with Enríquez her occupation of a special place among the ranks of
Spanish dramatists and the indomitability that denies efforts to destroy
and silence her voice:

> Ricos campos Sabeos singulares,
> unica es vuestra Fenix, que oy nos distes
> en los nuestros Elysios, do se anida.
>   FIN [48v]

CONCLUSION

There were other women dramatists in seventeenth-century Spain whose works have not been considered in this study, among them Bernarda Ferreira de Lacerda (*Cazador del cielo*); Sor María do Ceo (*En la cara va la fecha, Preguntarlo a las estrellas, En la más oscura noche,* and several *autos* such as *Mayor fineza de amor, Amor y fe,* and *Las lágrimas de Roma*); María Egual (*Los prodigios de Tesalia* and *Triunfos de amor en el aire*); and Juana Teodora de Sousa (*El gran prodigio de España, y lealtad de un amigo*). In addition, Mariana de Carvajal y Saavedra, who, like Zayas, published a collection of short *novelas* in the seventeenth century, claims in her salutory words "A lector" to have composed as well "un libro de doce comedias" (5). And Rodrigo Caro's reference to Ana Caro's many *comedias* written and performed in her home city of Seville tempt further speculation about her larger dramatic output.

The omission of these works from consideration in this book or inclusion in my anthology *Women's Acts* is due only to lack of access to them. They inspire the hope that they are not lost but merely undiscovered. Like the five authors studied here, these other dramatists and their works have suffered neglect as a result of literary canonization that relegates them to female silence for want of avenues of publication and re-edition.

The simultaneous theoretical positioning within the early modern period across feminist relational and individualist models—evident in the plays examined here—finds a reflection in the impulse behind projects such as my own. Starting from the essentializing move to study only women writers, my attempt is nevertheless to show that Spain's Siglo de Oro was shaped and reacted to by humans of both genders. The feminist relational balance that has been lost because of unbalanced patriarchal relational exclusion from circles of publication, reading, and performance now demands the redress of an individualist scholarly step: critical analysis of the plays in question to provide evidence of how competent the women were and in what ways they contributed to the art, letters, and intellectual pursuits that were both source and product of the social construction of gender.

The unavailability of a professional space for women authors in seventeenth-century Spanish society is reflected in the dramas of Azevedo, Caro, Cueva, Enríquez, and Zayas. The impossible situations in which their characters struggle to locate themselves socially reflect the sense of unresolved discomfort that a talented female writer must have felt about her place among the male authors, whose right to write was not problematized in the same way. The force of the female double bind underlies the dramatized experiences of the female characters. As argued in Chapter 2, Caro's Empress Rosaura (*El conde Partinuplés*) believes that she cannot save her realm or herself; she has been taught since birth that if she marries, a husband will be the instrument of ruination, yet her subjects cannot accept her as an undomesticated female monarch. With her final acceptance of the demand to privilege her body natural, she finds her social space at the side and, seemingly, in the shadow of her royal husband—yet he is still potentially the predicted agent of ruin for her reign and her empire. The play closes with wedding plans which Rosaura's subjects celebrate but which deny her the voluntary celibacy that she would have preferred.

Cueva's female courtier Armesinda (*La firmeza en la ausencia*) is able to prevail in her loyalty to an absent lover precisely because, as a woman, she occupies no spot in the power hierarchy that legitimates the military and political commands of one man to another. She is nevertheless confined and objectified by male authority, able to assume the wifely role she prefers only after the men around her have negotiated among themselves for this outcome. As Azevedo also dramatizes, the course toward matrimony and life after marriage is fraught with danger and difficulties for women. In particular, she focuses on women who have obeyed all the social rules for propriety—enclosure, silence, chastity—but for whom patriarchal commodification (*Dicha y desdicha del juego*) and the moral laxness of the men they marry or trust (*La margarita del Tajo*) disrupt what society's rules promise will be domestic harmony.

Caro's *Valor, agravio y mujer* and Azevedo's *El muerto disimulado*, contributing to the conventions of cross-dressed figures, emphasize the desperate need of their female protagonists to find access to the male circles of communication ordinarily closed to them. This is possible only if they erase themselves from the text as women and convince their cohorts that they are men and thus deserve to be heard. Azevedo takes the further theatrical step of including the cross-dressed Clarindo, a figure whose female disguise as Clarinda enhances the individualist insistence on the instability of sexed identity. But his charade is not so much a ploy to gain agency (as is the case for the cross-dressed woman) as a matter of curiosity and convenience; being taken for a woman affords him no important advantage in his quest to resolve a dilemma. His masquerade helps emphasize the fluidity of gendered identity but reiterates that the greater sociopolitical privilege is enjoyed by those recognized as male. Zayas's contribution to this convention is the cross-gendered Fenisa (*La traición en la amistad*), who assumes questionable male courtship behavior. Without a male disguise, however, she is always perceived as out of place and transgressive, and she ends up exiled from the social world she has challenged.

Finally, Enríquez clearly expresses her sense of exclusion from the male-dominated authorial ranks through her disruption of the conventions of play composition, both those associated with classical precepts and those of the Lopean *comedia nueva*. She anticipates by over four hundred years the French feminists' invocation of the *écriture féminine* that rewrites and poses alternatives to the patriarchal discourse traditionally recognized as the basis of communication and representation. She articulates the separation of her works from the mainstream in terms of their inappropriateness for representation in the space of the professional stage. She takes issue with, parodies, and ultimately internalizes the restriction that her female colleagues face by validating the private reading circles of the educated upper class as the site of reception for her works.

Commanding the attention of the theatrical public is the task that all these women were ultimately unable to accomplish in a lasting way. My efforts are directed to this end in their name. In closing this study, I return to the words of an introductory passage in Zayas's first collection of prose works. Here her narrational voice addresses the need to link the successful commercialization of texts with the public's receptive responsibility to those texts. In the second of two introductory sections, titled "Prólogo de un desapasionado," she praises her own undertaking in the third person and draws attention to her worth as a woman author: "Por dama, por ingeniosa y por docta, debes ¡oh lector!, mirar con respeto sus agudos pensamientos, desnudo del afecto envidioso, con que censuras otros que no traen este salvoconducto debido a las damas." She proceeds, moreover: "Y no sólo debes hacer esto, mas anhelar por la noticia de su autora a no estar sin su libro tu estudio, no pidiéndolo prestado, sino costándote tu dinero, que aunque fuese mucho, le darás por bien empleado" (*Tres novelas* 52).

Zayas then provides a catalogue of illegitimate readers. Some are freeloaders who

> se van a las librerías, y por no gastar una miseria que vale el precio de un libro, le engullen a toda priesa con los ojos, echándose en los tableros de sus tiendas, pasando por sus inteligencias como gatos por brasas, y así es después las censuras que dellos hacen; allí puestos no les ofende el ser pisados de los que pasan, el darles encuentros los que entran a comprar libros en la tienda, el enfadado semblante del librero en verle allí embarazar, ni los rebufos de sus oficiales; que por todo pasa a trueque de leer de estafa y estudiar de mogollón por no gastar. [52-53]

Still others, depending on the good nature of the bookseller, "le piden prestados los libros que vienen nuevos, y cuando lo antigüen, en vez de alabar su obra, la vituperan con decir mal del libro" (53). The legitimation of the book read is thus turned to focus on the legitimation of its reader in economic terms, since neither, it is implied, is taken seriously if money has not changed hands. Zayas also casts doubt on readers who simply borrow books from acquaintances who have finished reading them, again because she questions the ability of the parasite—having caused a disruption in market dynamics both for the retailer and, by implication, for the published author—to read meaningfully: "Y lo que resulta desto es que, si son ignorantes o no han entendido la materia o no les ha dado gusto, desacreditan el libro y quitan al librero la venta" (53). In an age before copyright laws and the lawsuits that today question photocopied sections of another's work,

Zayas insists that taking a woman's writing seriously requires willingness on the book merchant's part to market that writing and on the public's part to buy it.

The stakes are still the same in the efforts by members of the current academic community to refashion the canon, allowing space for editions and critical studies of the many women whose work has lain unrecognized and relegated to silence by the conditions of their own lives and cultures or by subsequent male-centered reading lists. I end, then, in the name of Angela Azevedo, Ana Caro Mallén de Soto, Leonor de la Cueva y Silva, Feliciana Enríquez de Guzmán, and María de Zayas y Sotomayor by repeating to my readers Zayas's exhortation to hers: "Sea, pues, oh carísimos lectores, este libro exento destos lances" (53).

NOTES

Introduction

1. For further information about their lives and works, see Chapter 1 and the individual discussion of each dramatist preceding the text(s) of her play(s) in my anthology (T. Soufas, *Women's Acts*).

2. This information is found in Serrano y Sanz's entry on Azevedo (268: 10). It coincides in information and brevity with the passage about her in Froes Perim's eigtheenth-century study of famous women (2: 493) and Barrera y Leirado (4).

3. See de Armas, "Ana Caro"; Kaminsky, 86-87; Lundelius, 228-32; Simón; and T. Soufas, "Ana Caro's Re-evaluation," 85-86.

4. De Armas believes her to have been born during the last decades of the sixteenth century ("Ana Caro," 66).

5. Cited in Lundelius (229) and Serrano y Sanz (268: 179). See also Luna, "Ana Caro, una escritora" for further discussion and citations from Caro's contemporaries about her "fama inusitada, . . . fama excepcional en una mujer, que llega a trascender los ámbitos privados para transportarla textualmente al espacio público de la historiografía" (11).

6. Most of Caro's *autos* do not survive, but in addition to *La puerta de la Macarena* performed in 1641, another known *auto* title is *La cuesta de Castilleja,* both composed for the Corpus Christi festival in Seville (Kaminsky, 86). Lundelius furnishes more detailed information about the dates and conditions of performance of these pieces (231); see also Luna, "Ana Caro, una escritora," 15-17.

7. In her *novela* now titled, "Tarde llega el desengño," for instance, Zayas includes Caro in a list of illustrious women intellectuals of her day (*Desengaños,* 230). Caro likewise contributes a sonnet in praise of her friend in the prefatory pages of Zayas's collection *Novelas amorosas y ejemplares.*

8. See Lundelius (230) and Kaminsky (86-87).

9. See Lundelius (231), Willard King (215), and Sánchez Arjona (328).

10. Some information about Cueva's life can also be found in Barrera y Leirado, 121; González Santamera and Doménech, 221-22; Janés, 210; Olivares and Boyce, 48-49, 105; Serrano y Sanz, 268: 300-301; and T. Soufas, "Leonor de la Cueva y Silva," 125-26.

11. They also add: "'Tales poemas nos sugieren la existencia en Medina del Campo de un círculo o tertulia literaria, de una sociología del amor donde la conducta amorosa imitaría la ficción, pero tan sólo en la medida en que el discurso femenino se atuviera a criterios de la sociedad y del género literario" (Olivares and Boyce, 48).

12. See also T. Soufas, "Leonor de la Cueva."

13. Pérez speculates about Enríquez's decision to marry at this point and, as with other elements of her life, bases his conclusions about her thoughts, attitudes, and activities on what he considers an autobiographical dimension to her plays. See, e.g., the rather facile conclusions about the conflation of life and art in Pérez, *Dramatic Works,* 1, 3, 8-11, 25.

14. Silva iii, quoted in Serrano y Sanz, 269: 356-57. See also Pérez *Dramatic Works,* 5-6.

15. See Pérez, *Dramatic Works,* 5-8, for discussion of those critics who have studied Enríquez or mention her briefly in their works on Golden Age theater.

16. Pérez (*Dramatic Works*) devotes all his endnote references to variants between the two seventeenth-century editions of Enríquez's play.

17. See Welles and Gossy, 509; and Cocozella, 190, for Zayas's life after 1639.

18. See Welles and Gossy, 508; and Olivares and Boyce, 210-11. There is also speculation that Zayas entered a convent; see, e.g., Welles and Gossy, 507-8; and the introductions to editions of Zayas's works by Redondo Goicoechea (Zayas, *Tres novelas,* 11-12) and Yllera (Zayas, *Desengaños,* 19-20; n. 49).

19. In the presentation of material in this book, I use the MLA system of citation and referencing. With the exception of certain pieces by Enríquez, quotations from the plays are taken from my anthology (T. Soufas, *Women's Acts*) and identified by line number in the text. The second part of Enríquez's interlude for *Segunda Parte* is written in prose and is therefore quoted by page number from the anthology. For her *Primera Parte* and its two-part interlude, I have quoted from the 1627 text, identified by folio number in the text.

1. Comedia, *Gender, Convention*

1. See Foucault, 17-44; Reiss, 21-54; C. Soufas, "Thinking"; and T. Soufas, *Melancholy,* x-xi, 1-36.

2. Among the many scholars to consult on the issues of essentialism and constructionism are Adams and Brown, Butler, Cixous and Clément, de Lauretis, Epstein, Heath, Irigaray, Kamuf, Kaplan, A. Jardine, Lesselier, Miller, Moi, Rich, Schor, "Dreaming" and "Reading", Sedgwick, Showalter, Spivak, Stimpson, and Wittig.

3. See Soufas and Soufas, "*Vida.*"

4. See Kelso, 3-4.

5. With regard to the Renaissance medical notion that the female was an imperfect version of the male, Orgel argues specifically that "analogously, and logically, many cases were recorded of women becoming men through the pressure of some great excitement or activity. The crucial point is, however, that those transformations that are attested to as scientific fact work in only one direction, from female to male, which is conceived to be upward, toward completion. . . . The frightening part of the teleology for the Renaissance mind, however, is precisely the fantasy of its reversal, the conviction that men can turn into—or be turned into—women; or perhaps more exactly, can be turned *back* into women, losing the strength that enabled the male potential to be realized in the first place" ("Nobody's Perfect," 13-14).

6. Merry E. Wiesner notes of Renaissance thought on public roles for women: "Philosophical discussions of 'freedom' as it was defined by male authorities may be leading us somewhat astray, however. While Renaissance women used a variety of philosophical, legal, rational, and religious justifications to argue their case, they in fact had a much more pragmatic definition of the word: 'freedom' to them meant the ability to participate in public life. Their voices tell us a great deal about female self-conception during the Renaissance, which never emerges when listening to male voices alone. It is true that women's sphere in most cultures has been defined by men, as have the limits of what is considered 'public' and what 'private'; but women have often objected to or ignored those limitations, and at no time more than during the Renaissance when they were aware that restrictions on them were increasing" (3). Thus, in exemplary fashion, our five seventeenth-century women playwrights participate in the composition of dramas that, even if not performed, were accessible in reading circles populated by their male peers.

7. Such antitheatrical discourse does not, as Peter Stallybrass points out, address "the local mechanisms of social control, differentiated by both class and region, to which women were subject, nor women's resistances to them both collectively and individually, but the production of a normative "Woman" within the discursive practices of the ruling elite" ("Patriarchal Territories," 127).

8. See T. Soufas, "Writing Wives Out," for further discussion of this issue.

9. See also Orgel, "Nobody's Perfect," 14-15. In discussing the morals controversy in Golden Age theater, McKendrick adds about the critics: "Such was the *corrales'* effect on Spain's military health, they concluded, that they might as well be a weapon of the Turk or the English" (*Theatre*, 202).

10. See Orgel, "Nobody's Perfect," 28 n. 1.

11. See Luna's discussion of similar issues ("Ana Caro, una escritora," 18-20).

2. Bodies of Authority

1. Among the studies helpful in my arguments on authority are those of Arendt, Flathman (*Practice*), Gailbraith, Jankowski, K. Jones, Sennett, and Simon.

2. See A. Jones, "Surprising Fame," 74-81; and Stallybrass, "Patriarchal Territories," 127-29. See also Bergmann, 126-27.

3. See J. Wilson, 60.

4. Margaret Wilson reiterates that if Elizabeth "had . . . married, she might have borne an heir. But had she married, she would have fallen under the influence of a male consort. Instead, a complete dyad in herself, she took no husband and declared herself married to England. Her heroic virginity, more in the pattern of the great saints than of a modern woman, set her apart from the other women of her realm who continued to marry and dwell within the family" (158-59). Among other recent studies on the gendering of Elizabeth I, see Axton, L. Jardine, Levin, Marcus, Neale, Stallybrass ("Patriarchal Territories"), Scalingi, Weimann, and Yates.

5. Quotations from Caro's and Cueva's plays are cited in the text by line number from T. Soufas, *Women's Acts*.

6. See T. Soufas, "Repetitive Patterns."

7. See Jankowski's discussion (133-38) of John Lyly's character Dido in his *Dido, Queen of Carthage*, who is portrayed as facing a dramatically different choice between love and duty. A famous confrontation of such demands in the Spanish *comedia* is found in Calderón's *La vida es sueño*, in which the prince Segismundo privileges his body politic over his love and desire for that play's Rosaura.

8. See T. Soufas, "Marrying Off the *Parthenos*."

9. See Kaminsky's comments on this same point (93).

10. See also Jordan, 22-25. For an early feminist challenge to the Genesis story, see the information in Schiesari, 154-59, on St. Hildegard of Bingen's reading of Adam and Eve's responsibility for sin.

11. For additional discussion of this play, which has not received much critical attention, see also T. Soufas, "Regarding the Woman's Response."

Chapter 3. Marriage Dilemmas

1. See also Lynch, *Spain 1516-1598* (ch. 4) and *The Hispanic World* (chs. 3, 6, 7); and Vázquez de Prada, 330-34.

2. Prejudice in favor of sons entailed inheritance of the family fortune and, at the highest social level, questions of succession to the throne. Thus, it is not surprising to find in a letter written by Philip II to his own beloved daughter Catalina Micaela upon the birth of her first child and his first grandchild: "Antes de responder a vuestras cartas os diré lo que he holgado de la buena nueva que he tenido de vuestro alumbramiento, que ha sido para mí el mayor acontecimiento que podrá ser. Y así estoy alegrísimo della y también de que sea hijo . . . aunque . . . de que vos estéis muy buena tomaría muy en paciencia que fuera nieta; mas estando vos buena como lo espero, muy bien está que sea nieto, y también por el contentamiento que su padre tendrá dello" (quoted in Fernández Alvarez, 252). Fernández Alvarez judges this passage as indication that the monarch reveals himself "muy por encima de los necios prejuicios de la época que veían con tan malos ojos el parto de niñas" (252). It is possible to read it otherwise, however, for the very fact that the king seems to feel the need to justify—by reference to concern for his daughter's health—a hypothetical positive appraisal had his grandchild been female does not suggest an attitude transcending this prejudice.

3. See also M. King, 48-50. For a different view, see McKendrick, *Woman and Society*, 47.

4. Advising about such matters in *La perfecta casada*, Fray Luis de León recommends: "Porque cierto es que la casada que fuere tan tasada en sus gastos y tan no curiosa por una parte, y por otra tan casera y veladora y aprovechada, no sólo conservará lo que su marido adquiriere, sino también ella lo acrescentará por su parte" (123). In his "Formación de la mujer cristiana," Vives also urges the worth of the Aristotelian counsel that "en el régimen doméstico, los hombres deben ganar y las mujeres deben ser guardadosas de lo ganado" (1129); see also 1031-32.

5. Quotations from Azevedo's plays are cited in the text by line numbers from T. Soufas, *Women's Acts*.

6. Vigil includes this quotation in her discussion of the tensions generated by

moralistic diatribes against marriages based on love instead of familial arrangement (80; see her fuller discussion of these issues, 78-80).

7. Stallybrass comments on the implications for class distinctions of the misogynstic universalization of women: "To emphasize gender is to construct women-as-the-same: women are constituted as a single category, set over against the category of men. To emphasize class is to differentiate *between* women, dividing them into distinct social groups. Insofar as women are differentiated, those in the dominant social classes are allocated privileges they can confer (status, wealth). In societies where heterosexuality and marriage are prescribed, those privileges can only be conferred back on *men,* so the differentiation of women simultaneously establishes or reinforces the differentiation of men. The deployment of women into different classes, then, is in the interests of the ruling elite, because it helps to perpetuate and to naturalize class structure. . . . But when the elimination of class boundaries is produced by the collapsing of women into a single undifferentiated group, that elimination is commonly articulated within misogynistic discourse" ("Patriarchal Territories," 133).

8. See Lynch, *Hispanic World,* ch. 7; and Vázquez de Prada, 653-55, 717-21.

9. The gender dilemma she dramatizes offers a parallel with the disastrous economic conditions in Spain. Vázquez de Prada's assessment of seventeenth-century Spain's economic decline is suggestive: "La inflación del vellón en el siglo XVII prolongó la inflación de los precios provocada en el XVI por la abundancia de plata americana. Pero mientras esta última tuvo algunos aspectos positivos para el desarrollo económico castellano, la del vellón no tuvo más que incidencias negativas. Hamilton se atreve a afirmar que la inflación del vellón fue uno de los factores que mayor incidencia tuvieron en la decadencia económica de Castilla" (655).

10. With regard to Tirso de Molina in this context, see also Kennedy, 211-14.

11. See Stallybrass ("Patriarchal Territories," esp. 128-31) for a cogent discussion of the conflation of natural geographies and women's bodies in Renaissance England.

12. Among the moralists critiquing the national decline were such figures as Juan de Mariana and Jerónimo Pujades, whom Elliott includes in a larger group writing against such purported evils as "addiction to the theatre and to games of chance" (245).

13. See Warner for a full discussion of *marianismo.*

14. For information on the controversy in the early seventeenth century over St. James or St. Teresa as patron saint of Spain and the gender implications of a male or female spiritual advocate, see Kendrick, ch. 4; and Elliott, 260-61.

15. For more information about the celebrated Portuguese Santa Iria or Irene upon whose life and martyrdom this play is based, see Garrett, 189-93; and Rosa, 26-29.

16. For further discussion of this dimension of convent life, see Arenal, 149; and Arenal and Schlau, 3.

17. Love as a malady in need of cure—primarily the affection of the one desired—has enjoyed a long history of scholarly, medical, and artistic attention. The bibliography on this topic is lengthy, and thus the following list is merely a beginning: Babb, 128-74; Burton; de Armas, "*La Celestina*"; Beecher and Ciarolella, *Eros and Anteros;* Ferrand; Heiple; Jackson, ch. 15; Lowes; Lyons, 24-26; Osborn; T. Soufas, *Melancholy,* ch. 4.

18. In her discussion of such notions, Jordan explains the medieval and Renaissance determination that "while woman, like man, is a human being (*homo*) and therefore cre-

ated in God's image, as a woman (*femina*) she lacks the essential feature of that divine image, rationality, which is reflected only in man (*vir*)" (26-27).

19. See also M. King, 93-95, 192, who also quotes the Spaniard Diego Pérez de Valdivia about virginity: "Zeal for holy chastity and virginity makes a weak young woman or woman of whatever sort stronger than many men, and than the whole world, and than all hell; and when men see such extreme energy and force, they are afraid and jump back dismayed" (94).

20. This passage, from St. Jerome's *Commentarius in Epistolam ad Ephesios,* is quoted in M. King, 192.

21. See McNamara, 105; and Schulenberg, 32-39.

22. Wiesner calls attention to the secular celibacy assumed by or imposed upon the learned woman scholar/writer: "Those who chose the life of learning were generally forced to give up a normal family life. Most lived chaste lives of scholarly solitude in 'book-lined cells.' They chose celibacy because their desire for learning required it; their male admirers—and there were many—applauded that decision as they felt no woman could be both learned and sexually active. By becoming learned, she had penetrated a male preserve, which was only tolerable if she simultaneously rejected the world of women. As Margaret King noted, 'Chastity was at once expressive . . . of the learned woman's defiance of the established natural order and of the learned man's attempt to constrain her energies by making her mind the prison for her body'" (13).

23. The issue of chastity is a thorny one, for even if a woman had to be re-gendered in order to be celibate in secular life, clerics and religious philosophers offered many praises of virginity. Vives, for example, cited religious authors such as Saints Ambrose, Augustine, and Jerome in support even of suicide as a woman's measure to preserve her virginity (1035-36). See also Schulenberg, 38.

24. Vives dedicated considerable room in his advice to wives about the need to accept their husbands' infidelities, even to the point of furthering this privilege of the double standard by honoring their spouses' mistresses and under no conditions challenging or accusing the men in question (1114).

25. With regard to the physical and intellectual autonomy that the convent afforded women, see Arenal, 149; Arenal and Schlau, 5-6; and M. King, 93-103.

26. Vives's pronouncements exemplify the humanists' qualifications on women as educated citizens and as educators. On the latter topic, he reiterates to women the exhortation to silence, approves of a woman as teacher only for young women students, and later adds: "Pues no parece bien que la mujer regente escuelas" (1001).

27. See Sánchez Ortega for the traditional connection between women and magic love spells.

4. Carnivalesque Implications

1. See T. Soufas, "Carnival, Spectacle," for further discussion of this phenomenon, embodied in the Golden Age *gracioso* who stands in briefly for the king at the end of a number of well-known *comedias.*

2. The many cross-dressed women characters in the male-authored *comedias*—thoroughly catalogued and described by, e.g., McKendrick (*Women and Society*)—also

exemplify this desperation, since it is frequently an honor dilemma that motivates their disguise. The women authors discussed here, however, develop their cross-dressed characters in somewhat different ways, albeit still within the larger context of such a characterization: Caro invests the masquerading female protagonist with more agency than do her male colleagues; Azevedo pairs her cross-dressed woman with a cross-dressed man; and Zayas experiments with the necessity of the disguise itself. I consider these women writers, therefore, to be collaborators with the more canonical male dramatic authors in establishing, challenging, and representing such theatrical conventions.

3. See studies such as those by Babcock, Davis ("Reasons"; *Society and Culture*), Dollimore (*Radical Tragedy*), Howard, Montrose, Orgel (*llusion*; "Nobody's Perfect"); and White.

4. See Elliott, 247, 251-52, and 265. The Spanish sumptuary laws enacted in 1639 at the behest of Queen Isabel de Borbón, for instance, sought to limit the use of veils and the large capes known as *guardainfantes,* items of apparel associated with prostitutes and their lascivious assignations, which these garments helped to effect. The law was more or less ignored by women of the middle and upper classes, and their dismissal of it erased "la distinción pública entre dama decente, cortesana y prostituta" (Olivares and Boyce, 267 n. 23).

5. This sort of complaint is complicated further in some of the antitheatrical tracts that deride women actors because, despite their presumed lack of morals, lascivious lifestyles, and scorn for propriety and tradition, they portray a range of religious characters, including the Virgin Mary and saintly figures. Lupercio Leonardo de Argensola, writing in 1598, offers an example: "De manera, que el cebo de que el demonio usó . . . fué el cantar, bailar, el danzar y traje exquisito, y diferencia de personas que cada día hacen, vistiéndose como reinas, como diosas, como pastoras, como hombres. Y lo que apenas se puede decir ni escribir que el traje y representación de la purísima Reina de los ángeles ha sido profanado por estas y por estos miserables instrumentos de torpeza" (Cotarelo y Mori, 67).

6. Ignacio de Camargo's late seventeenth-century attack on the Spanish theater for promoting female lasciviousness and male effeminacy is representative of the Spanish self-criticism that Elliott documents (247, 251, 265) and that Jordan discusses (126-27) with regard to Renaissance gender ideology in general. Camargo writes: "¿Qué escándalos no se ven en todas las repúblicas donde entra por su desgracia una de estas diabólicas compañías, que es como si entrara una legión de demonios. . . . La modestia y recato de una doncella, se vitupera como rústico encogimiento y se celebra la liviandad como discreta y cortesana bizarría. . . . ¿quién jamás pensara ver á los hombres nacidos sólo para nobles y varoniles empresas abatidos á tan bajos y afeminados empleos, que apenas se distinguen de las mugeres? ¿Entregados totalmente á fiestas profanas, á músicas, á paseos, á los amores lascivos, á conversaciones ociosas, á juegos y divertimientos vanos, á peinar, trenzar y teñir el pelo, á rizar la cabellera postiza, á pulir y componer el vestido con tanta proligidad y melindres como la dama más delicada? ¿De dónde pueden nacer estos viles y afeminados afectos sino del centro de las delicias sensuales, que son los patios de las comedias, fuente universal de todos los vicios?" (Cotarelo y Mori, 126-27).

7. Elliott quotes a diarist's entry from 1627 asserting that such effeminacy was a

"contagion from England" (247). Zayas's narrative voice likewise targets national identity and defense as elements placed in jeopardy by the effeminizing influence of foreigners, this time the French: "¡Que esto hagan pechos españoles! ¡Que esto sufran ánimos castellanos Bien dice un héroe bien entendido que los franceses os han hurtado el valor, y vosotros a ellos, los trajes" (*Desengaños,* 506).

8. About such dramatic phenomena, Loomba first quotes Catherine Belsey's remark—"Predictably, these creatures who speak with voices which are not their own are unfixed, inconstant, unable to personate masculine virtue through to the end"—and then concludes: "Their very attempts to transgress their limitations rob them of a unified subjectivity and express their self-negation, so typical in the psyche of the colonized: with their female skins and male masks, they approximate the splitting of colonial subject whom Fanon describes as oscillating between black skin and white mask" (94).

9. See the discussion of this double standard in Vives, 1069, 1070.

10. See T. Soufas, "Ana Caro's Re-evaluation," 96.

11. Vives augmented his moral lecture with examples of women from antiquity who, he claimed, were deserving victims of physical violence and death at the hands of retaliatory male relatives in such situations (1008-9).

12. The three plays in this chapter are cited in the text by line number from T. Soufas, *Women's Acts.*

13. See T. Soufas, "Ana Caro's Re-evaluation," 99-101.

14. See also Ordoñez.

15. The women named are ancient figures noted for their learning and literary talents. Argentaria (Pola Argentaria), a Roman, is purported to have helped her husband, the epic poet Marcus Annaeus Lucan, to write portions of his *Pharsalia.* Sofoareta seems to be the gracioso's confused combination of the two names Safo (Sappho—the famous Greek lyric poet) and Areta (renowned teacher of ancient Cyrene). Blesilla was a Roman widow known for her good works and eventually canonized.

16. Concerning the license and intimacy with which clown and fools interact with aristocratic figures, see Close, Kaiser, T. Soufas ("Carnival, Spectacle"), and Welsford.

17. Eve Sedgwick has persuasively described the locus of these tensions as the homosocial desire that relegates the female to the position of medium of transfer for eroticism between males (ch. 1). Certainly, Alvaro has penetrated Clarindo's body with his dagger in his moment of advantage in their rivalry for the body of Jacinta. See also Dollimore, "Subjectivity," 76-77.

18. In her *Desengaños,* Zayas's narrator Filis proclaims to her interior audience at one point: "Bueno fuera que si una mujer ciñera espada, sufriera que la agraviara un hombre en ninguna ocasión" (228). Later she adds: "¡Ea, dejemos las galas, rosas y rizos, y volvamos por nosotras: unas, con el entendimiento, y otras, con las armas!" (231).

19. Among recent studies of this play and their interpretations of Fenisa, Wilkins also considers carnivalesque elements (116); Stroud regards Fenisa as "in short, a kind of Doña Juana" (543); and Oakey contends that Fenisa is developed in the context of McKendrick's defined "mujer varonil" (63). See also Melloni, "María de Zayas."

20. See T. Soufas, "María de Zayas's (Un)Conventional Play," 153-54.

21. Among the complaints about the allegedly dissolute life-style of traveling acting

companies, the Jesuit Pedro Puente Hurtado de Mendoza's in 1630 is representative: "Que viven mezclados hombres y mujeres; ellos muchas veces jóvenes desenfrenados; día y noche meditando amores y encomendando a la memoria versos amatorios. Mujeres casi siempre impúdicas, en libre contacto con ellos, pues las mujeres no están en lugares distintos; a las que ven los hombres vestirse y desnudarse; ya en el lecho, ya semi-desnudas y siempre provocativas" (Cotarelo y Mori, 364). See also, in Cotarelo y Mori's collection of excerpts from tracts on the theater, Juan González de Critana (326), Juan de Mariana (432), Fr. Alonso de Mendoza (467), and Fr. Alonso de Ribera (521).

5. Locales of Dramaturgy

1. See also Alice Jardine's important essay "Gynesis" and its commentary on the difference between Anglo-American and French feminisms.

2. Conservative national interests underlay such suspicions. Maravall adds, for instance: "Novedad es cambio; por consiguiente, alteración, y, en fin de cuentas, un encadenamiento de trastornos. Equivale, pues, a una amenaza contra el sistema establecido, por lo menos cuanto afecta a los aspector fundamentales del mismo. . . . Se comprende, entonces, que fuera ésta una inclinación vigilada y controlada por quienes se hallaron interesados en el mantenimiento y conservación del orden vigente" (270-71).

3. See Johnson on the tension surrounding the debates over the new and the traditional in dramatic composition and theatrical consumption. See also the studies by Entrambasaguas, Soufas and Soufas ("Dialectics"), Prades, Stern, and Zimic.

4. Enriquez's "Carta ejecutoria" and "A los lectores" are cited by page number (as indicated in this paragraph) from T. Soufas, *Women's Acts*. For her *Tragicomedia*, citations in the text refer by folio number to the 1627 edition for *Primera parte*, and by line number to *Women's Acts* for *Segunda parte*.

5. See Pérez's discussion of Enríquez's theoretical positions (*Dramatic Works*, 8-10). Menéndez Pelayo likewise comments on this dimension in Enríquez's work: "Escribe un prólogo en verso suelto que parece la antítesis del *Arte nuevo de hacer comedias*" (290).

6. See Pérez, *Dramatic Works*, 10, and Newels, 148, concerning Enríquez's reasons for eliminating the term *jornada*.

7. Pérez, *Dramatic Works*, 37 n. 3, claims that Enríquez's use of the term *entreacto* instead of the more common *entremés* reflects an attitude of superiority, since she says in her "Carta": "Y así mismo no se entendía con las de los entreactos, que el llama sátyros, dichos vulgarmente entremeses" (p. 261).

8. Pérez draws attention to the uniqueness in Golden Age drama of Enríquez's *loas* and *entremeses* accompanying the principal plays. He cites Jean-Louis Flecniakoska with regard to the *loa*: "Desgraciadamente, no poseemos ningún programa completo y detallado, no sabemos qué loa, qué entremés y qué baile acompañaban tal o cual comedia de Lope, de Mira de Amescua"(*Dramatic Works*, 37 n. 33). Such an observation registers our unfortunate lack of evidence about what pieces were performed together, but it also indicates that Enríquez's works can, if recognized, help to fill this gap in our knowledge.

WORKS CITED AND CONSULTED

Adams, Parveen, and Beverly Brown. "The Feminine Body and Feminist Politics." *m/f* 3 (1979): 35-50.

Agnew, Jean-Christophe. *Worlds Apart: The Market and the Theater, 1500-1750.* Cambridge: Cambridge UP, 1986.

Anderson, Bonnie S., and Judith P. Zinsser. *A History of Their Own: Women in Europe from Prehistory to the Present.* Vol. 1. New York: Harper & Row, 1988.

Arenal, Electa. "The Convent as Catalyst for Autonomy: Two Hispanic Nuns of the Seventeenth Century." In *Women in Hispanic Literature: Icons and Fallen Idols.* Ed. Beth Miller. Berkeley: U of California P, 1983. 147-83.

Arenal, Electa, and Stacet Schlau. *Untold Sisters: Hispanic Nuns in Their Own Works.* Albuquerque: U of New Mexico P, 1989.

Arendt, Hannah. "What Is Authority." In *Between Past and Future.* New York: Viking, 1968. 91-141.

Axton, Marie. *The Queen's Two Bodies: Drama and the Elizabethan Succession.* London: Royal Historical Society, 1977.

Azevedo, Angela. *Dicha y desdicha del juego.* Ms. 21435. Biblioteca Nacional de Madrid.

———. *Dicha y desdicha del juego.* In T. Soufas, *Women's Acts.* 4-44.

———. *La margarita del Tajo que dio nombre a Santarén.* Ms. 33142. Biblioteca Nacional de Madrid.

———. *La margarita del Tajo que dio nombre a Santarén.* In *Women's Acts.* 45-90.

———. *El muerto disimulado.* Ms. 19049. Biblioteca Nacional de Madrid.

———. *El muerto disimulado.* In T. Soufas, *Women's Acts.* 91-132.

Babb, Lawrence. *The Elizabethan Malady.* East Lansing: Michigan State College P, 1951.

Babcock, Barbara. *The Reversible World: Symbolic Inversion in Art and Society.* Ithaca, N.Y.: Cornell UP, 1978.

Barbeito Carneiro, María Isabel. *Escritoras madrileñas del siglo XVII.* Estudio bibliográfico-crítico. Vol. 1. Madrid: Editorial de la Universidad de Madrid, 1986.

Barboso Machado, Diogo. *Bibliothece Lusitana.* 4 vols. Vol. 1. Lisbon, 1741-1759.

Barrera y Leirado, Cayetano Alberto de la. *Catálogo bibliográfico y biográfico del teatro antiguo desde sus orígenes hasta mediados del siglo XVII.* Madrid: Rivadeneira, 1860.

Beecher, Donald A., and Massimo Ciavolella, eds. *Eros and Anteros: The Medical Traditions of Love in the Renaissance.* Ottawa: Dovehouse, 1992.

Belsey, Catherine. *The Subject Is Tragedy.* New York: Methuen, 1985.

Bergmann, Emilie. "The Exclusion of the Feminine in the Cultural Discourse of the Golden Age: Juan Luis Vives and Fray Luis de León." In *Religion, Body and Gender in Early Modern Spain.* Ed. Alain Saint-Saëns. San Francisco: Mellen Research UP, 1991. 124-36.

Bernáldez, Andrés. *Historia de los Reyes Católicos.* Madrid: Biblioteca de Autores Españoles, 1959.

Beverley, John R. "On the Concept of the Spanish Literary Baroque." In Cruz and Perry, 216-30.

Blecua, Alberto. *Manual de crítica textual.* Madrid: Castalia, 1987.

Blue, William R. *Comedia: Art and History.* New York: Peter Lang, 1989.

Bristol, Michael D. *Carnival and Theater: Plebian Culture and the Structure of Authority in Renaissance England.* New York: Methuen, 1985.

Burton, Robert. *The Anatomy of Melancholy.* Ed. Floyd Dell and Paul Jordan Smith. New York: Tudor, 1948.

Butler, Judith. *Bodies That Matter: On the Discursive Limits of "Sex."* New York: Routledge, 1993.

Callaghan, Dympna. *Woman and Gender in Renaissance Tragedy.* Atlantic Highlands, N.J.: Humanities Press International, 1989.

Caro, Ana. *Ana Caro: El conde Partinuplés.* Ed. Lola Luna. Kassel: Reichenberger, 1993.

————. *Ana Caro: Valor, agravio y mujer.* Ed. Lola Luna. Madrid: Castalia, 1993.

————. *Comedia famosa el conde Partinuplés.* Mss. 17.189, Biblioteca Nacional de Madrid.

————. *El conde Partinuplés.* In *Dramáticos posteriores a Lope de Vega.* Vol. 2. Ed. R. Mesonero Romanos. Madrid: Rivadeneira, 1859. 125-38.

————. *El conde Partinuplés.* In *Laurel de comedias. Quarta parte de diferenctes autores.* Madrid: Real, 1653.

————. *El conde Partinuplés.* In T. Soufas, *Women's Acts,* 137-62.

————. *Valor, agravio y mujer.* Mss. 18.620, Biblioteca Nacional de Madrid.

————. *Valor, agravio y mujer.* In Serrano y Sanz, 268:179-212.

————. *Valor, agravio y mujer.* In T. Soufas, *Women's Acts.* 163-94.

Caro, Rodrigo. *Varones insignes en letras naturales de la ilustrísima ciudad de Sevilla.* Ed. Santiago Montoto. Seville: Real Academia Sevillana de Buenas Letras, 1915.

Calderón de la Barca, Pedro. *El médico de su honra.* Ed. D.W. Cruickshank. Madrid: Castalia, 1981.

Carvajal y Saavedra, Mariana de. *Navidades de Madrid y noches entretenidas, en ocho novelas.* Ed. Catherine Soriano. Madrid: Consejería de Educación y Cultura, 1993.

Case, Sue-Ellen. *Feminism and Theatre.* New York: Methuen, 1988.

Case, Sue-Ellen, and Janelle Reinelt, eds. *The Performance of Power: Theatrical Discourse and Politics.* Iowa City: U of Iowa P, 1991.

Case, Sue-Ellen, ed. *Performing Feminisms: Feminist Critical Theory and Theatre.* Baltimore: Johns Hopkins UP, 1990.

Castiglione, Baldassare. *The Book of the Courtier.* Trans. Sir Thomas Hoby. London, 1561; rpt. London: H.M. Dent, 1974.

Ciavolella, Massimo. "Eros and the Phantasms of *Hereos.*" In Beecher and Ciavolella, 75-85.

Cixous, Hélène. "The Laugh of the Medusa." In *Critical Theory since 1965.* Ed. Hazard Adams and Leroy Searle. Tallahassee: Florida State UP, 1992. 309-20.

Cixous, Hélène, and Catherine Clément. *The Newly Born Woman.* Minneapolis: U of Minnesota P, 1986.

Close, Anthony. "Sancho Panza: Wise Fool." *Modern Language Notes* 68 (1973): 344-57.

Cocozzella, Peter. "María de Zayas y Sotomayor: Writer of the Baroque *Novela Ejemplar.*" In Wilson and Warnke, 189-227.

Cohen, Walter. *Drama of a Nation: Public Theater in Renaissance England and Spain.* Ithaca: Cornell UP, 1985.

Cotarelo y Mori, Emilio, ed. *Bibliografía de las controversias sobre la licitud del teatro en España.* Madrid: Revista de Archivos, Bibliotecas y Museos, 1904.

Cotton, Nancy. *Women Playwrights in England 1363-1750.* London: Associated University Presses, 1980.

Cruz, Anne J., and Mary Elizabeth Perry, ed. *Culture and Control in Counter-Reformation Spain.* Minneapolis: U of Minnesota P, 1992.

Cueva y Silva, Leonor de la. *La firmeza en la ausencia.* Mss. 17234, Biblioteca Nacional de Madrid.

———. *La firmeza en la ausencia.* In Serrano y Sanz, 268:302-28.

———. *La firmeza en la ausencia.* In González Santamera and Doménech, 231-336.

———. *La firmeza en la ausencia.* In T. Soufas, *Women's Acts,* 198-224.

Dadson, Trevor J., ed. *Avisos a un cortesano: An Anthology of Seventeenth-Century Moral-Political Poetry.* Exeter, England: U of Exeter, 1985.

Daly, Mary. *Gyn/Ecology: The MetaEthics of Radical Feminism.* London: Women's Press, 1978.

Davis, Natalie Zemon. "The Reasons of Misrule: Youth Groups and Charivaris in Sixteenth Century France." *Past and Present* 50 (1971): 49-75.

———. *Society and Culture in Early Modern France.* Stanford, Calif.: Stanford UP, 1975.

De Armas, Frederick. "Ana Caro Mallén de Soto." In *Women Writers of Spain: An Annotated Bio-bibliographical Guide.* Ed. Carolyn L. Galerstein. New York: Greenwood, 1986. 66-67.

———. "*La Celestina:* An Example of Love Melancholy." *Romanic Review* 66 (1978): 288-95.

———. *The Invisible Mistress: Aspects of Feminism and Fantasy in the Golden Age.* Charlottesville, Va.: Biblioteca Siglo de Oro, 1976.

De Lauretis, Teresa. *Feminist Studies/Critical Studies.* Bloomington: Indiana UP, 1986.

———. *The Technologies of Gender: Essays on Theory, Film, and Fiction.* Bloomington: Indiana UP, 1987.

Derrida, Jacques. "Women in the Beehive: A Seminar with Jacques Derrida." In *Men in Feminism.* Ed. Alice Jardine and Paul Smith. New York: Methuen, 1987. 189-203.

Dollimore, Jonathan. *Radical Tragedy: Religion, Ideology and Power in the Drama of Shakespeare and His Contemporaries.* Brighton, England: Harvester, 1984.

———. "Subjectivity, Sexuality, and Transgression: The Jacobean Connection." *Renaissance Drama* ns 17 (1986): 53-81.

Duffy, Maureen. *The Passionate Shepherdess.* London: Jonathan Cape, 1977.

Eagleton, Terry. *Walter Benjamin: Towards a Revolutionary Criticism.* London: Verso, 1981.

Elliott, J.H. *Spain and Its World, 1500-1700.* New Haven: Yale UP, 1989.

Enríquez de Guzmán, Feliciana. *Entreactos de la primera parte de la Tragicomedia de los jardines y campos sabeos.* In González Santamera and Doménech, 173-217.

———. *Segunda parte de la Tragicomedia los jardines y campos sabeos* (with *Entreactos I and II;* "Carta ejecutoria;" and "A los lectores"). In T. Soufas, *Women's Acts,* 229-71.

———. *Tragicomedia los jardines y campos sabeos. Primera y segunda parte con diez coros y cuatro entreactos.* Coimbra, 1624.

————. *Tragicomedia de los jardines y campos sabeos: Primera y segunda parte con diez coros y cuatro entreactos.* Lisbon, 1627.

————. *Tragicomedia de los jardines y campos sabeos.* In *The Dramatic Works of Feliciana Enríquez de Guzmán.* Ed. Louis C. Pérez. Valencia: Albatrós, 1988.

————. *Tragicomedia de los jardines y campos sabeos* (Acts 1, 2, and 5 of *Primera Entreactos de la Primera parte;* and "Carta ejecutoria"). In Serrano y Sanz, 269:358-87.

Entrambasaguas y Peña, Joaquín de. *Una guerra literaria del Siglo de Oro: Lope de Vega y los preceptistas aristotélicos.* Madrid: Olózaga, 1932.

Epstein, Steven. "Gay Politics, Ethnic Identity: The Limits of Social Constructionism." *Socialist Review* 17 (1987): 9-54.

Espinosa, Juan de. *Diálogo en laude de las mujeres.* Ed. Angela González Simón. Madrid: Consejo Superior de Investigaciones Científicas, 1946.

Fernández Alvarez, Manuel. *La sociedad española en el Siglo de Oro.* Madrid: Editora Nacional, 1983.

Ferrand, Jacques. *A Treatise on Lovesickness.* Trans. and ed. Donald A. Beecher and Massimo Ciavolella. Syracuse: Syracuse UP, 1990.

Flathman, Richard E. *Concepts in Social and Political Philosophy.* New York: Macmillan, 1973.

————. *The Practice of Political Authority: Authority and the Authoritative.* Chicago: U of Chicago P, 1980.

Foucault, Michel. *The Order of Things.* New York: Vintage, 1971.

Fox, Dian. *Kings in Calderón: A Study in Characterization and Political Theory.* London: Tamesis, 1986.

Friedman, Richard B. "On the Concept of Authority in Political Philosophy." In Flathman, *The Practice of Political Authority: Authority and the Authoritative.* Chicago: U of Chicago P, 1980. 121-46.

Froes Perim, Damiao de. *Theatro heroino, abecedario historico, e catalogo das mulheres illustres em armas, letras, acçoens heroicas, e artes liberaes.* Vol. 2. Lisbon: Academia Real, 1740.

Fuss, Diana. *Essentially Speaking: Feminism, Nature and Difference.* New York: Routledge, 1989.

Galbraith, John Kenneth. *The Anatomy of Power.* Boston: Houghton Mifflin, 1983.

Garrett, Almeida. *Viagens na minha terra.* Oporto: Libraria Arnado, 1977.

Gibson, Joan. "Educating for Silence: Renaissance Women and the Language Arts." *Hypatia* 4 (1989): 9-27.

González Santamera, Felicidad, and Fernando Doménech, eds. *Teatro de mujeres del barroco.* Madrid: Asociación de Directores de Escena de España, 1994.

Gossy, Mary S. *The Untold Story: Women and Theory in Golden Age Texts.* Ann Arbor: U of Michigan P, 1989.

Hamilton, Bernice. *Political Thought in Sixteenth-Century Spain: A Study of the Political Ideas of Vitoria, De Soto, Suárez and Molina.* Oxford: Clarendon, 1963.

Heath, Stephen. "Difference." *Screen* 19 (1978): 50-112.

Heiple, Daniel L. "The 'Accidens Amoris' in Lyric Poetry." *Neophilologus* 67 (1983): 55-64.

Howard, Jean. "Scripts and/versus Playhouses: Ideological Production and the Renaissance Public Stage." *Renaissance Drama* 20 (1989): 31-49.

Ingram, Angela J.C. *In the Posture of a Whore: Changing Attitudes to "Bad" Women in Elizabethan and Jacobean Drama.* 2 vols. Salzburg: Universitat Salzburg, 1984.

Irigaray, Luce. *This Sex Which Is Not One.* Trans. Catherine Porter with Carolyn Burke. Ithaca, N.Y.: Cornell UP, 1985.

Issacharoff, Michael. *Discourse as Performance.* Stanford, Calif.: Stanford UP, 1989.

Jackson, Stanley W. *Melancholia and Depression from Hippocratic Times to Modern Times.* New Haven: Yale UP, 1986.

Janés, Clara, ed. *Las primeras poetisas en lengua castellana.* Madrid: Ayuso, 1986.

Jankowski, Theodora A. *Women in Power in the Early Modern Drama.* Urbana: U of Illinois P, 1992.

Jardine, Alice. "Gynesis." *Diacritics* 12 (1982): 54-65.

Jardine, Lisa. *Still Harping on Daughters: Women and Drama in the Age of Shakespeare.* Totowa, N.J.: Barnes & Noble, 1983.

Johnson, Carroll B. "El arte viejo de hacer teatro: Lope de Rueda, Lope de Vega y Cervantes." In *Lope de Vega y los orígenes del teatro español.* Ed. Manuel Criado de Val. Madrid: EDI-6, 1981. 95-102.

Jones, Ann Rosalind. "Surprising Fame: Renaissance Gender Ideologies and Women's Lyric." In Miller, *Poetics,* 74-95.

———. "Writing the Body: Toward an Understanding of 'l'Ecriture féminine.'" In *The New Feminist Criticism: Essays on Women, Literature and Theory.* Ed. Elaine Showalter. New York: Pantheon, 1985. 361-77.

Jones, Kathleen B. "On Authority; Or, Why Women Are Not Entitled to Speak." In *Feminism and Foucault: Reflections on Resistance.* Ed. Irene Diamond and Lee Quinby. Boston: Northeastern UP, 1988. 119-33.

Jordan, Constance. *Renaissance Feminism: Literary Texts and Political Models.* Ithaca, N.Y.: Cornell UP, 1990.

Kaiser, Walter. *Praisers of Folly.* Cambridge: Harvard UP, 1963.

Kaminsky, Amy. "Ana Caro Mallén de Soto (Seventeenth Century)." In Levine, Marson, and Waldman, 86-97.

Kamuf, Peggy. "Replacing Feminist Criticism." *Diacritics* 12 (1982): 42-47.

Kantorowicz, Ernst H. *The King's Two Bodies: A Study in Medieval Political Theology.* Princeton, N.J.: Princeton UP, 1981.

Kaplan, E. Ann. "Feminist Criticism and Television." In *Channels of Discourse: Television and Contemporary Criticism.* Ed. Robert C. Allen. Chapel Hill: U of North Carolina P, 1987.

Kaston, David Scott, and Peter Stallybrass, ed. *Staging the Renaissance: Reinterpretations of Elizabethan and Jacobean Drama.* New York: Routledge, 1991.

Kelly, Joan. *Women, History, and Theory: The Essays of Joan Kelly.* Chicago: U of Chicago P, 1984.

Kelso, Ruth. *Doctrine for the Lady of the Renaissance.* Urbana: U of Illinois P, 1978.

Kendrick, T.D. *Saint James in Spain.* London, 1960.

Kennedy, Ruth Lee. *Studies in Tirso, 1: The Dramatists and His Competitors, 1620-1626.* Chapel Hill: U of North Carolina P, 1974.

King, Margaret. *Women of the Renaissance.* Chicago: U of Chicago P, 1991.

King, Willard. *Prosa novelística y academias literarias en el siglo XVII.* Vol. 10. Madrid: Anejos del Boletín de la Real Academia Española, 1963.

Laqueur, Thomas. *Making Sex: Body and Gender from the Greeks to Freud.* Cambridge, Mass.: Harvard UP, 1990.

León, Fray Luis de. *La perfecta casada.* Madrid: Espasa Calpe, 1992.

Lesselier, Claudie. "Social Categorizations and Construction of a Lesbian Subject." *Feminist Issues,* Spring 1987: 89-94.

Levin, Carole. "John Foxe and the Responsibilities of Queenship." In *Women in the Middle Ages and the Renaissance: Literary and Historical Perspectives.* Ed. Mary Beth Rose. Syracuse: Syracuse UP, 1986. 113-33.

Levine, Linda Gould, Ellen Engelson Marson, and Gloria Feiman Waldman, eds. *Spanish Women Writers: A Bio-Bibliographical Source Book.* Westport, Conn.: Greenwood, 1993.

Loomba, Ania. *Gender, Race, Renaissance Drama.* Manchester, England: Manchester UP, 1989.

Lowes, John L. "The Loveres Maladye of Hereos." *Modern Philology* 11 (1914): 491-546.

Luna, Lola, ed. *Ana Caro: "El conde Partinuplés."* Kassel: Reichenberger, 1993.

————. "Ana Caro, una escritora 'de oficio' del Siglo de Oro." *Bulletin of Hispanic Studies* 72 (1995): 11-26.

————, ed. *Ana Caro: "Valor, agravio y mujer."* Madrid: Castalia, 1993.

Lundelius, Ruth. "Ana Caro: Spanish Poet and Dramatist." In Wilson and Warnke, 228-50.

————. "Tirso's View of Women in *El burlador de Sevilla." Bulletin of the Comediantes* 27 (1975): 5-14.

Lynch, John. *The Hispanic World in Crisis and Change: 1598-1700.* Cambridge: Blackwell, 1992.

————. *Spain, 1516-1598: From Nation State to World Empire.* Cambridge: Blackwell, 1992.

Lyons, Bridget Gellert. *Voices of Melancholy: Studies in Literary Treatments of Melancholy in Renaissance England.* New York: W.W. Norton, 1975.

Maclean, Ian. *The Renaissance Notion of Woman: A Study in the Fortunes of Scholasticism and Medical Science in European Intellectual Life.* Cambridge: Cambridge UP, 1980.

Maravall, José Antonio. *La cultura del Barroco: Análisis de una estructura histórica.* Barcelona: Ariel, 1975.

Marcus, Leah S. "Shakespeare's Comic Heroines, Elizabeth I, and the Political Uses of Androgyny." In *Women in the Middle Ages and the Renaissance: Literary and Historical Perspectives.* Ed. Mary Beth Rose. Syracuse: Syracuse UP, 1986. 135-53.

McKendrick, Melveena. *Theatre in Spain, 1490-1700.* Cambridge: Cambridge UP, 1989.

————. *Woman and Society in Golden-Age Spanish Drama: A Study of the "mujer varonil".* London: Cambridge UP, 1974.

McLuskie, Kthleen. *Renaissance Dramatists.* Atlantic Highlands, N.J.: Humanities Press International, 1989.

McNamara, JoAnn. *A New Song: Celibate Women in the First Three Christian Centuries.* New York: Harrington Park, 1985.

Melloni, Alessandra. "María de Zayas fra *comedia* e *novela." In Actas del coloquio Teoría y realidad en el teatro español del siglo XVII: La influencia italiana.* Rome: Instituto Español de Cultura y de Literatura de Roma, 1981. 485-505.

————, ed. *María de Zayas: "La traición en la amistad."* Verona: Universita degli studi di Verona, 1983.

Menéndez Pelayo, Marcelino. *Historia de las ideas estéticas.* Vol. 2. Madrid: CSIC, 1962.

Messer-Davidow, Ellen. "The Philosophical Bases of Feminist Literary Criticisms." *New Literary History* 19 (1987): 65-103.

Miller, Nancy K., ed. *The Poetics of Gender.* New York: Columbia UP, 1986.

————. "The Text's Heroine: A Feminist Critic and Her Fictions." *Diacritics* 12 (1982): 48-53.

Moi, Toril. *Sexual/Textual Politics: Feminist Literary Theory.* New York: Methuen, 1985.

Monaghan, Peter. "Reviving the Work of Woman Composers." *Chronicle of Higher Education* 41.7 (1945): A5.

Montoto de Sedas, Santiago. *Doña Feliciana Enríquez de Guzmán.* Seville: Deputación Provincial, 1915.

Montrose, Louis A. "The Purpose of Playing: Reflections on a Shakespearian Anthropology." *Helios* 7 (1980): 5-12.

Morgan, Fidelis. *The Female Wits.* London: Virago, 1981.

Munzer, Jerónimo. "Relación del viaje." In *Viajes de extranjeros por España y Portugal.* Ed. Barcía Mercadal. Madrid: Aguilar, 1952.

Navarro, Emilia. "Manual Control: 'Regulatory Fictions' and Their Discontents." *Cervantes* 13 (1993): 17-35.

Neale, J.E. *Elizabeth and Her Parliaments, 1559-1581.* London: Jonathan Cape, 1953.

Newels, Margarete. *Los géneros dramáticos en las poéticas del Siglo de Oro.* Trans. Amado Solé-Leris. London: Tamesis, 1974.

Novy, Marianne L. *Love's Argument: Gender Relations in Shakespeare.* Chapel Hill: U of North Carolina P, 1984.

Oakey, Valerie Hesgtrom. "The Fallacy of the False Dichotomy in María de Zayas's *La traición en la amistad.*" *Bulletin of the Comediantes* 46 (1994): 59-70.

Offen, Karen. "Defining Feminism: A Comparative Historical Approach." *Signs: Journal of Women in Culture and Society* 14 (1988): 119-57.

Olivares, Julián, and Elizabeth S. Boyce. *Tras el espejo la musa escribe: Lírica feminina de los Siglos de Oro.* Madrid: Siglo XXI, 1993.

Ordoñez, Elizabeth. "Woman and Her Text in the Works of María de Zayas and Ana Caro." *Revista de Estudios Hispánicos* 19 (1985): 3-15.

Orgel, Stephen. *The Illusion of Power: Political Theater in the Renaissance.* Berkeley: U of California P, 1975.

———. "Nobody's Perfect; Or, Why Did the English Stage Take Boys for Women?" *South Atlantic Quarterly* 88 (1989): 7-29.

———. "Prospero's Wife." In *Rewriting the Renaissance: The Discourse of Sexual Difference in Early Modern Europe.* Ed. Margaret W. Ferguson, Maureen Quilligan, and Nancy J. Vickers. Chicago: U of Chicago P, 1986. 50-64.

Osborn, Scott C. "Heroical Love in Dryden's Heroic Drama." *PMLA* 73 (1958): 480-90.

Pérez, Louis C. "A Classicist of the Golden Age: Feliciana Enríquez de Guzmán." *Atenea* (Mayaguez) 7 (1987): 61-69.

————, ed. *The Dramatic Works of Feliciana Enríquez de Guzmán*. Valencia: Albatrós, 1988.

Pérez de Montalbán, Juan. *Para todos*. Madrid: 1632.

Perry, Mary Elizabeth. *Gender and Disorder in Early Modern Seville*. Princeton, N.J.: Princeton UP, 1990.

Pigeaud, Jackie. "Reflections on Love Melancholy in Robert Burton." In Beecher and Ciavolella, *Eros and Anteros: The Medical Traditions of Love in the Renaissance*. Ottawa: Dovehouse, 1992, 211-31.

Postlewait, Thomas, and Bruce A. McConachie, eds. *Interpreting the Theatrical Past: Essays in the Historiography of Performance*. Iowa City: U of Iowa P, 1989.

Prades, Juana de José. ed. *Lope de Vega: "El arte nuevo de hacer comedias en este tiempo."* Madrid: Consejo Superior de Investigaciones Cientif, cosi 1971.

Pye, Christopher. "The Sovereign, the Theater, and the Kingdome of Darknesse: Hobbes and the Spectacle of Power." *Representations* 8 (1984): 85-106.

Reiss, Timothy J. *The Discourse of Modernism*. Ithaca, N.Y.: Cornell UP, 1982.

Rich, Adrienne. "Compulsory Heterosexuality and Lesbian Existence." In *Powers of Desire*. Ed. Ann Snitow, Christine Stansell, and Sharon Thompson. New York: Monthly Review, 1983. 177-205.

Robertson, Roland, and Burkart Holzner. *Identity and Authority: Explorations in the Theory of Society*. New York: St. Martin's, 1979.

Rosa, Amorim. *Historia de Tomar.* Tomar: Gabinete de Estudos Tomarenses,1965.

Rubin, Gayle. "The Traffic in Women: Notes on the 'Political Economy' of Sex." In *Toward an Anthropology of Women*. Rayna R. Reiter, ed. New York: Monthly Review, 1976. 150-210.

Sánchez Arjona, José. *Noticias referentes a los anales del teatro en Sevilla desde Lope de Rueda hasta fines del siglo XVII*. Seville: E. Rasco, 1898.

Sánchez Ortega, María Helena. "Woman as Source of 'Evil' in Counter-Reformation Spain." In Cruz and Perry. 196-215.

Scalingi, Paula Louise. "The Scepter or the Distaff: The Question of Female Sovereignty, 1516-1607." *Historian* 41 (1978): 59-75.

Schiesari, Juliana. *The Gendering of Melancholia: Feminism, Psychoanalysis, and the Symbolics of Loss in Renaissance Literature*. Ithaca, N.Y.: Cornell UP, 1992.

Schor, Naomi. "Dreaming Dissymmetry: Barthes, Foucault, and Sexual Difference." In *Men in Feminism*, ed. Alice Jardine and Paul Smith. New York: Methuen, 1987. 98-110.

————. "Reading Double: Sand's Difference." In *The Poetics of Gender*. Ed. Nancy K. Miller. New York: Columbia UP, 1986. 248-69.

Schulenberg, Jane Tibbetts. "The Heroics of Virginity: Brides of Christ and Sacrificial Mutilation." In *Women in the Middle Ages and the Renaissance*. Ed. Mary Beth Rose. Syracuse, N.Y.: Syracuse UP, 1986. 29-72.

Scolnicov, Hanna, and Peter Holland, eds. *Reading Plays: Interpretation and Reception*. Cambridge: Cambridge UP, 1991.

Sedgwick, Eve Kosofsky. *Between Men: English Literature and Male Homosocial Desire*. New York: Columbia UP, 1985.

Sennett, Richard. *Authority*. New York: Knopf, 1980.

Serrano y Sanz, Manuel, ed. *Apuntes para una biblioteca de escritoras españolas desde el año 1401 al 1833*. Vols. 268, 269, 271. Madrid: Rivadeneira, 1975.

Showalter, Elaine. "Feminist Criticism in the Wilderness." In *Writing and Sexual Difference*. Chicago: U of Chicago P, 1982. 9-36.

Sidorsky, David. "Spinoza: Freedom of Thought and Speech." In *The Liberal Tradition in European Thought*. New York: Putnam, 1970. 31-38.

Simón, José. "Caro de Mallén, Ana." In *Bibliografía de la literatura hispánica*. Vol. 7. Madrid: Consejo Superior de Investigaciones Científicas, 1967. 494-96.

Simon, Yves R. *A General Theory of Authority*. Notre Dame, Ind.: U of Notre Dame P, 1980.

Skinner, John E. *The Meaning of Authority*. Washington, D.C.: UP of America, 1983.

Smith, Paul Julian. *The Body Hispanic*. Oxford: Clarendon, 1990.

————. *Discerning the Subject*. Minneapolis: U of Minnesota P, 1988.

————. "Writing Women in Golden Age Spain: Saint Teresa and María de Zayas." *Modern Language Notes* 102 (1987): 220-40.

Snow, Edward. "Theorizing the Male Gaze: Some Problems." *Representations* 25 (1989): 30-41.

Soufas, C. Christopher, Jr. "Thinking in *La vida es sueño*." *PMLA* 100 (1985): 287-99.

Soufas, C. Christopher, and Teresa Scott Soufas. "The Dialectics of Dramatic Form in Lope's *El caballero de Olmedo*." *Romance Quarterly* 37 (1990): 441-53.

————. "*La vida es sueño* and Post-Modern Sensibilities." In *Studies in Honor of Bruce W. Wardropper*. Ed. Dian Fox, Harry Sieber, and Ter Horst. Newark, Del.: Juan de la Cuesta, 1989. 291-303.

Soufas, Teresa S. "Ana Caro's Re-evaluation of the *Mujer varonil* and Her Theatrics in *Valor, agravio y mujer*." In Stoll and Smith, 85-106.

————. "Carnival, Spectacle, and the *Gracioso*'s Theatrics of Dissent." *Revista Canadiense de Estudios Hispánicos* 14 (1990): 315-30.

————. "Leonor de la Cueva y Silva." In Levine, Marson, and Waldman, 125-30.

————. "María de Zayas's (Un)Conventional Play, *La traición en la amistad.*" In *The Golden Age "Comedia": Text, Theory, and Performance.* Ed. Charles Ganelin and Howard Mancing. West Lafayette, Ind.: Purdue UP, 1994. 148-64.

————. *Melancholy and the Secular Mind in Spanish Golden Age Literature.* Columbia: U of Missouri P, 1990.

————. "Regarding the Woman's Response: Leonor de la Cueva y Silva's *La firmeza en la ausencia.*" *Romance Languages Annual* 1 (1989): 625-30.

————. "Repetitive Patterns: Marrying Off the 'Parthenos' in Ana Caro's *El conde Partinuplés.*" In *Engendering the Early Modern Stage: Women Playwrights of the Spanish Enspire.* Ed. Valerie Hegstrom Oakey and Amy Williamsen, forthcoming.

————. "Writing Wives Out of the *Comedia.*" In *New Historicism and the "Comedia."* Ed. José Antonio Madrigal. Boulder: SSASS, forthcoming.

————, ed. *Women's Acts: Plays by Women Dramatists of Spain's Golden Age.* Lexington: UP of Kentucky, 1997.

Spivak, Gayatri Chakravorty. *In Other Worlds: Essays in Cultural Politics.* New York: Methuen, 1987.

Stallybrass, Peter. "Patriarchal Territories: The Body Enclosed." In *Rewriting the Renaissance: The Discourses of Sexual Difference in Early Modern Europe.* Ed. Margaret W. Ferguson, Maureen Quilligan, and Nancy J. Vickers. Chicago: U of Chicago P, 1986. 123-42.

————. "The World Turned Upside Down: Inversion, Gender and the State." In *The Matter of Difference: Materialist Feminist Criticism of Shakespeare.* Ed. Valerie Wayne. Ithaca, N.Y.: Cornell UP, 1991. 201-20.

Stallybrass, Peter, and Allon White. *The Politics and Poetics of Transgression.* Ithaca: Cornell UP, 1986.

Stamm, Robert. "On the Carnivalesque." *Wedge* 1 (1982): 47-55.

Stimpson, Catharine R. "Zero Degree Deviancy: The Lesbian Novel in English." In *Writing and Sexual Difference.* Ed. Elizabeth Abel. Chicago: U of Chicago P, 1982. 243-59.

Stoll, Anita K., and Dawn L. Smith, eds. *The Perception of Women in Spanish Theater of the Golden Age.* Lewisburg, Pa.: Bucknell UP, 1991.

Stroud, Matthew D. "Love, Friendship, and Deceit in *La traición en la amistad* by María de Zayas." *Neophilologus* 69 (1985): 539-47.

Varey, John E. "La edición de textos dramáticos del Siglo de Oro." In *La edición de textos: Actas del Congreso Internacional de Hispanistas del Siglo de Oro.* Ed. Pablo Jauralde Pou, D. Noguera, and A. Rey. London: Tamesis, 1990. 99-109.

Vázquez de Prada, Valentín. *Historia económica y social de Espana.* Vol. 3. Madrid: Confederación Española de Cajas de Ahorros, 1978.

Vigil, Mariló. *La vida de las mujeres en los siglos XVI y XVII.* Madrid: Siglo Veintiuno, 1986.

Vives, Juan Luis. ""Formación de la mujer cristiana." In *Obras completas.* Vol. 1. Ed. and trans. Lorenzo Riber. Madrid: Aguilar, 1947. 985-1175.

Walthaus, Rina. "La comedia de Doña Ana Caro Mallén de Soto." In *Estudios sobre escritoras hispánicas en honor de Georgina Sabat-Rivers.* Ed. Lou Charnon-Deutsch. Madrid: Castalia, 1992. 326-40.

Warner, Marina. *Alone of All Her Sex: The Myth and the Cult of the Virgin Mary.* New York: Random House, 1976.

Wayne, Valerie. *The Matter of Difference: Materialist Feminist Criticism of Shakespeare.* Ithaca, N.Y.: Cornell UP, 1991.

Weimann, Robert. *Shakespeare and the Popular Tradition in the Theater.* Baltimore, Md.: Johns Hopkins UP, 1978.

Welles, Marcia L., and Mary S. Gossy. "María de Zayas y Sotomayor." In Levine, Marson, and Waldman, 507-19.

Welsford, Enid. *The Fool: His Social and Literary History.* London: Faber and Faber, 1968.

White, Allon. "Pigs and Pierrots: Politics of Transgression in Modern Fiction." *Raritan* 2 (1983): 51-70.

Wiesner, Merry E. "Women's Defense of Their Public Role." In *Women in the Middle Ages and the Renaissance: Literary and Historical Perspectives,* ed. Mary Beth Rose. Syracuse: Syracuse UP, 1986: 1-27.

Wilkins, Constance. "Subversion through Comedy?: Two Plays by Sor Juana Inés de la Cruz and María de Zayas." In Stoll and Smith, 107-20.

Wilson, Edward M., and Duncan Moir. *A Literary History of Spain: The Golden Age Drama, 1492-1700.* London: Ernest Benn, 1971.

Wilson, Jean. *Entertainments for Elizabeth.* Totowa, N.J.: Rowman and Littlefield, 1980.

Wilson, Katharina M., and Frank J. Warnke, eds. *Women Writers of the Seventeenth Century.* Athens: U of Georgia P, 1989.

Wilson, Margaret. *Spanish Drama of the Golden Age.* Oxford: Oxford UP, 1969.

Wittig, Monique. "The Mark of Gender." In Miller, 63-73.

Woodbridge, Linda. *Women and the English Renaissance: Literature and the Nature of Womankind.* Brighton, England; Harvester, 1984.

Yates, Frances A. *Astrea.* London: Routledge and Kegan Paul, 1975.

Zayas, María de. *Comedia famosa de La traición en la amistad.* Mss. Res. 173. Biblioteca Nacional de Madrid.

———. *Comedia famosa de La traición en la amistad.* In González Santamera and Doménech, 31-172.

———. *Desengaños amorosos.* Ed. Alicia Yllera. Madrid: Cátedra., 1983.

———. *Maria de Zayas: La traición en la amistad.* Ed. Alessandra Melloni. Verona: Universitá degli studi de Verona, 1983.

———. *La traición en la amistad.* In Serrano y Sanz, 271:590-620.

———. *La traición en la amistad.* In T. Soufas, *Women's Acts,* 277-308.

———. *Tres novelas amorosas y tres desengaños amorosos.* Ed. Alicia Redondo Goicoechea. Madrid: Castalia, 1989.

Zimic, Stanislav. "Cervantes frente a Lope y la comedia nueva." *Meridiano 70* (1976).

Ziomek, Henryk. *A History of Spanish Golden Age Drama.* Lexington: UP of Kentucky, 1984.

INDEX